Changing Perceptions of Thomas Mann's Doctor Faustus

Ever since its appearance in 1947, Thomas Mann's novel *Doctor Faustus* has generated heated reactions among critics. Whereas initial ideological differences stemming from the Cold War and the division of Germany have abated following the reunification of 1990, diverse opinions and controversies persist about Mann's daring treatment of the Faust theme.

These include such topics as the political stance of the author and the historical dimensions of the novel; the biographical and autobiographical backgrounds of the work—especially in light of the subsequent publication of Mann's diaries and private notebooks; the writer's sexual and psychological proclivities; the thorny issues of montage, collage, and intertextuality; musical concerns such as the extent to which the novel's protagonist appropriates as his own Arnold Schönberg's twelve-tone system of composition or the role of Mann's fellow exile and mentor, Theodor W. Adorno, in indoctrinating his "pupil" into avant-garde musical techniques; the degree to which the novel exhibits structural features of the music on which the narrative focuses; and the function of certain mythic prototypes for this modern parody in fashioning the fortunes and fate of Adrian Leverkühn.

A provocative and still unresolved question centers on the precise role played by Goethe's *Faust* in the conception and execution of *Doctor Faustus*, in spite of Mann's assertion that his version of the legend had "nothing in common" with the work of his famous predecessor. Finally, the presence of strong visual elements in the novel leads to an assessment of the critical reception accorded Franz Seitz's film adaptation of *Doctor Faustus* (1982), a dicey subject in Mann circles, since few filmed versions of his novellas or novels have enjoyed an unsullied reputation.

JOHN F. FETZER is Professor of German Emeritus at the University of California, Davis.

Studies in German Literature, Linguistics, and Culture:
Literary Criticism in Perspective

About *Literary Criticism in Perspective*

Books in the series *Literary Criticism in Perspective* trace literary scholarship and criticism on major and neglected writers alike, or on a single major work, a group of writers, a literary school or movement. In so doing the authors — authorities on the topic in question who are also well-versed in the principles and history of literary criticism — address a readership consisting of scholars, students of literature at the graduate and undergraduate level, and the general reader. One of the primary purposes of the series is to illuminate the nature of literary criticism itself, to gauge the influence of social and historic currents on aesthetic judgments once thought objective and normative.

JOHN F. FETZER

CHANGING PERCEPTIONS OF THOMAS MANN'S DOCTOR FAUSTUS

Criticism 1947–1992

CAMDEN HOUSE
Rochester, New York

Copyright © 1996 by CAMDEN HOUSE, INC.

All Rights Reserved. Except as permitted under current legislation, no part of this work may be photocopied, stored in a retrieval system, published, performed in public, adapted, broadcast, transmitted, recorded, or reproduced in any form or by any means, without the prior permission of the copyright owner.

First published 1996 by Camden House
Transferred to digital printing 2012

Camden House is an imprint of Boydell & Brewer Inc.
668 Mt. Hope Avenue, Rochester, NY 14620, USA
www.camden-house.com
and of Boydell & Brewer Limited
PO Box 9, Woodbridge, Suffolk IP12 3DF, UK
www.boydellandbrewer.com

ISBN-13: 978-1-57113-070-9
ISBN-10: 1-57113-070-5

Library of Congress Cataloging-in-Publication Data

Fetzer, John F.
  Changing perceptions of Thomas Mann's Doctor Faustus : criticism 1947–1992 / John F. Fetzer.
    p. cm. — (Studies in German literature, linguistics and culture. Literary criticism in perspective)
  Includes bibliographical references (p.) and index.
  ISBN 1-57113-070-5 (alk. paper)
  1. Mann, Thomas, 1875–1955. Doktor Faustus. I. Title. II. Series: Studies in German literature, linguistics, and culture (Unnumbered). Literary criticism in perspective.

PT2625.A44D6934 1995
833'.912—dc20
                                                                    95-368
                                                                      CIP

This publication is printed on acid-free paper.
Printed in the United States of America.

To Henriette, my wife, my best friend, and most respected critic:

"Ma fin est mon commencement et mon commencement ma fin." Guillaume de Machaut, Rondeau

"In my end is my beginning." Mary, Queen of Scots, Motto

"In my beginning is my end." T. S. Eliot, *Four Quartets*

Contents

Acknowledgments	ix
Preface	xi
1: Reception, Reactions, and Research (1947–1955)	1
2: Elucidation through Archival Discoveries (1955–1975)	18
3: Illumination by Biographical and Autobiographical Revelations (1975–1992)	58
Conclusions, Contentions, Conjectures	122
Works Cited	133
Index	179

Acknowledgments

My greatest debt of gratitude is due my wife, Henriette, who for five long years has endured the promise that as soon as this book is finished, we can relax, enjoy life, and perhaps even take an extended vacation. The first condition has now been fulfilled; the trio of codicils, however, has yet to become a reality. As a partial reward for her patience, tolerance, and understanding, however, I am dedicating my last book to her, as I did my first. I also wish to thank the German Department and the Research Office of the University of California, Davis, for their moral and financial support respectively during this long and arduous gestation period. In addition, the Inter-Library Loan section of the University deserves a hearty word of thanks for some Herculean efforts in locating rare texts and hard-to-find secondary sources. They have also stoically accepted many a complaint on my part concerning delayed procurements and the limited retention period of borrowed texts. To both James Hardin and Eitel Timm, the dynamic duo serving as editors and advisors for the series Literary Criticism in Perspective, I owe a great deal. I only wish that I had been able to incorporate some of their sage suggestions more skillfully into the final version of the text. Lastly, I should like to express my appreciation to my colleagues at Davis, first and foremost to Clifford A. Bernd, for their direct and indirect input into my research efforts during my thirty years at this University. By letter, telephone, and word of mouth during casual hallway conversations, their advice and admonitions over the course of my career have enabled me to avoid some, although not all, of the pitfalls threatening the literary scholar in an effort to interpret German literary texts and to assess textual criticism, from the Romantic to the modern and postmodern periods. It was an exciting and rewarding adventure, thanks to all the forces and factors enumerated above.

John Francis Fetzer
September 1995

Preface: *Doctor Faustus* and the Critics (1947-1992)

IN THE ERA immediately following the Second World War, the dominant focus of critical interest in Thomas Mann (1875–1955) centered on his most recent novel, a modern adaptation of the legend of the pact between the Renaissance necromancer and speculator in the elements, Dr. Johann Faustus, and the forces of the devil: *Doktor Faustus. Das Leben des Tonsetzers Adrian Leverkühn, erzählt von einem Freunde* (*Doctor Faustus. The Life of the German Composer Adrian Leverkühn as Told by a Friend*). Mann completed the book in 1947, and it appeared the same year in Sweden (published in German by Bermann-Fischer) and in Germany (Suhrkamp). The first and still only English translation, by Helen T. Lowe-Porter, was published in New York by Alfred A. Knopf in 1948. Between 1947 and the death of the author in 1955, investigations and interpretations of *Doctor Faustus* appeared covering virtually all those aspects of this complex and multifaceted novel that the subsequent decades would treat in greater depth and detail.

With the opening of the Thomas Mann Archive in Zurich to the scrutiny of researchers (in the early 1960s) and the publication of Mann's correspondence (beginning in 1959), new avenues of access to *Faustus* became available. These were further expanded by accessibility to Mann's notes on *Faustus*, his other notebooks, the revised manuscript versions of the novel, and personally annotated editions of source books in the author's private library. Finally, with the publication (Mendelssohn, beginning in 1977) of those diaries that Mann either inadvertently or deliberately failed to destroy before his death, subsequent generations of *Doctor Faustus* researchers have been able to examine more definitively topics that, from the outset, had piqued the curiosity of scholars but could be treated only speculatively or intuitively, based primarily on evidence adduced from the novel itself.

With reference to *Doctor Faustus*, the range of these topics of interest is broad in scope, encompassing such diverse areas as the following:

1. ideologically colored perspectives on the novel in a politically divided Germany (especially after the founding of the separate German states in 1949 and persisting until the unification of the two Germanies in the wake of the 1989 upheavals)

2. theological-religious issues or the philosophical implications of the text

3. the historical dimensions embodied in the work and correlated with the life of the protagonist (a panorama of the German past from medieval to

modern times, with special emphasis on the most recent past — the roots and rise of National Socialism and its disastrous consequences for the country)

4. the place of *Doctor Faustus* in the overall career and creativity of Thomas Mann (that is, the treatment of the novel in comprehensive studies of the author's life and works)

5. thematic, generic, and specific problem-oriented investigations

6. the systematic study of sources — both literary and nonliterary, intrinsic as well as extrinsic — for this "novel to end all novels" (including works prior to the Doctor Faustus chapbook of 1587, ties to its world-renowned namesake, Johann Wolfgang von Goethe's *Faust* of 1832, or to other nineteenth- and twentieth-century Faustian paradigms)

7. the biographical background and autobiographical foreground. The former entails examining the protagonist, the composer Adrian Leverkühn, with specific attention to possible real-life counterparts — above all, to Nietzsche and other reputedly syphilitically afflicted geniuses such as Beethoven, Schumann, Hugo Wolf, or to contemporary musical giants including Alban Berg, Gustav Mahler, and especially Arnold Schönberg. The autobiographical component pertains to Mann himself, since the author could not be totally excluded from the realm of potential prototypes for his artist-hero. And since Mann, in his 1949 account of the origins and sources of the work, *Die Entstehung des 'Doktor Faustus:' Roman eines Romans* (translated in 1961 as *The Story of a Novel. The Genesis of 'Doctor Faustus'*) underscored the hidden identity between Adrian Leverkühn and the narrator, Serenus Zeitblom, a teacher of classical languages and lifelong acquaintance of the composer, one would also have to examine this humanist figure in conjunction with the composer and a host of real and fictional characters in the novel.

8. the role of music, musicians, musicology, and music theory — subjects which had elicited attention from the outset. The focal points were, first and foremost, the evolution of music up to and including Schönberg's serial technique (from the 1920s) and the musings of the philosopher and social critic Theodor Wiesengrund Adorno on music theory and the crisis facing this art form in the twentieth century. During his exile years in California, Mann came into close contact with his fellow expatriate Adorno, and the latter's contributions to the genesis of the novel and to the final version were considerable. These and many more aspects of music history and theory were augmented by what might be termed the musicalization of literature (whereby the literary work, like all the other arts according to Walter Pater, aspires to — and seeks to emulate — the condition of music with regard to structural components, thematic development, the leitmotif, and other devices considered to be common property of both media).

9. the possible application to *Faustus* of the familiar formula "myth and psychology," coined by Mann to characterize one aspect of his work and later amended by critics to read "myth plus psychology"

10. the visual component. Leverkühn's addiction to Albrecht Dürer's works provides one clue, but there are numerous other elements in the novel that appeal to the eye, to the sense of sight and eidetic apperception. The film version of the novel in 1982 opened new dimensions of the issue, not the least of which were the nature of cinematic adaptation of literary works in general and the role of the camera as narrator in particular.

In a complex, multi-faceted novel such as *Doctor Faustus*, one fundamental premise of which reads "Beziehung ist alles" (Mann, 1947: 66; "relationship is everything," Lowe-Porter, 1948: 47) and which makes extensive use of the combinatory principles of montage or collage, none of the above topics can really exist in a hermetically sealed vacuum. Relationship and interrelationship of ideas and images become an inevitable fact of fictional life when one investigates the artistic techniques, the dominant themes, and other intrinsic or extrinsic features of the work. But for the purpose of discussing analytically different critical approaches to Mann's novel, this study will isolate a prime component of each individual interpretation cited with reference to some aspect of the above ten categories. However, not even all three chapters of this overview of critical literature will contain the full complement of these topics in equal proportion, since shifts of interest over time dictate that certain aspects of a work come prominently to the fore at one period and recede into the shadows during the next. Yet there are enough constants in the cluster of topics to insure that a degree of continuity is maintained in spite of changes in focus and emphasis.

As early as the mid-1960s, the lament had already arisen that the critical literature dealing with *Doctor Faustus* alone was assuming vast proportions. This plight of plenty was then exacerbated by such events as the centennial of Mann's birth in 1975, when a new wave of celebratory homage to the author spawned a host of scholarly symposia commemorating one hundred years of Thomas Mannia, together with a plethora of dissertations and monographs destined for eventual publication. The upshot of this inundation of criticism in Germany and other countries was that the standard Thomas Mann bibliographies (Jonas, 1955, 1967; Bürgin, 1959; Matter, 1972) had to be augmented by periodic bibliographical sources if one wished to keep abreast of the latest developments. Supplemental reference works included such updated publications as *Germanistik, Bibliographie der deutschen Literaturwissenschaft* (after 1968 entitled *Bibliographie der deutschen Sprach- und Literaturwissenschaft*), and the yearly bibliography of the Modern Language Association. There were also sporadic reports of research on Mann to be consulted, by Hatfield

(1956), Lehnert (1969; 1977a, b; 1992), Gollnick (1977), Kurzke (1977; 1985a, b), Sautermeister (1977), Dvoretzky (1979), Vaget (1980), Orlowski (1981), Koopmann (1990d), Wißkirchen (in Koopmann,1990b), Wagener (in Koopmann,1990b) and others. The result of such bibliographical quests was the pinpointing of hundreds of essays, articles, monographs, and books dealing in some fashion with *Doctor Faustus*. Such a flood of printed material can be an unnerving prospect for the incipient scholar who seeks to be thorough in covering the field, and the situation grows more intimidating with each passing year.

Today Mann's novel still stands as a focal point of scholarly interest and investigation. The abundance of critical research material on *Faustus* continues to grow with each passing year, sometimes at an exponential rate. Therefore, any attempt to synthesize trends in criticism or to summarize the diverse treatments of *Doctor Faustus* must be selective rather than comprehensive — restricted to studies in which this novel plays a seminal rather than peripheral role. Such a criterion leads to the inclusion of certain studies and the exclusion of others, a procedure that may seem arbitrary to some readers. But exclusion is a necessary fact of intellectual life, even — or especially — in literary criticism because of the flood of information that constantly inundates the field. This exclusionary process is particularly necessary when one considers that many publications on *Faustus* are in languages beyond the ken of the average reader, and certainly not at the disposal of all literary scholars or Germanists either: Hungarian, Finnish, Japanese, Polish, to name just a few examples. Other texts in French, Italian, Spanish, or Russian, though linguistically more accessible, had to be excluded from this overview because of the limitations of space and overall scope of this study.

With regard to the chronological framework of the three chapters 1947–1955; 1955–1975; 1975–1992 — another seemingly arbitrary or at least artificial periodization — the basis for this particular divisional format is as follows:

Chapter 1: 1947–1955. The first nonacademic reviews of the novel and assessments by professional scholars of German literature began to appear already in 1947. By the time of Mann's death in 1955, secondary literature covering some aspect of the ten topics listed above — even though in preliminary and at times rudimentary form — had appeared in print.

Chapter 2: 1955–1975. In the wake of Mann's death, a number of major studies were published (such as Erich Heller's The *Ironic German* of 1958) that sought to profile the œuvre of the author and put his writings into some larger context. The increasing archival accessibility of material previously unavailable led to the correction — or qualification — of subjects treated earlier on the basis of less definitive sources. The prime example of this trend toward careful source research is Gunilla Bergsten's *Thomas Manns 'Doktor Faustus.' Untersuchungen zu den Quellen und zur Struktur des Romans* of 1963 (translated into English as *Thomas Mann's 'Doctor Faustus.' The Sources and Structure of the Novel* in 1969). This pioneering investigation (second revised edition 1974) was subsequently augmented by Lieselotte Voss's seminal book of 1975 and by numerous publications of Hans Wysling, which will be cited later in the text.

The close of the Thomas Mann centenary in 1975, twenty years after the author's death, seemed to provide a natural cæsura after the tremendous influx of critical commentary up to that date. One qualification, however, has to be made with regard to this time restriction: not infrequently, collections of essays stemming from the symposia and conferences of 1975 were published one, two, or, sometimes three years after the actual event had taken place. In spite of the delayed appearance of these anthologies, they were subsumed under the listings for 1955-1975, unless other valid reasons dictated inclusion in the 1975–1992 segment.

Chapter 3: 1975–1992. This is a period of further refinement in the study of specific aspects of *Faustus* and in the perception of certain thematic constellations (especially Mann's political views and his attitude toward the erotic and homoerotic). That *Doctor Faustus* still stands at the forefront of Mann research during this period is apparent when one notes that 1988 brought a symposium of international scope to the University of California at Irvine devoted exclusively to an examination of this single novel "at the margin of modernism," as the title of the conference indicated. The *Thomas-Mann-Jahrbuch* for 1989 included selected essays in German from this conference, while a volume in English containing a majority of the lectures and the rejoinders of respondents was subsequently published by Camden House (Lehnert and Pfeiffer, 1991). This concentrated effort either to arrive at a consensus or to air divergent opinions concerning *Doctor Faustus* seemed, at first glance, to provide an appropriate termination point for this overview of critical trends in the secondary literature, though there was, as always, a degree of arbitrariness involved in setting specific time limits. On the other hand, the publication in 1994 of the volume of the *Bibliographie der deutschen Sprach- und Literaturwissenschaft* covering the year 1992 made this subsequent date an even more suitable terminus ad quem, though 1992 does not mark any specific occasion or other significant commemorative anniversary with regard to either the author's career or to *Doctor Faustus*. Had the editor of the series decided to make 1997 the cut-off point for the survey, then a title such as *Thomas Mann's 'Doctor Faustus:' Fifty Years of Criticism* could have lent this enterprise a more sharply delineated chronological profile. By the same token, the amount of secondary literature by that juncture might have grown to truly unwieldy proportions, so that the earlier date would, in retrospect, seem preferable as well as practical.

The series Literary Criticism in Perspective usually deals in strictly chronological order with patterns of criticism for an author's entire œuvre or those for a single major work of that writer. This is the case, for instance, with Hugh Ridley's recent book *The Problematic Bourgeois: Twentieth-Century Criticism on Thomas Mann's 'Buddenbrooks' and 'The Magic Mountain'* (1994). On the other hand, the present critical overview of the secondary literature on *Doctor Faustus* modifies this standard approach to some extent, in that within the thematic rubrics enumerated above, a chronology will be maintained for that topic in each of the three major time-blocks. For example, on each occasion when "sources" are the prime target of the discussion, whether in Chapter 1 (1947–1955), Chapter 2 (1955–1975), or Chapter 3 (1975–1992), the section dealing with questions of source will have a chronological overlay. Thus the reader can gain some impression of how that topic has been treated during the particular time period; or, if the "source" sections alone in each of the respective chapters are read in sequence, a clearer idea of the evolution of that topic from 1947 to 1992 should emerge.

English translations of German titles as well as of excerpts from books and other secondary literature are, unless otherwise indicated, my own.

1: Reception, Reactions, and Research (1947–1955)

> *"For now we see through a glass, darkly...."*
> (Corinthians 1: 13)

Setting the Scene

THOMAS MANN began writing *Doctor Faustus* on May 23, 1943, during his exile in California's Pacific Palisades near Los Angeles, and he completed the novel there on January 29, 1947. According to his notebooks, the impetus for this monumental work goes back to some ideas he had outlined as early as 1904. His original intention had been to transform the myth of the daring Renaissance pseudoscientist and dabbler in the black arts, Dr. Johann Faust, found in the chapbook *Historia vom Dr. Johann Fausten, dem weitbeschreyten Zauberer und Schwarzkünstler* (The History of Dr. Johann Faust, The Widely Decried Magician and Necromancer, 1587, of which Mann acquired an edition of 1911), into the tale of a syphilitic artist who, like his predecessor, conspires with the devil. A sexually transmitted disease contracted in the bargain stimulates Faustus's creative fantasies to the extent that, under the aegis of this diabolically induced infection, the artist is able to create startlingly new and innovative works. However, when paralysis ultimately sets in, it becomes clear that Satan is finally claiming his part of the wager (Wysling and Fischer, 1981: 7–8).

In the wake of his experiences in the Second World War and his lifelong interest in music, Mann expanded the original design of the work to accommodate these historical and musical dimensions. The Faustian protagonist of the novel, Adrian Leverkühn (1885–1940), is now transformed into a modern composer faced with the challenge of creating a form of music that would not be burdened by the ballast of outworn techniques and outmoded traditions from the past. Aspects of the conflict raging in Europe are incorporated into the narration by Serenus Zeitblom, the pedestrian companion of Leverkühn's youth, a lifelong schoolmaster and humanistically trained scholar, who recounts the events in the novel from his perspective. Serenus admires Adrian's creative talents but has qualms about the composer's alliance with the satanic, Dionysian forces of the depths and darkness. Nevertheless, as the war comes to a traumatic close (1943–1945), Zeitblom faithfully records the course and tragic outcome of his friend's career, along with the downfall of Germany. The biographical account ends with Leverkühn succumbing to the ravages of syphilis after a span of twenty-four years (1906–1930), a period marked by moments of uninhibited, euphoric creativity but superseded by a decade of senility and second childhood (1930–1940). The demise of the composer of avant-garde, Schönbergian serial music is correlated with a sporadic recording of the rise and fall of Germany, a culturally privileged country that, in the Hitler era, had also blundered into a kind of alliance with the forces of the devil and darkness. Therefore, at the end of the work, Serenus can bid farewell to both his feared yet revered acquaintance Adrian Leverkühn as well as to his once prosperous and now prostrate Germany with the alliterative invocation "God be merciful to thy poor soul, my friend, my Fatherland" (L-P: 510).

Ideological Perspectives

In the period immediately following its publication in Germany (1947) until approximately 1950, *Doctor Faustus* was the object of bitter polemics and often contrary as well as contradictory opinions. This resulted not only from the religious-theological orientation of the work itself but also from the growing ideological bifurcation of the country into what amounted to capitalist and communist camps, a development coming on the heels of the National Socialist reign of terror (1933–1945). In the wake of the latter phenomenon, however, many Germans wondered how Mann, who had emigrated in 1933 and spent the war years safely ensconced first in an American university community (Princeton — where he taught, among other things, a course in *Faust*) and then in a sunny California retreat far removed from European soil, could have the audacity to comment on what had transpired in Germany. And what was even worse: how could he condemn his country for having made what seemed to be a Faustian pact with a fascist dictator of diabolic proportions in order to "break through" to world power? What was often neglected amid this bitter controversy over extrinsic concerns about the genesis of the work were its intrinsic, aesthetic qualities. Form and style, together with the plight of Leverkühn, the modern musician struggling to overcome a kind of compositional paralysis or creative impasse, took a back seat to the convenient yet oversimplified axiom Leverkühn = Germany. Such interpretive shortsightedness was rectified — or at least modified — by researchers only during decades following the death of the author, as the debacle of National Socialism receded into the past and one could examine the novel with greater objectivity and aesthetic distance.

In Germany, the critical reaction to the exile's novel was characterized by the polarization of the cold-war era. German critics in both the East and West sectors subscribed, in their politically differentiated fashion, to the linking of Leverkühn's fate with that of Germany's remote and recent history (from the Renaissance to 1945). Eastern bloc literary historians, together with their confreres in the German Democratic Republic and with other leftist-leaning intellectuals in various countries, detected in the work the demise of the bourgeois, capitalist-imperialist credo. The Hungarian Marxist Georg Lukács, in several articles as well as in his monograph on Mann, situated the novel within the context of the "tragedy of modern art" (1949). Predictably, he singled out as the root cause of the problem the isolation of the bourgeois-humanistic artist in a small, hermetically sealed world, alienated from the larger sphere of sociopolitical responsibility and allied to reactionary, mystifyingly demagogic forces under the sway of monopolistic capitalism. The portrayal of the devil serves as a caricature of imperialistic self-destruction. More positive, on the other hand, were Lukács's assessments of the musical dimensions of the novel and his interpretation of Adrian's final rational comments, which, according to this critic, reveal that the composer had ultimately forsaken his ultrasubjective inwardness with its concomitant regression into fascism (reflected by the barbarism of his later musical compositions), and found the path to — of all people — Karl Marx. Another proponent of socialist doctrine, Hans Mayer, was at this time still comfortably ensconced in the confines of the German Democratic Republic. His ideologically oriented treatment of the novel (1950) reflects similar gloom and doom for the capitalist enterprise, even though the interpretation he presents is replete with insightful literary observations and correlations. The same holds true for Paul Rilla (1948), who likewise demonstrates that adherence to the codified school of leftist criticism does not necessarily preclude literary interpretations of depth and perspicacity. Ernst Fischer (1949), likewise of the Marxist persuasion, while not necessarily subscribing to the parallelism of the fates of Leverkühn and Germany, nevertheless discovers in the pact with the devil a convenient scapegoat with which Mann is able to gloss over the real causes of the catastrophe of National Socialism. Since Mann fails to show the various echelons of German society during the imperialistic Wilhelminian era in all their subtle interplay —

there are, for example, no workers, no capitalistic big-business moguls or large land holders depicted — a social vacuum results and Mann must have recourse to the vague and somewhat Romanticized myth of an inevitable tragic Germanic fate with a Faustian aura. Adrian appears sometimes as a unique pathological case; on other occasions he is the embodiment of the entire declining bourgeoisie (exhibiting by his cold demeanor the ice age of the soul), while, toward the end of the work, he becomes a representative of decaying capitalism per se.

Religious-Theological-Philosophical Issues

Whereas critics of the Socialist-Marxist cast spoke with a fairly conformist voice with regard to the novel's aim and in generally positive terms of its aesthetic merits, those in West Germany were sharply divided into two camps, based at the outset on more or less religious-theological premises of Protestant versus Catholic provenance (Montesi, 1948; Rochocz, 1949; Hartwig, 1954). One of the most vociferous and influential of the West German critics of the novel was Hans Egon Holthusen, whose essay "Die Welt ohne Transzendenz" (1949), by virtue of its provocative title alone (The World without Transcendence), set the polemical guidelines for the immediate postwar period. As early as 1948, the cultural critic Erich Kahler had postulated the "secularization of the devil" in *Doctor Faustus,* implying that in this "terminal book," in which all intellectual and aesthetic practices are called into question, even the diabolic acquires a terrestrial ambience. Kahler saw this in a positive light, however, since Mann had thereby succeeded in bringing the Faustian dilemma "down to earth," as it were, in contrast to Goethe's lofty portrayal which, from the beginning to the end, basked in a cosmic perspective from above. Holthusen, however, was not to be reconciled with Mann's secularization of the myth. First of all, by linking the devil with music — an art form, that to Holthusen's mind, should be considered divine rather than diabolic — Mann had made a fundamental error. This was compounded by the blunder that in the novel there is no deific counterforce to the satanic. Instead of underscoring true religion and absolute values, the author, through his mouthpiece Zeitblom, makes a case for relativism and timid religiosity. The secularized demonic as the impetus behind genius, aided and abetted by sex and sickness (concisely formulated in German by the compound term for venereal disease "Geschlechtskrankheit"), leads to the demise of what Holthusen felt was the hallmark of any genial art: the eternal, noble, and, above all, transcendental. In Christian theology, original sin derives from arrogance and rebellion against God, not from acts of passion, and thus Mann's view also deviates sharply from traditional religious dogma. Finally, Leverkühn, by the affirmation of his descent into hell, renounces any hope for grace; he does not even appear to want to find salvation. Consequently, this Faustus, to Holthusen's mind, is not a suitable representative of the German spirit. After all, where is Weimar classicism in all this? What role do the humane and rational sides of the German character, the piety of the Middle Ages, and a host of other positive attributes play here?

What provokes Holthusen most seems to be Mann's refusal to supply definitive answers, unequivocal truths; instead, the writer prefers to wallow in tantalizing ironies, ambiguities, and ambivalences, and this irritates a critic who is anchored in a religiously stable world view. What Holthusen frequently fails to do is to distinguish the chaff from the wheat, to differentiate between the isolated views of figures in a fictional text, in an aesthetic context, and either the author's personal opinions expressed elsewhere (which also may change in the course of time) or the actual "facts" of history (to the extent to which these can ever be ascertained).

Whereas Holthusen elicited some qualified support in West Germany for his frontal assault (Schulz, 1951) and even echoed similar complaints from Catholic quarters (Becher, for whom Mann is "the writer of a declining world destined for decline," 1948: 221), there were nevertheless serious reservations from other factions (for instance, Christian E. Lewalter and Hans Paeschke, the former calling upon Kierkegaard's dialectical theology in defense of the book against the charge of an absent transcendence, 1949), including those otherwise in accord with his basic premise (Braun, 1949). The latter, for instance, argued against Holthusen's overwhelming nihilism and negation, finding at least a modicum of hope in such features as the final high G of the cello at the end of Leverkühn's last composition, *Dr. Fausti Weheklag'* (*The Lamentation of Dr. Faustus*) or some positive value in Adrian's heartfelt love for his nephew, the angelic boy Nepomuk (Echo). If Holthusen denied transcendence for Mann's novel, Walter Boehlich, in a very perceptive assessment, even deprived it of any claim to its nominal lineage ("Faust, der Nichtfaustische," "Faust, the non-Faustian," 1948: 593) finding paternal roots neither in the Volksbuch nor in Goethe. Peter de Mendelssohn, on the other hand, who in 1975 was to publish the first volume of a monumental Thomas Mann biography (which, because of the death of the biographer in 1982, remained fragmentary), addressed three letters concerning *Doctor Faustus* to a friend in Switzerland

(1948), in which he was extremely laudatory of both the form and content of the novel. In keeping with his overall adulatory attitude toward the author, Mendelssohn felt the novel might even serve the Germans as both a moral and a political guide, and this was certainly a far cry from Holthusen's harsh religious and ethical indictment of the book. Unabashed adulation of Mann and of the craft of his fiction in *Doctor Faustus* also characterizes Jonas Lesser's monograph on the life and works of the author (1952). Werner Milch (1948), on the other hand, takes a more jaundiced view, sharply criticizing the symbolic playfulness of the novel, which he believes bordered in some instances on pure kitsch.

More in the vein of half book review, half critical commentary on *Doctor Faustus* is the 1948 article of Iring Fetscher, which has no particular theological or political axe to grind and consequently is less polemic and more even-tempered in tone. Written for a West German student publication, this article constitutes part of a cluster of early attempts to introduce *Doctor Faustus* to the younger student generation. In this case, the introduction stems from "one of their own" in contrast to a similar goal of a general orientation pursued by professional educators for the controversial novel from either a pedagogical standpoint (Kielmeyer, 1949) or that of a literary scholar who analyzes techniques of fiction for prospective teachers on the level of the German gymnasium (Klein, 1951).

The International Response: Interpretations in Larger Contexts

The polyphony of critical voices greeting the appearance of *Doctor Faustus* was from the very outset by no means exclusively German but rather international in scope. Elsewhere in Europe, for example, the Swiss, who had been affected only indirectly by aberrations of the National Socialist regime, reacted objectively and dispassionately, even though the novel represented to Emil Staiger, the most eloquent literary spokesman of that nation, a "poisoning of the German spirit" (1947: 180). Robert Faesi, on the other hand, writing with much more chronological and critical distance intervening (1955), produces a comprehensive, balanced appreciation of the novel in the hands of this "master of narrative art," in spite of the "signature (or signs) of finality" ("Endeszeichen," 159) embedded in the work by the author himself.

In England, James M. Lindsay (1954), who traces chronologically a cluster of central topics (such as the artist in conflict with the burgher, humanism and democracy, sickness and death, and so on) in his general study of Mann, found that these themes reach their apex of development in *Doctor Faustus,* thus marking a certain culminating point and lending coherence to the author's total creative œuvre. But Lindsay's study is typical of most analyses of *Faustus* in the larger context of a lifework overview in that it disregards questions of style and structure almost totally. More influential than these thematically oriented interpretations of the novel was the work of the émigré Erich Heller, who, with an occasional essay on Mann (1954), was even at this early juncture laying the foundation for his major publication of 1958, *The Ironic German.* In the late 1950s, Heller's provocative book would cause as much of a furor among critics as had Holthusen's controversial piece during the late 1940s. In the United States, the publication in 1948 of Helen T. Lowe-Porter's translation of *Doctor Faustus,* together with the appearance of a pocket guide to the novel for American readers, edited and published by Alfred A. Knopf in 1949, helped Mann's work become in this country what might be termed commercially a modest best seller, though professional book critics here had been at best lukewarm in their initial responses — much to Mann's chagrin. This was similar to the situation in England, where the anonymous reviewer for the *Times Literary Supplement* (1949) was anything but favorable, so that the cudgel had to be taken up there as well as in the United States by the university community of literary scholars.

On the American side of the Atlantic, Holthusen's theologically based and religiously biased hostility toward *Doctor Faustus* was shared by Ramón J. Sender ("not the book the Germans need at this moment," 1953: 206), not so much on religious grounds but because of its ultimately apologetic tone toward "Germanism." Holthusen's broadsides were defused somewhat by Wolfgang Seiferth's commonsense article of 1949, which argued that only select facets of the Teutonic character and German history had been presented in the novel, so one should not consider Adrian's fate the whole truth and nothing but the truth. Already in 1948, André von Gronicka, who was subsequently to become one of the leading authorities on Mann in America, had published a sympathetic prolegomenon to an interpretation of the novel (as did Sell, 1948), which stressed the concept of a "breakthrough" in music and literature. In a brief analysis, Joan Merrick (1949) launched on a very modest scale the practice of intertextuality (at that time still considered in terms of influence or the montage principle) by tracing ties between a passage in the novel and a parallel paragraph from Heine's prose. John Henry Raleigh's analysis of Mann's "double vision" (1953) pits the innate ambiguities, ambivalences and "fantastic equivocations" (382) of the world of "disordered extremes" (386) in *Faustus* against the "integrating spirit" of the intact medieval universe found in *The Holy Sinner,* a work already foreshadowed in the earlier novel. In Canada, Hans Eichner assessed the status of *Doctor Faustus* in the context of Mann's total oeuvre (1948; as did Hans A. Maier in the same year). Later, in his 1953 introductory monograph on Mann, Eichner traces a sequentially triadic pattern in the chronology of the writer's life, which moved from an early penchant for dichotomy to the gradual evolution of a sense for synthesis and finally to a level of balance and maturity. This schematic design would relegate *Faustus,* Mann's "real debate with fascism" (94), to that final stage of equanimity, which is perhaps an overly facile pigeonholing of a work so multi-stratified in nature (Enright, 1950). Another early introductory study in English dealing with the totality of Mann's creative output is Henry Hatfield's book of 1951, which regards the writer as a seismograph of Western culture and attempts to address issues of the craft of fiction with regard to *Faustus*. But this goal is particularly difficult to attain when the critic is writing about phenomena in a foreign language, a literary text in a linguistic medium that English-speaking readers may not even understand in the original. On a pragmatic level, James Fellows White (1951) examines abridged passages in *Doctor Faustus* (for instance, the "overindulgence in Brentano songs" that was tempered by Mann's daughter, Erika, 377), in addition to uncovering omissions (including one of Echo's prayers, White, 1950) and some odd excisions which occurred in the English translation of 1948.

With regard to the issue of stylistic criteria, one might mention several different attempts to broach this issue with regard to *Doctor Faustus*. The earliest of these deals with the interesting topic of the Anglicisms that may have crept into Mann's German style as a result of his American sojourn (Suhl, 1948); the second probes the conscious use of archaisms in the text (Orton, 1950); while the third, from a much later date but highly relevant for this early period, treats the difficulties of translation which confronted Helen T. Lowe-Porter in her Herculean efforts to make the novel accessible to English-speaking audiences (Thirlwall, 1966). Unfortunately, a stylistic study by a German critic — the essay on Mann as a verbal artist by Eberhard Hilscher (1955) — suffers from basic methodological defects: Hilscher is more concerned with the mechanical cataloguing and categorizing of data than with any analysis or interpretation of what he has compiled. More relevant with regard to the issue of Mann's stylistic prowess is Marianne Bonwit's essay "Babel in Modern Fiction" (1950), which spotlights the opposite end of the philological spectrum — the breakdown of language as a vehicle of communication in the novel, a pertinent twentieth-century topic ever since Hofmannsthal's 1901 letter to "Lord Chandos." Bonwit points out how Leverkühn's ability to speak declines as his illness progresses. Of course, one might interject that it took an artist of Mann's caliber to depict the demise of the verbal idiom so convincingly. It is also noteworthy that Serenus leaves it to music in its "speaking unspokenness" (L-P: 490; "mit der sprechenden Unausgesprochenheit," Mann: 650) to convey the final message of hope beyond hopelessness once the closing tones of the *Dr. Fausti Weheklag'* have faded in the distance. This passage seems to imply that music might ultimately impart what words, in the final analysis, cannot now or never could convey. By the same token, Serenus clearly prepares and, to a certain extent, prejudices, the reader by informing him what this closing sound possibly signifies rather than leaving the gist of that mysterious message to the interpretive powers of the unbiased listener.

The approaches to *Doctor Faustus* touched upon up to this point (marking the years from the initial appearance of the novel until the death of its author) might be said to subsume the following topics outlined in the introductory section of this study: ideological issues; theological-religious questions (this branch of the history of ideas school of interpretation was still in vogue in 1940s, as Erich Brock demonstrates, 1949); historical dimensions (deriving from the facile but problematic equation Leverkühn = Deutschland); and general interpretations within the framework of larger contexts (Mann's life and work), including some rudimentary attempts at stylistic analysis. Naturally, because there had been so little time for critics to gain what is usually termed aesthetic distance from the work, some of the avenues of interpretation taken at the outset proved to be detours from the artistic truth of *Doctor Faustus* rather than genuine access routes of understanding. Later scholars would have the advantage of consulting extensive archival holdings; of perusing the full spectrum of the author's notes on the novel, his other notebooks, correspondence, and myriad personal documents; and of digesting the ever-burgeoning mass of secondary critical literature. This advantageous sequence of events enabled later critics and scholars to refine, expand, or in some cases, correct with hindsight what their predecessors had conjectured with foresight but on the basis of less substantive evidence.

Searching for Sources and Biographical-Autobiographical Links

One field of research that flourished soon after *Doctor Faustus* was published and that subsequently reaped an abundant harvest with the opening of the Zurich archives was the quest for sources of the novel — general, specific, literary, non-literary, biographical and autobiographical. This trend became especially apparent as a result of the publication of Mann's own account of the gestation period — the sometimes informative, occasionally evasive and even deceptive, but always provocative "novel of a novel" *Die Entstehung des 'Doktor Faustus.' Roman eines Romans* (1949; *The Story of a Novel. The Genesis of 'Doctor Faustus,'* 1961). Subsequently, with the publication of Mann's diaries and correspondence, certain covert autobiographical elements latent in the work came prominently to the fore.

There are a number of obvious German literary landmarks to which one might have recourse when searching for immediate fictional models for Mann's *Doctor Faustus* without even indulging in archival rummaging. First, the chapbook of 1587 comes to mind (Butler, 1949; Bianquis, 1950; Reed, 1952; Diersen, 1955) as do Goethe's, Christian Grabbe's and Nikolaus Lenau's Faust figures, Heinrich Heine's Faustina, or even E. T. A. Hoffmann's deranged composer-conductor, Johannes Kreisler. In addition, several works from the annals of world literature feature the infamous Renaissance necromancer — for example, Marlowe's *Tragical History of Dr. Faustus* or Valéry's "Mon Faust" (Leonard, 1950) — which, by virtue of the nominal protagonist alone, automatically become candidates for consideration and comparison. Among those historical personages whose lives were felt to parallel that of Adrian Leverkühn most closely was, as Mann readily acknowledged, the philosopher Friedrich Nietzsche. But aspects of the novel were also indebted to a host of less profiled but equally prominent figures from the world of romantic and modern music — Beethoven, Schumann, Hugo Wolf, Gustav Mahler, Alban Berg — as well as the medieval magician-scientist Simon Magnus (Hennings, 1953). There were even biblical ancestors stretching as far back as Adam (Kahler, 1957), who could lay claim to having served, in some capacity, as real-life or mythic role models for Leverkühn.

One of the pioneers in examining the biographical potential of a Nietzsche-Leverkühn connection was John C. Blankenagel (1948), who based his case on Mann's essay of 1947, "Nietzsche's Philosophy in the Light of Our Experience," and on an account of the Cologne bordello experience of the philosopher as recorded in Paul Deussen's memoirs of 1901. Nietzsche's conscious attempt to contract venereal disease as a kind of intellectual aphrodisiac is correlated by Blankenagel with Leverkühn's Hetæra Esmeralda experience and is undergirded by other external parallels in the lives of the fictional composer and this celebrated prototype (akin to Heintel, 1950). Anni Carlsson (1949), somewhat surprisingly, begins her essay, which features a prominent Nietzschean component, by sketching parallels with Goethe's *Faust*, even in the face of Mann's assertion that his novel had nothing to do with the masterpiece of the sage of Weimar. Some of Carlsson's correspondences (Euphorion-Echo, for instance) ring truer than do other correlatives (Gretchen-Esmeralda or Helena-Hyphialta). The ties of Leverkühn to Nietzsche, however, are seen not so much with respect to common details from their lives (as had been the case with Maurice Colleville, 1948) but rather in relation to their mutual artistic attitudes — especially concerning the phenomenon of decadence and the concept of the Dionysian lifestyle (against which Alfred von Martin later cautioned in a circumspect analysis of the Mann-Nietzsche affiliation, 1953).

In the wake of Mann's revelation in *The Story of a Novel* that a secret identity exists between the narrator of the novel, Serenus Zeitblom, and Adrian Leverkühn, the protagonist, especially in the implied sense that these contrasting figures represent different aspects of his (the author's) own ego, it is a foregone conclusion there would soon be attempts to examine the nature of the often bungling humanist and to pinpoint the essence of his idiosyncratic personality and problems (Lüders, 1949). This was the first in a long line of analyses which sought to measure the degree of accuracy in Mann's concession or confession.

A biographical link of much more tangential nature and much less encompassing than the connection to Nietzsche stems from Mann's indirect allusion (in figures like Professor Ehrenfried Kumpf) to the historical personage of Martin Luther. Whereas Werner Kohlschmidt (1950) is concerned with the historical veracity of the depiction of the Protestant reformer and his doctrines, Pierre-Paul Sagave (1954) prefers to see in the man who proclaimed, somewhat paradoxically, both spiritual freedom and political subservience, the secret villain of the novel and of German history itself. This initially negative assessment of Mann's attitude toward Luther was destined to be reviewed and ultimately revised, once the archival holding became accessible to later generations of researchers.

Several studies of sources from a literary perspective might be mentioned at this point, since they all focus on minor or episodic figures from the novel and were conducted without benefit of the full range of manuscript material later available in the Mann archive. Victor A. Oswald, for instance, established a solid reputation for his extremely brief but penetrating miniarticles containing major disclosures. This is evident most notably in his still seldom-challenged hypothesis of 1948 that the prostitute Hetæra Esmeralda and Adrian's unseen benefactress, Frau von Tolna, are one and the same person. Proceeding with detective-like precision, Oswald bases his identity thesis on textual evidence alone. In a second article (1949), which employs virtually the same ingenious sleuthing procedures, he traces two seminal episodes in the novel back to figures from the scientific community: the twentieth-century deep-sea diver William Beebe and the sixteenth-century Italian syphilologist Giovanni Manardi. This leads Oswald to the conclusion that the concept of a "strict form" with no free note ("strenger Satz," Mann: 256) holds for both Leverkühn's constructivist music and the construction of Mann's prose text. This conjecture has not remained as immune from critical assault as has the Esmeralda-von Tolna theory. Undaunted, however, Oswald adopted a similar tactic in an equally brief investigation of Hans Christian Andersen's little mermaid (1950), whose fate is recapitulated periodically throughout the novel, especially in the closing pages of the work. Based on Mann's deployment of this figure, Oswald draws structural conclusions which transcend the limits of straightforward source hunting (as other critics, such as Carlsson, 1954 had practiced). Hans J. Mette (1951) compares the motifs of Leverkühn's descent into hell (and into the sea) and his heavenward flight with comparable adventures in the late Greek romance of Alexander, maintaining that Mann admonishes against such hubristic feats. Finally, Alfredo Dornheim (1952) argues effectively that the angelic Echo and Goethe's Mignon are embodiments of the archetypal "divine child" as postulated by the philologist-theologian Károly Kerényi, with whom Mann maintained a lively correspondence. But then Dornheim goes a bit too far in his speculations by postulating an elective affinity between Nepo and such mythical figures as Hermes and Eros. The roots of Echo's prayers are traced by James F. White back to Mann's second-hand knowledge of medieval texts as well as to Shakespeare's *Tempest* (1950). One final note with regard to the bio-autobiographical sources of another minor figure: the Pentateuch scholar Chaim Breisacher, whose highly unflattering portrayal is subjected to careful scrutiny by Jacob Taubes (1954). The critic draws the conclusion that the rabbi must have been fashioned after Dr. Oskar Goldberg, a rabid, antirationalistic interpreter of myths, whose dogmatic and monolithic theories both fascinated and repulsed Mann. On the periphery of such an analysis lurks the question of Mann's stance toward the Jews in general — was he an anti-Semite or, as he sometimes proclaimed, a philo-Semite? The answer has proven to be complex and still may be open to debate today in spite of a plethora of new revelations in the interim.

Questions of a broader scope that emerge from specific source studies like those above involve issues such as to what extent Mann is actually indebted to the works he cites or paraphrases — that is to say, was his knowledge of these sources firsthand or derivative, based on opinions of friends or authorities? And how successfully did he integrate such gleanings into his own work — aesthetically speaking? (The issues of montage-collage and intertextuality would later come to hold dominant positions in the field of Mann research). Are the portraits of fictitious characters actually and accurately fashioned after real-life models? And perhaps the most important issue: how does the precision or distortion in the portrayal of an original prototype from the "real" world in the fictional context add to or detract from our appreciation of the work itself? These queries, together with incipient interest in the extent of the author's Goethe *imitatio*, Mann's growing identification with this illustrious predecessor, and the involvement of the author with mythological models as a kind of pattern of eternal recurrence became aspects of source appropriation that grew in scope and depth over the intervening years and have continued to occupy scholars' attention down to the present day.

Mann's Man of Music

To anyone who has even perused *Doctor Faustus*, it is obvious that music as both a theme and a structural principle in the novel was bound to arouse critical attention from the outset, given that the protagonist was a modern composer caught in the throes of creative stagnation yet bent upon finding some means to overcome this crisis of creativity. In addition, Mann had once made the provocative (but hardly provable) declaration that his novel had to become that about which it spoke — namely, constructivist music (meaning serial or twelve-tone music on the model of Arnold Schönberg). Such a daring assertion had implications for the structural features of Mann's novel as well as for the rhetoric of his fiction, and it became a topic of considerable critical debate that still elicits heated response.

After several preliminary assessments of Leverkühn's music and his musicianship had paved the way (Herz, 1948; Zuckerkandl, 1948; Pringsheim, 1949a, b), Jack M. Stein presented a systematic and informed résumé of the composer's compositions (1950) marred only by the omission of reference to the man who was later to be regarded as Mann's guru in musical matters and a major force in determining the ultimate form and content of key compositions in the novel: Theodor Wiesengrund Adorno. The lacuna in Stein's account was filled to some extent by Erich Doflein (1949) and John L. Stewart (1951), who isolated Adorno as the source of Adrian's inspiration and of Mann's knowledge of modern music. An interpretation of Leverkühn's last composition, *Dr. Fausti Weheklag'*, from a philosophical rather than musicological standpoint was offered in 1949 by Fritz Kaufmann (who was later to publish a monograph on Mann's relation to Schopenhauer's concepts of the world as Will and Representation), in which the roots of the composer's damnation are deemed to be the same as those that inspire veneration of him as an artist. This premise could be regarded as a preliminary variation of the concept of the "similarity of the dissimilar," a fundamental dialectic behind much of Leverkühn's later creations and a phenomenon that was beginning to attract increasing attention (Engel, 1949). For instance, Philip B. Rice (1949) isolates, as the central premise of this entire novel with myriad variations, the coalescence of opposites, without the loss of extremes of tension in the process.

As one might expect, critics of the now defunct German Democratic Republic such as Johannes Krey (1954) were inclined to underscore the societal and sociological aspects of Leverkühn's music, while in the West, a literary scholar with a strong musicological bent, Joseph Müller-Blattau inaugurated a long line of comparative musicoliterary studies (1949) by juxtaposing Adrian's compositions, produced in isolation, with those originating in the exclusive realm of Hermann Hesse's Kastalien and linked with the cryptic glass bead game in the 1943 novel *Magister Ludi*.

Whenever music is at issue, it seems inevitable that the name Beethoven must soon be invoked, as does Edward Engelberg's article (1955) juxtaposing Leverkühn's final confession to his assembled friends with his precursor's confessional "Heiligenstädter Testament" (Will Written at Heiligenstadt). Another fascinating conflation of musicology and biography in a fictional context can be found in the famous controversy between the author and the composer Arnold Schönberg — actually Mann's neighbor in Southern California at the time when the novel was written. The father of the twelve-tone (dodecaphonic) or serial technique of musical composition did not relish the parallels that he encountered in Mann's *Faustus* between Leverkühn's achievements and what he believed to have been his own contributions to the rise of the modern musical idiom. Besides, the pact of the fictional composer with the forces of the devil, resulting in syphilis and madness, was anything but flattering, and Schönberg took umbrage at the implications of any kinship in an indignant letter to the *Saturday Review of Literature* in 1949, to which Mann responded in a conciliatory tone in the same issue of the periodical. The jagged course of this involved verbal boxing match between intellectuals has been traced by Willi Schuh (1949). One wonders if the dispute was actually resolved by Mann's insistence that his open acknowledgment and account of Schönberg's contribution to the theoretical speculations of the novel's hero be appended as an explanatory "author's note" to any future editions of the work.

Given the fact that parody was an essential ingredient of Adrian Leverkühn's compositional arsenal, especially at the outset of his career, it is not surprising that critics at an early stage began to examine how the literary counterpart to this device manifested itself in the novel (Blackmur, 1950; Eichner, 1952; Hatfield, 1955). By the same token, the correlation of musical structures derived primarily from the serial technique, the twelve-tone row in its four variant modalities (forwards, backwards, upside down, upside down-backwards), together with the strict style of composing, which ostensibly permitted no free note, was soon to be deployed in order to establish a contemporary form of that reciprocal illumination of the arts that had taken wing in Germany during the Romantic era and continued to flourish in the nineteenth and twentieth centuries. Whereas the initial excursions into what might be termed this musicalization of literature with respect to *Faustus* were relatively conservative (Greiner, 1954), later attempts would become much more radical and fanciful, arousing skepticism even among devotees of Mann, who realized that his technical knowledge of music in general was at best derivative, while his understanding of the modern constructivist idiom, which he never really espoused aesthetically, was actually quite deficient.

Finally, two separate but ultimately interrelated aspects of this novel, in which, as noted previously, "relationship is everything," involve the role of sickness in the life of the artist and, concomitant with this (because Leverkühn's pact actually entails a sexually transmitted disease), the erotic in its full spectrum, from heterosexual to homosexual

forms. A preliminary step in this direction was taken in Frank Hirschbach's 1955 study of the role of love in Mann's works, an overview in which *Doctor Faustus* is discussed under the colorful rubric "Devil's Jig on Hallowed Ground." Hirschbach notes how the novel presents us with a complete catalogue of human relationships — shallow affairs, abnormal practices, hetero- and homosexual eroticism, coolly distanced ties, instinctual liaisons, prohibitions of love, self-imposed abstinence, caritas, and maternal bonding. We experience the whole gamut of Eros, with one glaring exception: a truly loving relationship. Can an artist like Leverkühn, cold and devoid of true affection, create anything emotionally moving in such a sterile and seemingly barren environment? This is a question that Hirschbach raises, but scrupulously avoids answering — except to point out that the novel concludes with a very tentative "no," for which there may never be a definitive "yes." In 1950 William Rey diagnosed the state of disease in Leverkühn stemming from his sexual relations with the prostitute; he also traced the sickness of the German nation and of Western civilization as a whole, manifest in the cultural malaise of the times. Mann labels the malady incurable — a grim prognosis, Rey finds, mitigated somewhat by an awareness of author's predilection for dialectical thought patterns. Therefore, the promise of a return to health may yet loom on the otherwise bleak horizon, akin to Zeitblom's concepts of "light in the night" or "hope beyond hopelessness" at the close of the *Dr. Fausti* cantata. On the other hand, a more clinical — one might even say cynical — perspective on disease is offered by Alfred Kaufmann in an article contained in the 1956 anthology of commemorative essays from the German Democratic Republic marking Mann's death in the preceding year. This sobering medical diagnosis might serve as a companion piece to the analysis of the psychological illnesses prevalent among the various echelons of society surrounding Adrian Leverkühn traced by P. M. Pickard in 1950. With regard to health of the psyche, the formulaic pronouncement regarding Mann's predilections for "myth plus psychology" (Gronicka, 1956) was to become a hallmark of scholarship for years to come, so that the increasing application of psychological analysis (or even of Freudian psychoanalysis) to the mythical Faust figure did not seem out of place.
Disease, death, the devil, dangerous liaisons, the demise of Western culture, and a deity *absconditus* — these are some of the main concentrations of research interest in *Doctor Faustus* during the era from 1947 to 1955. Since the impressions that emerge are rather dismal and seem slightly out of focus in spite of attempts at critical illumination, this initial section of the survey of secondary literature on the novel has been

given an epigraph from the thirteenth chapter of St. Paul's First Epistle to the Corinthians: "For now we see through a glass, darkly . . . . " Of course, the corollary to this pessimistic diagnosis (and one which follows immediately in the biblical text), is the prognosis that the future will bring greater clarification: "but then face to face: now I know in part; but then shall I know even as also I am known." The extent to which critical enlightenment was to shine upon and illuminate "face to face" the dark recesses of *Doctor Faustus* will become evident in the succeeding chapters. Whether or not our knowledge of the novel will ever attain the optimum level of complete elucidation predicted in the biblical passage above, however, seems destined to remain a moot point.

2: Elucidation through Archival Discoveries (1955–1975)

> *"I heard . . . the parable . . . of the man who carries a light on his back at night, which does not light him but lights up the path for those coming after."*
> (Doctor Faustus)

Setting the Scene

CRITICISM OF DOCTOR *Faustus* up to the death of the author in 1955 had been limited to either articles of a specialized nature or analyses of the work in the context of introductory studies of Mann's life and his overall œuvre. Helmut Koopmann (1990d: 950) makes the astute observation that there is a German academic tradition not to treat living authors, to which critical literature on Mann was certainly no exception. Therefore, scholarly research on this author in Germany began to acquire greater impetus and a more individual profile only after 1955. It was not until this date and the subsequent opening of the Zurich archive to scholars in the early 1960s that detailed monographs dealing exclusively with this novel in its own right began to appear — especially those concentrating on the investigation of sources, with special emphasis on Mann's techniques of montage or collage. In addition, in the late 1950s editions of the author's selected correspondence began to appear that would likewise open new vistas to *Doctor Faustus*. There come to mind in this regard the three volumes of Mann's letters edited by his daughter, Erika Mann (1962, 1963, 1965), as well as the publication of his correspondence with specific individuals during the years in which the novel was conceived and put to paper. Into the latter category fall Herbert Wegener's collection of Mann's letters to Paul Amann (1959), Inge Jens's edition of those to Ernst Bertram (1960), and Peter de Mendelssohn's compilation of the correspondence with the publisher Gottfried Bermann-Fischer (1973), to mention those with close ties to *Faustus*. One must also consider the discovery of a large packet of notes on the novel found in the author's home at Kilchberg in 1962 and dating from March through May of 1943, the initial months of the novel's gestation period. Even though

Mann's diaries, which also contained material relevant to the genesis of the novel, could legally be made public only after 1975, Hans Wysling did supply in 1965 a foretaste of what was to come later.

In addition to personal documentation noted above, comprehensive bibliographies of primary sources and secondary literature began to appear in 1959 (Bürgin), providing scholars convenient access to already published material as well as an overview of what their predecessors and contemporaries had written on a given aspect of *Faustus*. It was during this two-decade period prior to the centennial celebration of 1975 that several other seminal bibliographical compilations of Mann studies were published. Georg Wenzel catalogued the complete correspondence (1969); Klaus W. Jonas (1955) presented a very comprehensive account of Mann criticism from 1896–1955, organized chronologically by themes and genres; a second volume, compiled by Jonas with the assistance of Ilsedore B. Jonas, followed in 1967 and covered the period from 1954 to 1965 with a chronological listing of secondary works (also rectifying errors and filling some of the gaps from the earlier listing). For the German editions of his two bibliographies (1972, 1979), that extended coverage to 1975, Jonas employed a strictly chronological format throughout. In a compilation that appeared in the German Democratic Republic, Harry Matter recorded the secondary critical literature on Mann from 1896 to 1969 in two volumes (1972), and included many works from Eastern European sources. A third volume of Jonas's bibliography covering the period after 1975 and scheduled to be published in 1990, has not yet appeared in print.

Finally, one must also give at least partial credit for the tremendous upsurge of critical interest and activity surrounding Mann's *Doctor Faustus* from 1955 to 1975 to the competent and challenging surveys of scholarship published by Henry Hatfield (1956) and Herbert Lehnert (1969). On the other hand, the inventory of scholarship by Thomas Hollweck (1975) in the series bearing the auspicious title Literatur als Geschichte: Dokument und Forschung (Literature as History: Documentation and Research) was more general in approach and proved to be of less value for this specific account of *Faustus* criticism.

Religious-Theological-Philosophical Approaches

The theological-religious-metaphysical aspect that had stood at the forefront of early *Doctor Faustus* criticism because of Holthusen's pronounced condemnation of the novel's "world without transcendence" still occupied a place of prominence in the succeeding decades.

Holthusen himself subsequently modified and mollified his views somewhat in favor of other compelling features of the novel such as its depiction of homeland, homesickness and domestic disaster (alliterated effectively and etymologically in German by the phrase "Heimat, Heimweh und Heimsuchung," 1975: 95). The titles of selected essays make the persistence of the religious trend evident: "The Anti-Diabolic Faith. Thomas Mann's '*Doctor Faustus*'" (Enright, 1957); "The Theological Challenge of Mann's *Doctor Faustus*" (Simon, 1958); "The Role of Theological Themes in Thomas Mann's *Doctor Faustus*" (Peterson, 1966). Whereas Joachim Müller (1960) contends that the theological issue overrides the critique of the historicopolitical landscape in the novel, Herbert Lehnert (1966b) addresses the theological issue pragmatically with reference to two passages deleted from the original manuscript (for further deletions from the novel, see Blomster, 1964). Other studies confront different dimensions of the religious problem: "self-sacrifice of the spirit" by William Rey (1960), Gerd Schimansky's "angel of venom" and "anti-deific offer" (1962), Arieh Sachs's study of "religious despair of *Doctor Faustus*" (1964), and Hildegard D. Hannum's "self-sacrifice in *Doctor Faustus* (1974). Of course, demonic forces in the novel represent the obverse of the divine (Heller, 1959, 1962; Goll, 1975), but evil and Satan nevertheless constitute an integral and essential component of the theological design of the work. Even in the German Democratic Republic, a study such as Michael Schädlich's privately printed essay of 1964 on the ties between theology and music (later republished in an anthology of 1978) evinced abiding interest in religious-theological issues — a trend that abated in both East and West only in the post-1975 era.

From the philosophical-metaphysical perspective, two monographs deserve attention. The first of these, by Anna Hellersberg-Wendriner (1960), examines the entire corpus of Mann's work from the standpoint of man's essential aloofness or detachment from God, his nonparticipation in the divine essence, which leads to the depiction of a distorted world. But the critic uses a concept gleaned from *Doctor Faustus* — namely, that even apostasy can be construed as an act of faith — to shift the perspective into a positive mode. Since God is all-encompassing, He must incorporate even the breaking away from Him as a part of His all-embracing essence. Regarded in this light, Leverkühn's music, created in isolated subjectivity, might thus be considered a means of bridging the gap between the divine creator and the mundane creature. The strongly Catholic Hellersberg-Wendriner may be ascribing here a religiosity to the author above and beyond what he merits, since her seriousness of purpose prevents her from recognizing the significant role that irony occupies in Mann's scheme of things.

The second investigation is by Fritz Kaufmann, and the telltale subtitle, *The World as Will and Representation* (1957), reveals its ancestral roots in Schopenhauer. This is not a new premise by any means in the history of ideas, especially with regard to Mann, but Kaufmann is innovative in the manner in which he stringently applies Schopenhauer's antithetical concepts of Will (as a kind of immanent vitalism) and Representation (a transcendental absolutism), together with Mann's ironic mediation between them, to the chief figures in the author's major works. *Doctor Faustus* appears here under the rubric "Last Judgment," and the myth of a contemporary Faust is fused with the historical reality of the Third Reich, while the dilemmas facing Protestant theology become conflated with sinister demonology — premises that not every reader may be able to share without qualification.

Historical Perspectives

The allusion to the now almost clichéd concept of Leverkühn = Germany — or, in Kaufmann's even more radical and restrictive variation Leverkühn = Hitler's fascist Germany — calls to mind the historical rubric employed by numerous critics in coming to terms with Mann's novel. A pioneering voice in this direction was the historian and political scientist Kurt Sontheimer. In his book *Thomas Mann und die Deutschen* (Thomas Mann and the Germans, 1961), he sought to shed light on the conflict between the privileged exile who had basked in the California sunshine during the darkest days of the war and those inner émigrés who had experienced Germany's downfall firsthand (represented by such writers as Frank Thieß and Manfred Hausmann). Even though Sontheimer finds Mann's political concepts vague and oscillating, he maintains that the writer at least did not compound the problem by committing one blunder after another. The impression of Mann's totally misguided political stance arises because critics fail to distinguish between politically tinged statements in fictional texts as opposed to pronouncements on political topics in expository prose contexts or in personal documents — certainly a valid argument, but one that is not satisfactorily resolved by Sontheimer's exposé either.

There was a marked trend during the epoch of the 1960s and 70s (which witnessed the advent of student revolt at the universities in Germany as well as waves of terrorism directed at the establishment — political, social, educational, or whatever — followed by repressive governmental legislation to curb such dissent) to regard *Doctor Faustus* from the point or view of a Marxistically tinged dialectic. One might illustrate this tendency via Hans Mayer's (1959, 1966) clever chiasmus: "Endzeit des Romans" (the precarious modernity of the work signaling the "end of the novel") and "Roman einer Endzeit" ("the novel of an era coming to a close," with the work embodying the death throes of a moribund society, bound to the past but moving toward a brighter — socialist — future). The reciprocal interplay of dialectical forces was also articulated in terms of the tension between competing tendencies in the text (it is, for instance, both an artist novel and a novel about the age, Klussmann, 1978) or by means of a comparative-contrastive study of another postwar work such as Grass's *The Tin Drum* (Carlsson, 1964). The latter is felt to be a novel that tries to cope with the recent past in a different, more direct fashion.

There are numerous attempts to articulate, if not to resolve, other dichotomous reciprocities in *Doctor Faustus*; for instance, by regarding Leverkühn as either the representative of his epoch or the antipode to it (Michael Mann, 1965); realizing that the author's exegesis of his homeland's political demise may be more rhetorical than real (Trommler, 1970; Meixner, 1972); examining the "breakthrough" from a Romantic as well as chauvinistic perspective — and, consequently, in an ironic refraction (Siefken, 1971); viewing the historical process in terms of the traditional father-son conflict (Zeller, 1974); or interpreting specific incidents in the life of the musician as correlatives for key events in twentieth-century German history (Brode, 1973). In accordance with Brode's hypothesis, for instance, the composition of the *Apocalypsis cum figuris* (1919), following the apocalyptic war, would stand in analogy to the promulgation of the Weimar Constitution also of 1919, while Adrian's liaison with Marie Godeau (1925) could reflect the improving Franco-German relations after the Locarno Pact, which went into effect in 1925. These and other examples seek to make out of Leverkühn's personalized biography a personified German history. Not all the specific coincidences of chronology enumerated by Brode, however, prove convincing. Proceeding on a less specific basis, on the other hand, proves to be a more rewarding strategy, and Joseph. P. Stern (1975, 1979) examines the generalized concepts of history and allegory as they apply to *Doctor Faustus* . Stern maintains that history is a valid and integral component of literary study, and he uncovers metaphorical analogies for Germany's political developments in the "histories" of the musician and in the course of music history itself or that of Western culture as a whole. Stern regards the parallel pattern which derived from the original Faustian pact with the devil as a kind of consistent allegory for both politics and music. Yet even here, one grows suspicious of such overarching configurations when they are applied to diverse fields. The allegorical argument is at best approximate, not absolute. There are still too many ragged edges on Stern's otherwise well-made Procrustean bed. Finally, Dolf Sternberger, in a chiasmatic *salto mortale* entitled "Deutschland im *Doktor Faustus* und *Doktor Faustus* in Deutschland" (Germany in *Doctor Faustus* and *Doctor Faustus* in Germany: in Bludau, Heftrich, and Koopmann, 1977), a lecture given at the Munich symposium in the commemorative year, proceeds from Mann's own premise of a secret identity between Zeitblom and Leverkühn, noting that both figures also represent converging sides of German history and the German heritage. Sternberger makes the valid observation that "fatherland" is the final word of the novel and constitutes a verbal cipher that alliterates suggestively with the previously articulated "friend," thus forging an aural link between the two key entities — both in need of "grace" ("Gott sei euerer armen Seele gnädig, mein Freund, mein Vaterland," Mann: 676; "God be merciful to thy poor soul, my friend, my Fatherland," L-P: 510). Acknowledgment of the unholy alliance made by both the friend and the fatherland, however, does not necessarily preclude Zeitblom's love for either of them on the personal level — for the composer as well as for his country.

General Interpretations of Mann's Life and Works

In the wake of Mann's death in 1955 and the attempt to square the circle with regard to assessing his overall creative output, the number of major monographs increased dramatically. Hermann Kurzke reports in his incisive book *Thomas Mann. Epoche-Werk-Wirkung* (Thomas Mann. Epoch, Work, Influence, 1985b: 310) that, whereas only thirteen such comprehensive publications on Mann had appeared up to 1955, the number increased between 1955 and 1975 to seventy-four. This trend appears to be in keeping with that previously mentioned unwritten law cited by Koopmann (1990d) concerning taboos on critical accounts of living authors as opposed to open season with regard to deceased writers. The host of life-work studies was then complemented by several commemorative volumes of collected lectures, essays, and other contributions from the various scholarly symposia, conferences, congresses, and honorary celebrations held in 1975 (the results of which, however, were, in some cases, only published several years later). Between the chronological parameters of 1955 and 1975, there also appeared seminal monographs and investigations devoted exclusively to *Doctor Faustus*, especially with regard to sources — a development that has persisted to the present day and that does not seem to want to abate in our age of increasing specialization.

Heralding the numerous general surveys of Mann's life and works that began to appear in print immediately following the death of the writer was R. Hinton Thomas's short monograph of 1956, focusing on the major works from the standpoint of the "mediation of art." By this concept the critic presumably meant that the author mediated his vision via a precarious balance in his dualistic world view, hovering playfully (and ironically) above the contrasts and conflicts presented in his creative writing. The *Faustus* discussion, however, which also deals at length with Nietzsche's influence, does not seem to develop this central concern to any appreciable degree beyond that which others had already formulated. Hans M. Wolff, in his 1957 analysis written in the tradition of the history of ideas (which characteristically neglects the artistry and form of the work for the sake of its ideas, the intellectual content), traces the manner in which the writer overcame his initial nihilism as well as his Nietzschean bent. In this same vein, *Faustus* is seen as concluding on a brave note of defiance, preparing the way for "grace," which predominates in *The Holy Sinner*, and "love," which conquers all in *Felix Krull*. Thus *Faustus* is to be considered in terms of a continuum rather than in isolation — a valid and valuable insight.

Undoubtedly the single work on Mann that aroused the most critical attention during this time period — positive as well as negative — was Erich Heller's *The Ironic German* (1958), a provocative play with Nietzschean, Schopenhauerian, and Romantic ideas that nevertheless scrupulously avoids ever delineating its slippery central concern — the ironic stance ascribed to the writer. In an age of the "disinherited mind," Heller conjectures, man dwells in a fragmented, disintegrated universe and with no prospect of attaining absolute truth. Instead, he is forced to accept as a compromise subjective veracity and verification in order to make some sense out of the seeming senselessness of life. Under such compromising circumstances, art becomes for the protagonist of *Doctor Faustus* a means — indeed, the *only* means — of giving valid form to the hypercritical and divided modern consciousness. But the exhaustion of all artistic media in our modern age, together with the cultural sterility of this epoch, predispose an artist of Leverkühn's constitution for a pact with the devil, so that the transcendental vacuum (a concept that undoubtedly warmed the cockles of Holthusen's heart) is filled by the forces of evil, by the minions of Satan. The outcome can no longer be a Romanticized redemption of the world through the creative artist but is rather the damnation of that ill-fated artistic creator. Heller sees the tragedy of Leverkühn as being absolute, without even the hint of the transfiguration that Serenus, the benign narrator, perceives in the final high G of the cello at the conclusion of the *Weheklag*' or that Hans Wolff postulated via grace and love in Mann's subsequent novels.

Ingrid Diersen's analysis of the artist figure within the evolving realism of Mann's narrative (1959) reverberates with echoes of the Lukács-Fischer-Mayer school of socialist thought, though in much less subtle terms than those of her predecessors. According to this critical voice from the former German Democratic Republic, Goethe's Faust represents the prototypical individual of the rising capitalistic phase of society, whereas Mann's Leverkühn is the embodiment of the era of decline, the imperialistic Faust, whose pact has the paradigmatic function of signaling the downfall of capitalism and its class system. Diersen's subsequent monograph on Mann (1975), although a bit less heavy-handed, still toes the line of socialist realism in its basic formulations, dealing with the end of the bourgeois epoch and the critique of fascist-capitalist ideology. A similar situation obtains in the introductory study by Eike Middell (1966) and in the richly illustrated monograph of Theo Piana (1968), the latter doting on Mann's occasional positive statements on socialism and underplaying the actual complexity of his political stance. By the same token, Eberhard Hilscher's life-work account, published originally in 1965, initially had a strong socialist bent in the *Faustus* section, but the glancing blows against imperialism, capitalism, and megabusiness were progressively softened in successive editions so that by the ninth printing (1983), one can maintain that, as had been the case with Lukács and Mayer, adherence to Marxist doctrine is not necessarily incompatible with incisive literary criticism.

The tradition of the intrinsic or "close reading" approach to literature (according to which extrinsic factors such as authorial biography, philosophical trends, social forces, economic trends, and historical incidents are avoided in favor of the self-contained network of interrelationships articulated within the work itself), which came into vogue in the late 1940s under the aegis of the New Critics, still pervades the study of Mann's novels by Paul Altenberg (1961). Altenberg distills a cluster of recurring motifs (such as the hero as the "chosen" individual) and consistent formalistic principles (all derived from or related to musical concepts, as, for instance, the polyphonic interplay of motifs), which he traces through the entire corpus of Mann's major prose works, culminating in *Faustus*. But with Altenberg, the consequence of taking statements of fictional individuals as gospel truths instead of considering them in the overall context of the work in which they appear, proves a serious methodological drawback and results in conclusions that are pronounced apodictically but that, upon closer inspection, prove at best contradictory, at worst confusing. A decade later, Mann's novels were investigated by Herbert Anton (1972) in a fashion akin to that of Altenberg, using the terms "pattern" ("Schema") and "schemata" in place of the latter's "leading motif" ("Leitmotiv") or simply "motif." These schematic concepts are, in Anton's formulation, indicative of antithetical typologies: birth and death, promise and fulfillment, essence and appearance, myth and psychology, and many more. By operating between these contrasting pairs, however, the reality of life or "the real" makes itself manifest — an interesting premise that could well hold for *Faustus*, provided the reader can penetrate the dense, theoretical underpinnings of Anton's cerebral discussions. In Hermann Stresau's investigation of 1963, in which Mann is characterized as a perennial Grail seeker, the critic builds on ideational structures akin to those of the Altenberg-Anton school: major motifs such as the breakthrough to life are traced from early to late works. Indeed, the tendency to "break through" has long been acknowledged as a central concern in *Faustus* on various levels — politicohistorical, musical, and personal. In contrast to some earlier critics, Stresau regards this novel as far removed from Goethe (interesting in this regard also is Walter A. Berendsohn's article of 1967, "Thomas Manns Goethe-fernstes Werk *Doktor Faustus*," The Work of Thomas Mann Furthest Removed from Goethe: 'Doctor Faustus'), but Stresau scrupulously skirts the periphery of the author's political engagement, thereby relegating an important ingredient of Mann's work to an undeserved limbo. By way of contrast, Berendsohn's book of 1965 characterizes the author as an originally unpolitical writer who was compelled by circumstances to become a political advocate for humanity, especially in times of upheaval and unrest. *Faustus*, for instance, wages war against fascism, and Leverkühn's fate is unequivocally linked with the political destiny of the German people. Yet Berendsohn's justifiable concern for matters of form, which he examines by means of stylistic and structural analyses (sorely missed in most idea-based or thematically oriented studies up to now), paradoxically undermines his attempt to deal pragmatically for the fascist past — trying to understand the formalistic "how?" interferes with our appreciation of the ideational "what?"

Several monographs concentrating on Mann's career and creativity, such as that by Roman Karst (1970), prove to be either heavily biographical (in spite of Karst's provocative subtitle "Or the German Dichotomy,") or they are strictly introductory, written primarily for an audience seeking a general orientation (Stern, 1967; Feuerlicht, 1968). Other studies deal with certain problems in depth, but these may be topics that concern *Doctor Faustus* only peripherally (as, for instance, von Gronicka, 1970; but his collection of essays does include in the appendix, 181–83, a laudatory letter from Mann to von Gronicka in appreciation for the critic's aforementioned article of 1948 containing prolegomena to a reading of *Doctor Faustus*). Reginald J. Hollingdale, like Altenberg and Stresau, builds his study (1971) on a framework of recurrent motifs (decadence, irony, myth, crime, and sickness), but he also makes Nietzsche's nihilism and *amor fati* the centerpieces of the discussion. Nietzsche, of that fabled cosmic triumvirate or triadic constellation in Mann's life (the "Dreigestirn" which also included Schopenhauer and Wagner), exerted the most lasting influence, according to Hollingdale, so that *Faustus*, the "nihilistic monster" (45), readily falls into place under that rubric. Andrew White, in a succinct and unpretentious introductory monograph on Mann (1965), makes parody the common denominator of his discussion, a topic certainly not alien to *Faustus* research in spite of — or just *because* of — what White terms the novel's most serious theme: daring "speculation with sin as a way to win grace" (59).

The number of essays of a general nature dealing with *Doctor Faustus* that were published during the two decades from 1955 to 1975 was, if not exactly legion, then at least of sufficient quantity to receive only brief mention in a survey such as this. Some of these studies certainly have provocative titles: "The Greatest Dead Novel of our Age" (Welter, 1959) or "Art at the Edge of Impossibility" (Oates, 1969). Others either develop specialized problems already treated in earlier investigations, including the origins of the work (Mann, 1973; Kern, 1975; Hermsdorf, 1976), the crisis of the modern novel (Ruprecht, 1967), the reception of the work in a divided Germany (Pongs, 1966), or they are of a generalized nature (Wiemann, 1956; Buisonjé, 1957; Williams, 1959; Nemerov, 1960; Borcherdt, 1961; Poser, 1962; Willnauer, 1963; Tuska, 1965; Hwang, 1969). Valuable for its factual commentary is Georg Wenzel's postscript to the edition of *Doctor Faustus* published in the German Democratic Republic (1971). There are, as before, instructive articles suggesting how to teach *Doctor Faustus* on the advanced educational levels in Germany (Bantel, 1964), an issue that is not to be treated lightly or dismissed cavalierly, since that country was then, as now, struggling to come to grips with its recent past while awareness and acknowledgment of the full ramifications of the Holocaust experience — touched upon briefly but tellingly in the novel — still lay in Germany's future.

Themes, Genres, and Specialized Problem Areas

Not only did *Doctor Faustus* constitute an indispensable component in any general discussion of Mann's career, but the novel also found its way into studies that dealt (either in larger contexts or within the orbit of Mann himself) with thematic concepts, genre concerns, and specific problems (such as the extent of the author's indebtedness to tradition). Aside from books treating broad literary issues — Murray Krieger's probing of the tragic vision from a European perspective (1960), in which an entire chapter is devoted to *Faustus* — there are a number of stimulating thematic investigations of Mann in which the novel may sometimes play only an ancillary role, but one that augurs future potential. Such a work is George C. Schoolfield's compendium of musician figures in German literature (1956), in which Leverkühn's "appallingly tragic" fate (190) is compared and contrasted with that of his Romantic forerunners Berglinger and Kreisler. In the context of "great moral dilemmas," Henry Hatfield notes that Leverkühn could have compromised and saved his soul but, in the process, would have been untrue to himself: "Error and sin may be forgiven; a failure to live to the utmost of one's abilities would be the unforgivable, indeed, the inconceivable 'great refusal'" (1956; 97). In Ignace Feuerlicht's book on Mann and the boundaries of the ego (1966) the critic seeks to demonstrate ways in which these subjective limitations can be crossed, the frontiers of consciousness expanded, and the confines of the self transgressed. Among the remedies suggested are several that could be applied to *Faustus* to an even greater degree than Feuerlicht applies them: love (including its homoerotic variant in the Paul Ehrenberg-Rudi Schwerdtfeger connection), mythical identification (Leverkühn and his legendary progenitors), the notion of doubling (Adrian's mother, Elsbeth, and Mrs. Schweigestill), religion and mysticism, and role-playing. Klaus Hermsdorf's monograph on Mann's rogue figures and their contribution to the essence and structure of the comic element (1968) summarizes succinctly the plight of Leverkühn (in spite of sporadic dosages of socialist jargon and his claim that *Faustus* is essentially a rougueless work). Consequently, Hermsdorf's feeble attempt to link the protagonist with the rogue through Adrian's clever manipulations of the pact falls short of persuasive argumentation. Another thematic study based on a typological figure is that of Gisela Hoffmann (1974), who, like Altenberg before her, examines the "elect" or "chosen ones" among Mann's heroes but pays only lip service to Leverkühn as a candidate for this elite group, while weighing down her study with the outmoded jargon of "essentiality," frustratingly reminiscent of Heidegger's existentialist vocabulary.

Helmut Koopmann, who has published widely and well on Mann in general and on *Faustus* in particular but who, for valid reasons, omits this work from his early book on the development of Mann's "intellectual" novel with its "double optic" (1962), compensates partially for this lacuna with his later monograph (1975c) dealing with four "constants" in the author's works. In tracing one of these topics, the poet in exile, Koopmann concentrates on the dialogue with the devil in chapter 25 of *Doctor Faustus* as a means of showing how the horrors of the Nazi past might be dealt with in literature — since irrational behavior is not readily amenable to rational discourse. Koopmann makes the interesting point that Mann's dispute with National Socialism is invariably also a debate with his own German, middle-class, Romantic-aesthetic tradition. Perhaps this co-incidental overlap had been previously underplayed because of Mann's penchant for polyperspectivism, a technique compatible with his playfully serious urge to reveal and conceal simultaneously, to confide and to hide something at the same time. Another critic who was establishing an imposing reputation as a formidable Mann scholar, Eckhard Heftrich, published a major book in 1975 that, although focusing on the author's earlier novel — as its title *Zauberbergmusik* (The Music of the Magic Mountain) reveals — nevertheless paved the way for a full-fledged analysis of *Faustus* with the second volume, *Vom Verfall zur Apokalypse* (From the Decline to the Apocalypse), that appeared in 1982. The seminal concepts developed in the earlier study which have relevance for *Faustus* include "positive ambiguity" (200), the "Alexandrine novel of intellectual or spiritual development" (214) and the unique definition of literary musicality as a force through which ideas become integrated into a complex whole, a construct of universal relationships (3).

The genre issue with regard to Mann's novels in general and to *Doctor Faustus* in particular had been broached in 1967 by Jürgen Scharfschwerdt, who, as might be inferred from the title of his study of Thomas Mann and the tradition of the Bildungsroman, spoke of the work as a parody of this genre. In his view *Faustus* is to be regarded as a "negative fulfillment" of the form of the novel of intellectual and spiritual development (235) and as a deliberate "taking back" of such cultural landmarks as Goethe's *Faust* and *Wilhelm Meister* as well as of Mann's own earlier achievements in the field of the novel genre. If Scharfschwerdt predicts the demise or deconstruction of the longstanding Bildungsroman genre in *Faustus*, Gunter Reiss (1970) postulates for the same novel the restitution or rehabilitation of an older generic type, the allegory, but in a revised or renovated form that he labels "allegorization." In an age in which the coherence of things has been superseded by their dissolution and disintegration (in this regard, Heller's "disinherited mind" and Yeats's lament that "the center cannot hold" come to mind), the venerable Goethean concept of symbol has also been rendered invalid, since it presupposes a stable universe with correlations between the sign and signifier. Consequently, an appropriate substitute had to be found to suit the altered state of human consciousness. Rather than simply resuscitate "allegory" with its medieval or baroque ballast and the implication of disparity between signifier and the thing signified, Reiss proposes "allegorization." By this term he implies that the disjunction is certainly not completely eliminated but rather complemented by a reciprocity stemming from a narrative procedure deploying "structural musicalization" or a "musicalized structure" (anticipating Heftrich's later formulation). Quite often such an allegorizing procedure leads to an "autobiographical" narration, whereby the narrative ponders its own constitution and justification (a metafictional device reminiscent of the German Romantics' transcendental poetry). This latter technique definitely provides a fruitful approach to *Faustus* when one considers Zeitblom's recurrent excursions into the problems associated with the mere telling of his tale.

An entire monograph devoted to *Faustus* by Gérard Schmidt (1972) focuses on the unique, intrinsic "law of form" according to which the novel is constructed, as opposed to the approach of those who would interpret the structure of the work with reference to its biographical roots, to the historical framework, or to some even more extrinsic and idiosyncratic criteria. The formal key for Schmidt can be found in Adorno's negative dialectic, whereby Leverkühn's hyperreflectivity and his breakthrough experience actually represent a reversal, a falling back from enlightenment to myth. Therefore, this novel, which in mythical fashion relates the Faust-devil story, becomes itself an aesthetic critique of such remythicization: it is this kind of dialectical thrust and parry that constitutes the formal principle of the novel. The much-needed analysis of the formalistic laws underlying *Doctor Faustus* is, however, only minimally fulfilled by this densely textured, overly theoretical, and often terminologically opaque investigation in Adornoesque jargon. Like so many larger studies purportedly concentrating on a single facet of the work, Schmidt's monograph often loses sight of its central concern in an effort to cover a wide spectrum of interesting, but ultimately extraneous, matters (at least with regard to its announced topic). Gábor Bonyhai, on the other hand, undertakes a structural analysis of *Faustus* using semiotic principles and limiting the investigation to a consideration of the plot configurations and value systems presented in the novel (1974). The former encompass signs found early in Jonathan's experiments fusing the sensuous and intellectual, while the latter underscore the fact that the text endorses no absolutely positive nor negative values, but rather stresses the correlation of the relative and absolute. Robert Magliola (1974), building on the concept of the "magic square," seeks to link the thematic and formal structures of the novel to a dialectical mode of thinking which distinguishes genuine opposites (the purview of the humanist way of thinking) from the modality of an unmediated "polar unity" (whereby "truth embraces both poles simultaneously," 58).

In the early 1970s, two problem oriented works appeared that, in a sense, complement each other in their attempt to take stock of Mann's relationship to the traditions of the past by probing deeper than merely superficial ties. The earlier of these, Peter Pütz's anthology of 1971, reflects the views of diverse scholars and treats such subjects as the extent of Mann's indebtedness to his cosmic triumvirate or "Dreigestirn." This is certainly a germane issue for *Faustus* when one considers such questions as Schopenhauer's role in delineating the nature of mythical recurrence, the function of Nietzsche's cognitive perspectivism, and the evolution of Wagner's European image from that of decadent artist to a proto-Hitlerian figure, especially when the composer's persona is refracted through Nietzsche's skeptical lens. A related question pertains to the extent to which Mann's acquaintance with thinkers from the past is based on actual knowledge of their original works as opposed to his dependence on secondhand opinions, a filtered-down account mediated through critics and friends. Whereas the ties of Pütz's collection to *Faustus* are at best peripheral, those in Terence J. Reed's book on Mann's "uses of tradition" (1974) are seminal, even though *Faustus* forms only one building block in the critic's ambitious and imposing edifice: to examine the entire corpus of Mann's writings with reference to its roots in tradition and the manifestations of this literary legacy. Reed has pored over the Mann holdings of various archives with the proverbial fine-tooth comb in order to isolate the genetic process of evolution of works such as *Faustus* and to indicate just how the author used what he appropriated from the past to suit his own purposes. Reed goes far beyond mere source-hunting and identification, however. But his conclusions regarding *Faustus* — that it is the only one of Mann's works not to have undergone fundamental changes from its original conception in 1904 (except for the later interpolation of the political dimension) and that it deals less with the Faust myth than it does with disease and Dionysian intoxication (syphilitically induced euphoria producing an "apparently sacred transport," 402) — are daring. Some of Reed's bolder contentions may have proven vulnerable to the qualifications and criticisms they received in the press, but his book has weathered the storms of adversity well. Victor Lange's succinct but penetrating article on tradition and experiment in Mann (in Bludau, Heftrich, and Koopmann, 1977), delivered as a lecture in 1975 in Munich, isolates the author's mode of quotation as an interlacing array of cultural thought and beliefs, articulated in his sovereign but fundamentally traditional narrative voice. Lange finds this procedure different from that of Mann's avant-garde contemporaries who used quotations experimentally and primarily for their shock value.

The incorporation of quotations and other modes of intertextuality touches obliquely upon the unresolved question of language and style in *Doctor Faustus*. This is an issue that has proven both perplexing and frustrating for scholars, especially in view of such factors as Mann's ubiquitous gift for irony; his penchant for parody; and, in the case of this particular novel, the precarious status of the narrator, Serenus Zeitblom, a humanist who must deal in a humane fashion with an almost inhuman subject. Walter Müller-Seidel (1968) broaches the issue from the vantage point of language in its relationship to humanism in the novel, a topic that the intensive study of Mann's diction by Ulrich Dittmann (1969) also addresses in conjunction with the dilemma of the writer in an age of linguistic crisis and the breakdown of communication. Dittmann deals with our fading confidence in the verbal medium as an adequate or reliable means of expressing inner states of being or feeling ("Sprachbewußtsein") as opposed to our indulgence in preconfigured forms of speech ("Redeformen"). The latter do, indeed, articulate elements of common consensus, but they give rise in the individual to a state of tension stemming from his awareness of the discrepancy between such stereotypical verbal ciphers and any genuine expressions of emotion. What is puzzling about Dittmann's book is the contention that in *Faustus*, Mann overcomes his early skepticism toward language and finds a path to direct verbal articulation, culminating in an affirmation of genuine humanism in Zeitblom's closing lines. What about the narrator's periodic qualms and caveats concerning his ability — or inability — to tell his story? This complaint, which is announced on the opening page of the book, runs cantus firmus-like through the entire corpus of the work. The "last word" is yet to be spoken concerning the verbal craftsmanship of the author, an acknowledged virtuoso stylist par excellence of the German language, in this most complex work, one that forms the delicate nexus of so many conventions of Mann's style and convictions of his life.

The Study of Sources: Systematic and Speculative

Without a doubt, the most fertile field of research on *Doctor Faustus* during the decades from 1955 to 1975 was the discovery and dispensation of the extensive range of source works consulted by the author. Concomitant with this phase of scholarship, however, modifications arose toward his deployment of such devices as the montage technique. It was argued that rather than engaging in a noncreative, mechanical appropriation of material from extraneous sources, Mann carefully arranged and amalgamated what he borrowed into an aesthetically refined context. The period also saw some revamping of earlier lines of inquiry and investigation, as well as reinterpretation based on new evidence found in manuscript variants.

In the case of *Doctor Faustus*, there are clearly two studies that stand like sturdy pillars supporting the entire edifice of source-hunting and its proper place in the critical spectrum: Gunilla Bergsten's pioneering work of 1963 (subtitled in the English translation of 1969 *Sources and Structure of the Novel*) then reissued in a revised German edition of 1974, and Lieselotte Voss's *Die Entstehung von Thomas Manns Roman 'Doktor Faustus.' Dargestellt anhand von unveröffentlichten Vorarbeiten* (The Genesis of Thomas Mann's 'Doctor Faustus.' Illustrated on the Basis of Unpublished Preliminary Writings, 1975). Arching over this duo of seminal monographs dealing with the identification, evaluation, and disposition of sources are the initial volumes of the *Thomas-Mann-Studien* (Thomas Mann Studies), inaugurated by the first curator of the Zurich archive, Paul Scherrer (1967), in collaboration with Hans Wysling and continued by the latter when he became Scherrer's successor. The *Thomas-Mann-Studien* and their adjunct publications contribute to the unraveling of many a mystery surrounding Mann's integration of sources, even when they do not treat *Doctor Faustus* and its complex web of allusions per se (as is the case with Wysling, 1973; 1974).

When Gunilla Bergsten's Upsala dissertation was published in book form in 1963, it caused a sensation among Mann scholars. Having gained access to the actual books and documents in the author's personal library (many of them actually annotated by him), she was able to take giant strides in sorting out the bewildering maze of allusions and concealed quotations from, or paraphrases of, the eclectic array of texts incorporated into the novel. Bergsten also perused and commented on the 177 pages of typescript that had been omitted from the published version. Such meticulous detective work garnered for the researcher both accolades (for her pioneering efforts in uncovering and cataloguing correspondences) and negative reactions (Jørgensen, 1965, for example, believes she showed too slavish an adherence to archival data and acquiescence to the mechanics of the montage technique). By printing side by side excerpts from the sources and corresponding passages from the text of *Faustus*, Bergsten makes a persuasive case for the extent — if not the intent, the precise function or aesthetic significance — of the borrowings. But Bergsten does more than merely ferret out sources; she also offers a structural analysis of the novel and indulges in some interesting speculations. For instance, she is innovative in linking the musical structure of the entire work with the principle of the strict style. She demonstrates how Leverkühn's last composition, *Dr. Fausti Weheklag'*, which "reconstructs" two prehumanistic works (Monteverdi's *Lamento* and the chapbook of Dr. Faustus) and, at the same time "takes back" (or "deconstructs") two landmarks of the humanistic age (Beethoven's Ninth Symphony and Goethe's *Faust*), also functions as a symbolic replica in miniature of the entire novel. In the course of her investigation, Bergsten makes some discoveries that have staunchly stood the test of time — for example, how Adrian's life unfolds like a musical chord, akin to the chordal progression of the manifold time layers in the work. Not all of these theses were original insights by any means, as evidenced by Heinz Politzer's essay on time levels, for instance, which had appeared in 1959, and Frank C. Maatje's monograph on the duplication of time in the novel (1964), which was in press when Bergsten's book was in the process of publication. Other statements by Bergsten needed correction (the version of the chapbook used by Mann was not that of Scheible from 1841 but rather that of 1911, edited by Robert Petsch), modification (Zeitblom's allusion to himself as an old man — "ein alter Mann" — considered by Bergsten to be a concealed pun on the author's name), or clarification (for instance, what was meant by her off-hand use of such commonplace literary period designations as Naturalism?). Many of these were modified or eliminated in the second edition. Nevertheless, the Rubicon had been crossed; a foolproof case had been made for the categorical imperative of an obligatory research journey to the Zurich archive as the backbone for all future *Doctor Faustus* scholarship. In a word, research on this novel would never be the same after Gunilla Bergsten had left her imprint on the profession. As a matter of fact, the two major volumes discussed above by Pütz and Reed dealing with Thomas Mann and "tradition" might even be considered direct or indirect descendents of Bergsten's challenging excursion into the terrain from which the author's work had drawn its roots.

For her 1975 study of *Doctor Faustus*, Lieselotte Voss was able to consult considerably more archival material than had been previously available to Bergsten for her investigation (Mann's diaries, however, remained under lock and key until 1975 by a proviso in his will). For instance, Voss studied the author's two hundred pages of preparatory notes for the novel (discovered at Mann's Kilchberg residence in 1962 but not published until 1975) as well as pages excluded by Mann from his own not infrequently obfuscating 1949 account of the genesis of the novel. In her assessment of the sources of *Faustus*, Voss attempts to reconstruct how major components of the text were originally constructed, including such diverse aspects of the novel as geographical locations; major and minor figures; interrelated time planes; Adrian's key compositions; quintessential chapters such as the "pact" scene, the protagonist's "dialogue" with the devil, and Leverkühn's concluding confession. Voss's prime intention is to counter the old prejudice that Mann was primarily an uncreative craftsman, a calculating artisan (5) who simply incorporated material found in such "real" sources as reference books, newspapers, periodical essays, book reviews, literary articles, scientific reports, and even personal correspondence (Tillich, 1965) into a sophisticated German prose context. Instead of merely compiling his data in card-file fashion, juggling the file-cards, and inserting the excerpts into the text at the proper juncture, Mann, according to Voss, coordinated the various source materials associatively. He transposed them from one context to another and melded them intuitively into a multifaceted yet unified aesthetic totality — for which operation the bland concept "montage" proves inadequate. Although Voss does not substitute another term for this operation or its product, the designation "mosaic" might perhaps better suit this associative and intuitive operation. Some of Voss's findings border on the startling: for instance, her demonstration of how unreliable much of Mann's account in *The Story of a Novel* actually is, with certain statements comprising deliberate detours or stratagems of deception, while others purposely withhold essential information. By the same token, her own unflinching confidence in the complete veracity of what the Kilchberg notes contain (245) may itself be misplaced. Should one not assume that Mann intended these materials to be found and thus edited or emendated them accordingly? Otherwise, why did he not destroy them as he did portions of his correspondence and diaries? And, too, the notes cover a two-month period at the outset of the writing phase of *Faustus*; what about later changes in plans or articulation because of the intervention of technical advisers such as Adorno? At times, however, Voss's conjectures provide genuine food for thought. For example, her hypothesis that Mahler (who had used excerpts from Goethe's *Faust* for his Eighth Symphony and portions of Nietzsche's *Zarathustra* for his Third) might be a viable candidate for the Leverkühnian lineage, or the extent (unacknowledged by Mann) to which Igor Stravinsky's memoirs had been consulted and conscripted. These and other contentions elicited positive responses in later years (Guibertoni, 1978; Maar, 1989).

Ad Fontes: Other Source Seekers in the Age of Intertextuality

Already in the wake of Bergsten's book — not necessarily as a direct result of its approach but perhaps as an indirect by-product of its success — the number of *Faustus* source studies increased dramatically during the subsequent decades. Coincidentally, the year 1963 (in which Bergsten's investigation appeared) saw the advent of another monograph, by Sigrid Becker-Frank, which deals in part with the same general subject Bergsten treats — the integration of quotations into the novel (perhaps an offshoot of Herman Meyer's pioneering 1961 study of intertextuality) — but which pales in comparison with its rival for thoroughness and breadth of background research. Of course, the traditional quests for literary sources of influence by means of stylistic-thematic comparisons and parallels with other authors or specific works continued unabated. These include some old standbys already catalogued by Bergsten such as Goethe (Müller, 1961), Paul Valéry (Charney and Charney, 1962; Pfaff, 1975, 1976), Dostoyevsky (Seghers, 1963; Jehl, 1975), James Joyce (Egri, 1966), Hans Christian Andersen (Plard, 1967; Fass, 1972), and Kleist (Reiss, 1969), as well as fledgling nominees not directly traceable to Bergsten's impetus: Lessing (Stout, 1963), Jean Paul (Moses, 1956, 1972), Joseph Conrad (Kaye, 1957; Viswanathan, 1974), Gabriele Reuter (Kreuzer, 1963), Ibsen (Pache, 1973a), Oskar Panizza (Vaget, 1975), and Walter Benjamin (Martin Müller, 1973). The latter study, for instance, notes that Mann received as a gift from Adorno a copy of Benjamin's *Der Ursprung des deutschen Trauerspiels* (The Origin of the German Tragedy) in which such topics as the hellish stage laughter of the actor, the use of the echo effect in a baroque drama dealing with the martyr Johannes von Nepomuk, and the concept of the transcendency of despair are treated. All these subjects find resonance in *Faustus*. Such coincidences may constitute circumstantial evidence but they are compelling by virtue of the striking affinity they have to the intricate networking of motifs in *Doctor Faustus*.

Close scrutiny of names of the Halle figures in the novel such as Kumpf, Deutschlin, Arzt, and many others leads one source-seeking critic back to a book on the German Renaissance sculptor and woodcraftsman, Tilman Riemenschneider (Kolb, 1970). Hans-Joachim Schoeps (1970), a leader of a youth movement in the early 1930s and a principal writer for the periodical *Die freideutsche Position* (The Free-German Position) during that same period, confirms a suspicion of Bergsten (also expressed by Floquet, 1972) that this conservative newspaper provided one source (another being the previously noted Tillich letter published in 1965) for the musings of the Halle student group called Winfried. Yet Schoeps emphatically stresses Mann's "anachronistic" integration of this material, no doubt a facet of the author's manipulation of the montage-mosaic principle. Also, following up on a comment of Bergsten, Margaret Klare (1975) pursues what she terms a "literary reminiscence" — the thematic and narrational links of *Faustus* to André Gide's *Les Faux-Monnayeurs* of 1927. Klare isolates similarities as well as differences; she points out that both major books are accompanied by an explanatory volume by the respective authors that contains a personalized account of the origins and attending circumstances of the main work (but note that Mann's subtitle, "Roman eines Romans" or the "novel of a novel," implies the "fiction of fiction," not necessarily the "facts of fiction" or the facts of his life). Gide and Mann also employ a problematic self-reflective narrator; they both dote on diabolic overtones and figures, and their works even evince striking resemblances in specific verbal formulations.

Picking up on a passing reference to William Blake in Bergsten, Walter Pache (1973b) examines the eccentric English Romantic's strangely beautiful poetry ("The Sick Rose," "The Poison Tree," and so on) with reference to the images cited or verses quoted in the novel and their possible plot ramifications (such as the syphilitic infection constituting a deadly love poison). Mann's acquaintance with Blake was secondhand, transmitted via his son-in-law, W. H. Auden, and reenforced by a study of Gide by Klaus Mann, the author's son (*André Gide and the Crisis of Modern Thought*, 1943), which stressed the pervasive influence of Blake on contemporary writers. Bergsten's extensive treatment of Dante's works and their impact on *Faustus* builds on an earlier essay about the author of the *Divine Comedy* by Erich Berger (1957) and is itself augmented by Lea Ritter-Santini (in Bludau, Heftrich, and Koopmann, 1977), who argues that Dante's Christian cosmos is a key concept in the theological coordinate system of *Faustus*. However, as Vaget later comments in a survey of Mann scholarship (1980: 282), making the Catholic cosmic hierarchy central in a novel that is so thoroughly Protestant in spirit was no easy matter for the author and may be difficult for the critic to accept. Bergsten's probing of the impact of Shakespeare (in view of Mann's disclosure that he had read Frank Harris's *The Man Shakespeare and His Tragic Life Story* while working on *Faustus*), provided food for thought for other scholars, especially with reference to the early comedy *Love's Labour's Lost*, that is so significant for Adrian's development as a composer. Interestingly enough, a husband-and-wife team, Siegfried and E. M. Puknat, were among the first (1967) to examine this comedy about the amorous games people play and to pursue similarities between the careers of Adrian and the English bard ("a potential and possibly blasphemous equation," 149). Even though they are somewhat critical of Leverkühn's appropriation of the libretto for his opera (he wears a "borrowed halo,"149), the Puknats demonstrate effectively why this particular play was an ideal choice as a text by the composer: the dominant parodistic element — especially the parody of humanism together with the irony implicit in Zeitblom's eventual collaboration on a work that mocks the very humanistic tradition for which he stands. Shakespeare also develops the contrast between barbarism and humanism, and his recurrent references to the allure of the eye and to its malevolent counterpart, the "evil eye," have reverberations in *Faustus*. The same play with its constellation of characters and plot mechanisms (love triangles, proxy wooing, and the like), its themes (culture and barbarism, ironized in Shakespeare but treated with utmost gravity in Mann), and the stress placed on certain unique physical traits (black eyes, dark complexion) induced Jeffrey Meyers (1973b) to pursue the parallels in further detail. This line of inquiry continued to attract critical interest and retained a prominent place in the 1975–1992 phase of research.

Sometimes it is the smallest, seemingly most inconsequential textual detail rather than larger contextual components (such as in Sagave's 1970 comparison of the classical world and the modern mind in *Faustus*) that proves most captivating for the reader when a critic goes source hunting on the basis of either archival evidence or ingenious speculation. One might cite in support of this contention the aforementioned, incisive article by Victor Oswald that deciphered, apparently for all time, one of the novel's deepest mysteries of concealed identity (Hetæra = von Tolna). In that same vein, Calvin S. Brown uncovers an entomological source for the poisonous species of butterfly (1962), Hetæra's lepidopterous counterpart. Fresh insights into one aspect of the novel are provided by a bit of enterprising literary detective work in Wesley V. Blomster's article (1975), derived from textual evidence alone but supported by some clever deductions on the part of the critic-sleuth. He regards the scene depicting Frau Schweigestill holding the unconscious Leverkühn on her lap as a kind of literary rendition of the pietà, an iconographic concept that lends endorsement to the view that Christian grace does become a dominant force as the novel draws to a close. As some later critical forays based on ingenious conjectures will demonstrate (for instance, those of Oskar Seidlin, 1983a), it is often just this type of educated guessing or imaginative, associative thinking which sparks reader interest to a greater degree than the cut-and-dried search for sources in the realia of biographical data, in the mass of material from archives and the author's personal documentation, or even in the discovery of overt and covert literary parallels — as scholarly and scientific as these forms of source research might otherwise be.

The status of Mann's adaptation of the Faust legend in the vast panoply of Faustian world literature (Schwerte, 1962) and the standing of the novel within the corpus of twentieth-century versions of that tradition (Henning, 1963) continued to be topics of interest with strong source-related affiliations. But no other work in the spectrum of world or German literature could seriously challenge the original chapbook of 1587 as the focal point of concentration and comparison. Erich Heller, for instance, in an article which treats the "morality of knowledge" within the Faust tradition (1959a), claims that Leverkühn not only rewrites or, better, "unwrites" Beethoven's Ninth, but also that Mann actually revokes Goethe's *Faust*. The novel thus becomes a reflection of the original "damnation of Faust" and a refutation of Faust's intervening Goethean liberation. With minor exceptions (Birven, 1956), however, the prime mover in connecting the Dr. Faust of 1587 with Dr. Faustus of 1947 proved to be Dietrich Assmann, who initially, in a 1967 article, hurled down the gauntlet to scholars by challenging prevalent opinion and labeling the material Mann derived from the Volksbuch as mere "subordinate motifs." This view was substantiated to some extent by Käte Hamburger (1969), who found it anachronistic to apply aspects of the original Faust legend (reckless striving, sins against the theological world order, or falling away from God) to a modern composer whose psychic disposition and creative sterility are totally independent of the Faustian dilemma. The only concession Hamburger makes to the tradition is to admit that the novel does contain diabolic symbolism (but not the devil per se, as in earlier versions of the Faust tale), and she undergirds this thesis by noting that Mann himself quite often referred to the work as a novel of the devil ("Teufelsroman") rather than a Faust novel (147). Arguing from the opposite end of the spectrum, J. W. Smeed (1975) posits a convincing parallel between Dr. Faustus's speculating in the elements and the musical speculations of his modern counterpart. Smeed himself speculates as to why Mann may have abandoned Goethe in favor of the "naive model" (127): to escape from a Goethean dependence that had trammeled so many writers in the nineteenth century; to insure "that his Faust had none of the chauvinistic overtones that Goethe's had acquired, especially in the 1930s;" and to "disassociate himself from the optimistic message" of his predecessor (127). Assmann wrote a second essay treating "Faustus Junior," now from the standpoint of mythical identification with Faustus's forerunners (1971), and this was followed by the publication of his doctoral dissertation (1975), which did enumerate in detail links between Mann's novel and the Faust tradition, including — somewhat paradoxically, given his previous position — over a hundred pages on the novel's close ties to the *Faustbuch*. According to this critic, the motifs taken from the chapbook have basically a structural function for the novel (200), while thematically, the concept of grace — for which a Novalis quotation may have actually been the inspiration — becomes a dominant concern. One of the unique aspects of *Doctor Faustus* that distinguishes it from the chapbook, Assmann asserts, stems from the loss of clear-cut concepts and values ("Eindeutigkeit"). This definitiveness has been superseded by ambiguity and ambivalence ("Zweideutigkeit"), a condition that can even result in the paradoxical identity of opposites. Whereas the latter has proven to be a controversial issue (Kirsch, in Wenzel, 1962), one must concede that Mann himself did add fuel to the fire by speaking of the "secret of their identity" ("Geheimnis ihrer Identität") when alluding in the *Story of a Novel* to the Dionysian protagonist and his Apollonian biographer. In addition, the major original compositions of Adrian likewise operate on a principle of the "Geheimnis der Identität" (Mann: 502), a concept, which according to Mann's dialectical thought processes, maintains that every idea subsumes its converse: Kirsch's investigation into "making unlike the like" ("Verungleichung des Gleichen," Mann: 502) is a variant of this premise.

In a subsection of Bergsten's book entitled "Settings," this critic had inaugurated a trend to pinpointing actual geographical sources for some of the localities and landscapes depicted in *Doctor Faustus*. A short time before Bergsten (1962), Károly Kerényi (the Hungarian philologist and religious scholar, who ostensibly induced Mann to pursue the study of myth) had made the town of Palestrina the focal point of an attempt to uncover the biographical background for many details in the novel. A comprehensive account by Ilsedore Jonas (1969) of Mann's sojourns in Italy and his encounters with Italian intellectuals does not yield insights of any great magnitude for an understanding of the *Faustus* novel (aside from stressing the author's qualms about the seductive nature of southern climes as well as his lifelong susceptibility to this *bellezza*). But the trend to focus on topographical features had become an established modus operandi (for instance, Voss has a section called "constitution of scenes," 43–73) and was fostered especially by Hungarian critics bent upon disclosing Mann's ties to their homeland — Antal Mádl's study of two "Danubian chapters" of the novel (1971) and Istv·n Varga's exposé of the poverty-stricken Hungarian village near the lush estate of Frau von Tolna (1972) being cases in point. Perhaps it was the nurturing of this local interest together with Mann's popularity in Mádl's native land that later gave rise to a major anthology containing the contributions of that country's leading scholars *Thomas Mann und Ungarn* (1977), jointly edited by Mádl and Judit Györi. By the same token, the linking of Pfeiffering, where Leverkühn spends his most productive years, to the German verb "pfeifen" ("to whistle") by H. J. Dill (1971) seems at first glance inconsequential. But the numerous key instances of whistling in the text (Schwerdtfeger's skill in this activity, the summoning of the dog Kaschperl, whose very name has diabolic overtones — even calling to mind the sardonic whistling of the devil at the close of Boïto's *Mefistofele*) further contribute to the view of a fictional context in which there is "no free note" (36)

Biographical and Autobiographical Backgrounds

Certainly Bergsten was not the first nor Voss the last to argue in depth for Nietzsche as the main mythic-biographical prototype for Leverkühn. Virtually every study of the novel makes overt or covert reference to the philosopher in conjunction with the high- and lowlights of Adrian's career. In fact, the year of Bergsten's study also saw a major publication in this vein — Peter Pütz's book on verbal artistry and the artist's modus vivendi in Nietzsche and Mann (1963a), together with his article on the philosopher's aesthetically effective but morally irresponsible perspectivism as constituting a form of deviltry (1963b). Pütz's principal investigation examines how Nietzsche's epistemological or cognitive perspectivism (which accounted for so many of his contradictory pronouncements on the same subject) becomes, in Mann's hands from *Tonio Kröger* to *Doctor Faustus*, an aesthetic form of perspective, a changing optic affecting the manner of perceiving, describing, and narrating. *Faustus*, then, represents the apex of this technique, in which the author aims at creating an all-encompassing complex of interrelationships through a polyvalent narration, with Mann himself assuming the familiar medial stance, one that enables him to mediate between the otherwise rigid antinomies. Hubert Mainzer (1971), though casting doubt on whether or not *Faustus* is truly a Nietzsche novel, nevertheless takes up Pütz's line of argumentation by finding correlations between Nietzsche's doctrine of an epistemological perspectivism, which questions objective truth, and Mann's montage technique, which establishes coordinates of interrelations but defies definitive interpretation (the famous formulaic equation that relationship is the equivalent of ambiguity; "Beziehung = Zweideutigkeit," Mann: 66). Whether or not an "eternal recurrence" manifests itself in the Buchel-Pfeiffering parallel, however, as Mainzer implies, is a dubious point. Further refinements or modifications of the Nietzschean image as reflected in *Doctor Faustus* come to the fore in an essay by Elrud Kunne-Ibsch (1969), which finds elements of the philosopher's personality not only concentrated in Leverkühn, but also distributed between Zeitblom and the devil. This tripartite division justifies the designation of the work as a genuine Nietzsche novel. In fact, the critic suggests that the differences in the early stages of development between the philosopher-critic and the fictitious composer actually outweigh the similarities and that the ties of the young Nietzsche to Zeitblom are stronger. It is only later, when Leverkühn becomes diseased and isolated, that his lifestyle begins to parallel that of Mann's spiritual mentor, while many of the devil's pronouncements on art do resemble a Nietzschean "transvaluation of all values." Finally, Ferruccio Masini, at a 1975 symposium in Bochum (in Klussmann and Fechner, 1978), broached the subject of Mann's growing estrangement from Nietzsche's nihilistic views and his gradual espousal of ethics over aesthetics, of logocentrism (a humanistic credo embodied in Zeitblom) as opposed to melocentrism (the Dionysian temperament and creative force). However, Masini correctly qualifies his own neat pattern when he conjectures that even the bourgeois humanist Zeitblom has a proclivity to be seduced by the demonic nature of music, so that the hypothetically clear-cut dualism of logocentrism versus melocentrism is marked by that persistent ambiguity that invades and pervades virtually every other facet of the novel.

One of those nagging ambiguities, for instance, was the secret identity postulated by the author himself between his Faustian protagonist and the humanist-narrator. As a result of this contention, the stature and status of Zeitblom became focal points of scholarly concern (in this regard, an inauspicious note was sounded by Helmut R. Boeninger, who in 1959 labeled Serenus a spiritual descendent of Goethe's pedestrian academic, Wagner, and of the composer Wagner's pedantic Beckmesser), as did the question of his capability of telling his story effectively. Three larger studies from the 1960s treat the above issues with contrasting results. Two of these address the proximity of the demonic and the humanistic in the text. The first, by Ilse Metzler in 1960, argues that since Zeitblom and Adrian share a common identity, they both embody the decline in strength of German mental and spiritual values. The second study, by Hubert Orlowski (1969), disputes the authority of Zeitblom, who, rather than merely reporting on the false consciousness of Leverkühn, actually represents false consciousness. An entirely new and challenging dimension is then introduced when Orlowski conducts a structural analysis of the novel and discovers a number of links to the medieval hagiography or life of a saint. Evidence adduced for the hagiological substructure includes the appearance of stock rhetorical figures such as the *captatio benevolentiae* (for instance, feigned modesty on the part of the narrator), the stereotypical plot patterned on the vita of the holy figure, and the reverential attitude of Zeitblom toward his subject. The last of the trio of Zeitblom-oriented investigations is by Margrit Henning (1966), who examines the first-person narrative in a wider context, with *Faustus* serving as the line of demarcation between the older tradition (the concept of narration as a formal, compositional principle, a refractive procedure that creates tension and humorous effects or qualifies values) and the new (as an indispensable aesthetic principle and, in this instance, the sole means to achieve the aim of the work: "only through the refraction of Zeitblom can the impenetrable personality of Leverkühn gain form in all its shimmering ambiguity," 158).

Aside from these extensive examinations of Zeitblom as Leverkühn's (and Mann's) other self and his ultimate function in the novel, several shorter studies touch upon topics related to narratology (Heller, 1958b; Barbu and Deleanu in *Sinn und Form*, 1965; Henze, 1965; Honsa, 1974 and Hage, 1976), the most provocative of which is probably the last mentioned analysis. Volker Hage considers the novel as primarily Janus-faced: it is traditional insofar as it has a closed structure and uses montage in an antimodern fashion (a view akin to Lange's aforementioned juxtaposition of tradition and experiment). But it is modern to the extent that there is a deliberate ironizing of Zeitblom and his alleged objectivity (as in his verbatim accounts of long conversations at which he was never present). This tactic fundamentally undermines the notion of a completely trustworthy and reliable first-person narrator, one of the last bastions of a plausible narrative voice and a coherent view of the world. Far from being modern in the sense of *Ulysses*, however, *Faustus* looks backward conservatively to a greater degree than it looks forward innovatively.

The second historical personage (in addition to Nietzsche) who functions prominently in Bergsten's analysis of source figures and whose originally tarnished image in Mann's oeuvre ultimately improved with the passage of time was Martin Luther. Pierre-Paul Sagave offers a preliminary synoptic view of Lutheranism in *Faustus* (in *Sinn und Form*, 1965), but this was superseded in the same year by a sweeping account of Mann's attitude toward Luther by Herbert Lehnert in his major study (1965; the Luther section in this book was reprinted with slight changes to accommodate the format of an anthology of essays in the third volume of a series of Thomas Mann studies, published under the auspices of the East German Thomas Mann Circle, Lehnert 1966a). Lehnert is concerned with a clarification of the concepts of fiction, myth, and religion in Mann's work, toward which goal he spent endless hours of painstaking research among the documents in the Zurich archive. Under the rubric of religion (a term that, in Mann's case, was blurred by theological confusion), Lehnert focuses on the author's changing image of Luther from his depiction of him as "national" figure in the *Betrachtungen eines Unpolitischen* (Observations of a Non-Political Man) to the unfavorable portrayal of the reformer and representative of the German spirit in the essays after 1933 and finally, toward the end of Mann's life, to a more positive assessment. Predictably, it was Nietzsche who initially determined Mann's attitude, inducing him to see in Luther an uncouth individual, a genial yet stubborn boorish man. These and a host of other unflattering qualities dominate the author's initial portrayal of Luther, in spite of the fact that Mann had been conditioned in his youth by orthodox German Protestant thought. The negative opinion, which he acquired second-hand rather than from original research, persisted even in *Doctor Faustus* (as seen in Kumpf, among others, a cruel and crude caricature). It seemed to mellow only in the writer's final years, when Mann placed less stock in humanism and more in the concept of grace and, as a result, revised his attitude toward the reformer. At the time of his death, Mann was still working on a play, *Luthers Hochzeit* (Luther's Wedding), originally conceived as a comedy but subsequently made more serious in tone, in which the father of the Reformation was to appear in a more favorable light. The Luther section of Lehnert's study retains the difficult term — introduced earlier in his 1965 text — of "dynamic metaphysics," a kind of Nietzschean derivative which implies a critical disavowal of fixed orientations. This leads to doubts concerning the viability of absolute constituents and to the fostering of structural components with manifold and shifting relationships. The upshot of this procedure is a "literary work that regards itself as free of all normal orientation factors in the real world, as long as it remains within the framework of its self-delineated structures" (61).

Under the rubrics "Nietzsche and Inspiration through Disease" and "Further Diseased Geniuses," Bergsten had named a number of reputedly syphilitic composers — Beethoven, Schumann, Hugo Wolf — and other luminaries ostensibly infected by sexually transmitted illness — Nietzsche and Kierkegaard, among them — who might have served as full or partial models for Leverkühn's deliberately self-inflicted malady. As noted earlier, the alliance between sickness and art was nothing new in Mann's writing nor in *Faustus* research. However, the radical type of venereal incursion portrayed here together with its devastating effects on the body (but uplifting force for the mind) did constitute an innovative idea and had attracted attention at an early date (Rey, 1950; Alfred Kaufmann, 1956), even before Bergsten even broached the subject. But neither of the two post-Bergsten studies devoted to this issue — Cecil A. Noble's investigation of the nexus of sickness, crime, and creativity in Mann's work (1970) and Fernand Hoffmann's analysis of the author as a philosopher of disease (1974) — proved particularly edifying for *Faustus*. Noble is basically psychoanalytical in his Freudian approach, regarding Adrian as a neurotic artist who does not suppress his drives but rather sublimates them in a creative process that blurs any distinctions between the "healthy-divine" and the "diseased-diabolic" (210). Noble adds parenthetically that Mann himself was also suffering from a debilitating illness while completing the novel. Hoffmann belongs to the structuralist school of interpretation and correctly claims that questions dealing with the affinity between creativity and sickness must be answered within the fictional structure of the work itself. However, conclusions such as the following do not add substantially to our fund of knowledge: an artist of Leverkühnian proportions participates in both the darker forces from below and in the sources of light from above (206). Hoffmann simply falls short of resolving the issue he raises so provocatively.

Thomas Mann was not the type of author to write passionate love scenes; the essence of the erotic realm in the form of a torrid romance between a man and woman somehow eluded this writer's fictional grasp. The publication of Mann's diaries after a legally mandated twenty-year hiatus following his death gave some insight into why this might have been the case. Heterosexual love was haunted by the skeleton of homosexual proclivities in the closet of Mann's consciousness. Those researchers who ventured into this uncharted area without full knowledge of Mann's sexual orientation (Hirschbach, for example) did not exactly experience calm seas and a prosperous voyage. The results of these early excursions into Eros are, as far as *Doctor Faustus* is concerned, unrewarding. Of course, one might argue that in a novel of which a basic premise is that love and any form of the erotic that entails human warmth are forbidden to the protagonist, it would be quixotic to seek anything but unsatisfactory male-female relationships. Yet given the nature of Leverkühn's pact, it is clear that the stigma of disease of a sexual nature is an essential feature of the bargain. David Myers's broad survey of love ranging from the erotic to *caritas* in Mann (1969) does set the general parameters within which the author operates even in *Faustus*, but this short essay is only cursory and preliminary. On the other hand, Inta Ezergailis's detailed monograph (1975) on the dialectic of the male principle and female force operative in Mann's work (not simply as the interaction between men and women, but rather the essential interplay of masculinity and femininity) holds the promise of an analysis in depth. Ezergailis implies that this fundamental polarity should, under ideal circumstances, culminate in a reciprocal, mutually rewarding and enriching relationship. The metaphors from the novella *Death in Venice* of the clenched fist as opposed to the open hand might, as Ezergailis suggests, be taken as the objective correlatives for the masculine and feminine attitudes respectively. Mann's ideal sexual orientation, it would seem, turns out to be a kind of bisexuality or androgyny, but in his prose fiction he appears to prefer sexual ambivalence — the men will appear male in relation to one person, female in respect to another; a similar pattern, only in reverse, holds for women. With regard to *Doctor Faustus*, Leverkühn is considered by Ezergailis to be the embodiment of the male syndrome exclusively. Such total captivity in the domain of the masculine is bound to fail if love is at issue, since this human emotion requires a reciprocity of the two contrasting orientations in order to achieve a sense of fulfillment or completeness. Adrian was, to be sure, a clenched fist in many respects, but did that rigid hand gesture not relax in varying degrees with regard to Marie Godeau, Rudi Schwerdtfeger, and Nepomuk Schneidewein? And what about postulating some degree of latent affection even in the fleeting affair with Hetæra Esmeralda, or in the maternal ties binding Adrian to Elsbeth and her Bavarian surrogate? The manifest shortcomings of the investigations of Eros up to 1975 were more than compensated for in the 1980s by the flood of studies devoted to the phenomenon of love in every conceivable form.

Music, Musicians, Musicianship, Musicality, Musicalization

Even though two substantial monographs on the role of music in Mann and in *Doctor Faustus* appeared during the period from 1955 to 1975 (Zmegac 1959; Carnegy, 1973), it was again Gunilla Bergsten who could be considered the leading voice in the chorus of those dedicated to ascertaining the proper perspective from which to regard the significance of this art form in and for the novel. In 1959 she led a pioneering foray into the field by examining the musical symbolism in *Faustus* (Michael Mann's article of 1956 bears a similar title but is more of a personal reminiscence than an analytic study), presenting a statistical survey of the musicians, musical instruments, and musical epochs treated in the novel. Her main point, however, is that Beethoven represents the iconoclastic, Faustian man of the Romantic age, an heir to the Reformation's Dr. Faustus and a fitting progenitor of the modern musical Faust, Adrian Leverkühn. With the resolute phrase "it shall not be" ("es soll nicht sein," Mann: 634) Adrian vows to take back or "unwrite" the accomplishments of his predecessor's "it must be" ("es muß sein") (this view is expanded by Heller, in Bludau, Heftrich, and Koopmann, 1977). Bergsten has, once more, put her finger on the pulse of problems in an area germane to the prime concerns of Mann's work and to the predilections of his life. Therefore, in her major study of 1963, she found it expedient to expand on her previous musical findings by delving into such topics as the roles of musicians, real and fictitious; of musicology (the historical development of the art); of the theory of composition (especially in conjunction with mathematics, the magical arts, and modern serial techniques); of music practices (including the thorny issue of the "reciprocal illumination" of the tonal world by the verbal and vice versa); and the proper role of analyses of specific compositions or concert performances. It can be shown that the essence of music is, indeed, an ambivalence (or even polyvalence) of its component parts. On the simplest level, for instance, a chord, the vertical tonal cluster, can have multiple applications, functioning as the tonic of one key or as the dominant, subdominant or more remote harmonic component of a different key; a succession of individual tones in a horizontal sequence is a melody, but the same tones, when sounded simultaneously, form a chord, so there is an interchangeability factor involved between homophony (chord progression) and monody (a single melodic line). Consonance and dissonance, too, are only relative terms depending upon the total acoustical environment. These examples just scratch the surface of music's inherent ambivalences ("Zweideutigkeiten"), so it is not surprising to find the novel's fundamental dictum, "Relationship is everything," and its codicil that a more precise name for this is "ambiguity" (L-P: 47), invoked especially for this technical milieu. Whatever happens in the novel may also be said to have a musical correlative either concealed or revealed in a texture crafted in accordance with the principle of the strict style of composition, and in compliance with which no free note (that is, non-functional) is allowed to appear. Take, as an illustration of such interrelationships, the familiar "Dreigestirn" configuration or, on a different plane, the favorite literary device of the "ironic" German. Each member of the "Big Three" thinkers in the Nietzsche-Schopenhauer-Wagner triadic constellation has, in varying degrees, musical affiliations. Nietzsche not only theorized about the birth of tragedy from the spirit of music but he also composed pieces for the piano. To Schopenhauer's mind, music comes closest of all the arts to embodying the Will in its most pristine form. It is superfluous, of course, to mention Wagner's musical feats, but what is worth noting in the context of ambiguity is Mann's lifelong love-hate relationship with the creator of the music drama. Irony, too, like the single musical note or the isolated chord, arises at a point of intersection linking a number of potential "meanings" or inferences, and it is the surrounding context or the overall thrust of the passage that determines how the reader is to interpret the individual word, the phrase, paragraph, chapter, or, in some rare cases, the entire opus of this "ironic German" (Baumgart, 1964; Schaper, 1965; Koopmann, 1968).

One of the early technical studies of the role of music in Thomas Mann's life and work, the published Zagreb dissertation by Viktor Zmegac (1959), appeared prior to Bergsten's analysis and focused primarily on *Doctor Faustus*. The critic begins with an analysis of the triadic intellectual constellation mentioned above in order to document how Mann's initial fascination with the emotional, dangerously seductive inwardness of music (especially in the Wagnerian mold) later ceded precedence to a more sobering view of the art: music that is beneficial rather than detrimental to life (Zmegac's argumentation is bolstered by many Marxist trappings, but the validity of some of his arguments is not overshadowed by them). Such solid, antibourgeois musical fare can even find convincing expression in the modernist idiom — an attitude that was naturally grist for the socialist mill and struck a responsive chord among numerous East bloc critics (Mittenzwei, 1962; Dobbek, in Wenzel, 1962; Gisselbrecht, in *Sinn und Form*, 1965). Building on methods akin to those of Stein (1950), Zmegac differentiates between verbal "description" and prose "narration" of music, by which terms he distinguishes passages in fiction dealing with known compositions ("music described," such as the Wagner sections of the *Tristan* novella and found in other works prior to *Faustus*) and prose exegeses of fictitious compositions (primarily Adrian's), couched in technical vocabulary. In an extension of Zmegac's first premise, Steven P. Scher interprets Leverkühn's description of the prelude to Act 3 of *Meistersinger* (1967) as a symbolic foreshadowing of events in Adrian's later life. The contention of Hans Oesch (1972) based on indications in Mann's later correspondence that the musical focus in the novel may have actually played a decisive role in Schönberg's turning or returning to the twelve-tone technique is certainly challenging, even though highly debatable from a strictly chronological standpoint.

The second comprehensive musical investigation is by Patrick Carnegy (1973), at the time a writer for the *Times* in London, and deals specifically with the figure of Leverkühn as a practicing musician. Carnegy's monograph is refreshingly devoid of the accoutrements of formal scholarship and the jargon of literary criticism. He builds on Bergsten's theories about the role of Adorno and his writings (such as

Philosophie der neuen Musik — The Philosophy of New Music — and the essay on "Beethoven's Late Style") for the genesis and final form of the novel. Taking into consideration the Adorno speculations expressed by earlier critics (Stewart, 1951; Heimann, 1964; Buzga, 1965; Ute Jung, who dubbed Adorno "a fanatic of crises," 1969: 85; and Hansjörg Dörr, who labeled the theoretician Mann's "co-author" 1970: 288), Carnegy makes the philosopher-musicologist-sociologist of the Frankfurt School a focal point of his study. Subsequent accounts in the two decades after Mann's death concerning the Mann-Adorno collaboration either add nothing substantially new to the controversy (Mainika in Wiecker, 1975), or they simply clarify minor details of the cooperative enterprise. This situation is symptomatic of much — but certainly not of all — German research on Mann in particular as well as on other aspects of German literature in general: the failure to take into account the findings of scholars of other nationalities, especially those published in English such as Carnegy, leads to needless repetition or to the "discovery" of ideas which long ago may have seen the light of day. It is frequently the case that germane research by foreign critics is not even listed in the bibliography section of an investigation, giving the impression that such material has either been overlooked or is considered of inferior quality and hence not worthy of inclusion. Jürgen Maegard (in Wiecker, 1975), on the other hand, does argue innovatively that it was actually Adorno's idiosyncratic interpretation of the serial technique that riled Schönberg more than Mann's adaptation of this compositional device for the novel. Carnegy contends that Adorno filled the huge gaps in Mann's knowledge of modern music to a greater extent than the author even acknowledged in *The Story of a Novel* and that it was Mann's reading of the typescript of *Philosophie der neuen Musik*, lent to him by Adorno, that led to an understanding of how the musical paradigm also provides a pathology of twentieth-century civilization in crises (in politics as well as art). Adorno also made it clear how Schönberg's technique evolved from the relative formlessness of free atonality to the highly structured system of the twelve-tone row (and its prescribed forty-eight permutations) and how Stravinsky's archaism, primitivism, conformism, and even his neoclassicism could lead to the brink of fascism. But by asking rhetorically, "How valid is the musical metaphor for the political reality?" (137), Carnegy joins the ranks of the skeptics concerning the unequivocal axiom Leverkühn = Deutschland, since an artistic impasse resolved by strict adherence to serialism is not necessarily tantamount to the commitment of an entire nation to a totalitarian regime. A contrary opinion is rendered by the critic Hanjo

Kesting, who harbors a strong bias against Mann because of the author's self-proclaimed role as representative of the German spirit, tradition, and culture; Kesting still clings to the original premise (Leverkühn = Germany) when he speaks in the same breath of musical ideas and political ideology in the novel as comprising a "sickness unto death" (1976). Ján Albrecht (1971) had postulated a direct correspondence between all dictatorial systems that stifle individual initiative, and thus he relegated dodecaphony and fascism to the status of birds of a feather. East bloc critics, to be sure, had always proved receptive to the idea that Mann was bent on showing how both German art and German political institutions had "gone to the devil" in the twentieth century (Wilmont, 1960).

Considering the myriad array of musicians who appear, at least nominally, in *Doctor Faustus*, Erich Heller's (1958a) provocative and perceptive comment about the difficulty in establishing identities in the novel: "I know who Schildknapp is, but who is Bruno Walter?" (272) seems particularly apropos. What he may have meant by this clever quip is that because of the novel's detailed portrayal of a figure such as Schildknapp, the quixotic translator of English literature, the reader becomes thoroughly familiar with his fictional persona; but when a name such as that of the famous conductor Bruno Walter falls, we cannot be certain whether this is a reference to the actual living personage or whether it stands for some cryptic system of allusions, to a complex set of intratextual or extratextual inferences. For instance, it might pertain to the fact that the renowned conductor Bruno Walter, of German-Jewish extraction, spent years of exile in the United States just as Mann had done and — shades of Adrian's teacher Wendell Kretzschmar — had even lectured on Beethoven (Wysling, 1974).

From among the other historical music figures linked to the novel, whether these be Russians (Devoto, 1959), Romantics (Wooton, 1974), or independent geniuses of the calibre of a Wagner (Oplatka, 1965), none has proven as intriguing as that strange German-American Johann Conrad Beissel of the Ephrata religious community in Pennsylvania, who exists in a kind of limbo between fact and fiction (Briner, 1958). Apparently, the sole reference to this composer and cult leader at the author's disposal was an article in the *American-German Review* of 1943, which he adapted freely for incorporation into his text (Karst, 1968). But it is Mann's deviation from the original rather than his strict adherence to the source text that proves most challenging. This variation in the mechanics of the montage-collage technique, which Mann employed with such sovereign dexterity, might be made into a general rule of thumb: whether incorporating excerpts from external sources verbatim into his text or altering them to whatever degree he deems necessary, it remains Mann's deftness in the process of the intertextual transfer operation that matters and that should concern the critic, not the mere identification of the source text or the degree of fidelity to the original.

A brief but significant note concerning fictional predecessors of Leverkühn is supplied by Hans Ulrich Engelmann (1963) when he compares Wackenroder's Berglinger with Adrian from the standpoint of the contrasting motives of warmth and coldness respectively. The latter concept in conjunction with Leverkühn's life and his inability to love has been mentioned in virtually every study of the composer, ranging from socialist criticism of Western art (Golik, 1971) to the need of the Tasso-like, creative intellect for isolation as an essential component of the creative act, which requires a certain cooling down process (Gerhardt, 1975) — a theme which fascinated Mann ever since the days of *Tonio Kröger* (1903).

Since, as Bergsten and others have shown, *Doctor Faustus* dealt so extensively with the structure and construction of modern music (which, in turn, served as a surrogate for all the other arts), it comes as no great surprise to learn that critics have long sought to uncover the correlations between the structural features of the tonal medium and the verbal artifact. This quest ranges from unassuming studies of the interrelations between words and tones (Lyon, 1959; Frey, 1963; Rose, 1971) to the most daring attempts to postulate and then prove intricate structural kinships between complex musical forms and the formal patterns of narrative prose (Kross, 1967; Förster, 1975). It should be noted from the outset that these latter undertakings are fraught with problems of terminological obscurity. The wary reader sometimes stumbles over such vague interdisciplinary concepts as "epic symphonicism" ("epische Symphonik," Dück, 1970), which can be stretched to the breaking point in an effort to link the aural and syntactical qualities of words in certain contexts (onomatopoeia; sound symbolism; grammatical features such as hypotaxis and parataxis, all used in the descriptions of performances, in passages on music theory, or even in quotations from familiar musical works) with the abstract and non-referential "language" of music . Some, like Harald Vogel (1973), have endeavored to draw parallels between music and the time levels in the novel (akin to Bergsten's temporal "chords"). Vogel feels that the layers of time have been superimposed upon each other in a manner akin to that of the interplay of voices in musical polyphony; the management of these intertwining strands (like the control of the intersecting voices in polyphonic texture) lies completely in the hands of the narrator, Zeitblom, who assumes the role of a kind of composer in prose. But since when has Zeitblom, who complains constantly of his difficulties in writing and who confirms that his ties to the Dionysian arts such as music are scant, become such a verbal virtuoso? The results of this and similar structuralist undertakings (István Söter's "plot mosaic," 1957; Starzycki, 1964) arouse at best suspicions of overinterpretation with regard to metaphoric parallels in terminology and, at worst, of manipulation of musical or literary data to conform to some eccentric, preconceived hypothetical scheme of correspondences.

A similar dose of "the willing suspension of disbelief" is required to appreciate those investigations dealing with magic (Linder, 1975) and number symbolism (Pritzlaff, 1972), but a happy compromise is found by Henry Hatfield in examining the role of the magic square in the novel (1968). The format of the numerical columns constituting the square is so designed that each column, when added vertically, horizontally, or diagonally totals thirty-four. Further mathematical calculations yield the following results: $34 = 3 + 4$; $3 + 4 = 7$, and seven is Mann's favorite symbolic digit. Hatfield links this integer to seven pairs of contrasting concepts, which, to his mind, predominate in the novel. The seven are: breakthrough/stagnation, hope/despair, salvation/damnation, health (sanity)/sickness (madness), heat/cold, humanism/barbarism, and expressivity/control (sterility). In addition to the seven pairs of contrasts, Hatfield proposes seven levels of reference in the course of the novel's development, to which one might apply each contrasting pair: the Faust legend; music; politics; reminiscences of Nietzsche or Faustian figures— Dürer, Beethoven, and others; Leverkühn's life; autobiographical allusions; and religion or theology. Seven (contrasts) times seven (levels of reference) equals forty-nine, and by adding the forty-seven chapters of the novel (one of which is divided into three parts) together, Hatfield arrives at the sum total of forty-nine or seven times seven, seven squared or raised to a higher power. A clever bit of calculation, to be sure, but others have counted differently. For instance, in order to support some artfully contrived mathematical scheme, one might regard the three divisions of Chapter 34 together with the "Postscript" as a total of fifty, thereby promoting the dialogue with the devil (in Chapter 25, the mid-point of the narrative) to the status of centerpiece for the entire work.

However, not only the seven of the magic square serves Hatfield's purposes, but also the twelve (3×4) of Schönberg's dodecaphonic serial technique of composition. This cipher becomes a functional metaphor for the structure of the book — not in a prescriptive or literal fashion but rather in a suggestive and richly allusive way. Hatfield is neither fanatic nor dogmatic in applying his 7 x 7 system or his dodeca formulae in any rigidly prescribed fashion, and moderation renders his theory plausible and persuasive. But later critics delving into the intricacies of the magic square would not be as circumspect as Hatfield had been, and they ran the risk of stretching the boundaries of credulity to the breaking point — an unwilling suspension of disbelief became the order of the day.

Myth and Psychology. Myth Plus Psychology

Throughout the preceding discussions of Bergsten, Voss, and others, the terms "myth" and "psychology" have been used either in their primary forms or in derivative variations ("mythological," "mythology" and "psychological," "psychoanalytic"). The coupling of the two terms in the phrase "Myth and Psychology," was first used by Mann himself in his revised version of the essay of 1919 "Der alte Fontane" (Fontane in His Old Age) and it became a prime critical concept when André von Gronicka appropriated the formula "Myth plus Psychology" for the title of his groundbreaking article on *Death in Venice* (1956). Von Gronicka drew a distinction between the "poet," who deals with myth — the Romantically transcendent realm captured in lyrically intoned language — and the "writer," as one who delves into penetrating analyses of the minds of his characters in a psychologically realistic, carefully controlled linguistic idiom. The "plus" factor was indicative of an ideal fusion or amalgamation of the two elements, a bifocal vision (or "doppelte Optik," to use another favorite Mannian term) in the context of behavior that is both mythically prepatterned yet also psychologically unique.

Subsequent critics offer a variety of hypotheses about the significance of myth in Mann's oeuvre (Feuerlicht, 1963), as well as with specific reference to *Faustus*. Bengt Algot Sørensen (1958) saw a mythical element embodied in the German people per se. For Hellmuth Petriconi (1958), it was the ubiquitous aura of defeat and destruction that constituted the central myth in the novel. Birgit Nielsen (1965) regarded Leverkühn's entire career as a conscious mythical *imitatio* of the life of the original Dr. Faust, while Leslie L. Miller (1968) treats the tenuous interplay of myth and morality and the role of "mythic imitation" (208) in forming the deterministic course of the novel. In a comprehensive study of mythology in the modern novel (1971), John J. White also ponders the relation of "prefigurative patterning" techniques in *Faustus*. The novel establishes a correlative parallelism between Leverkühn's demise and the image of recent German history with its predetermined path of events and inevitable aura of tragedy.

Refining the amorphous contours of the concept of myth even further, Hans Wysling, in an essay of 1969, conceives the mythical in terms of the typical in mankind, of eternally recurrent, timeless human elements. He conjectures that in Mann's early works, the tendency toward "the psychological became ever stronger, while in his late writings the trend reversed itself: the psychologization of myth asserts itself" (19). Instead of myth constituting merely prepatterned forms, it subsequently encompassed the entire narrative in both its super- and substuctures. Manfred Dierks next took up the cause of the myth and psychology complex in a major investigation (1972), which made full use of the notes, sketches, and handwritten marginalia in the author's personal copies of books from his library (such as Bachofen's *The Myth of the Orient and Occident*), now housed in the Zurich archive. Dierks, who at this point concentrated more on myth than on psychology, treated *Doctor Faustus* only in passing, tracing the extent that Nietzsche, whose mythical prototype provides the not-so-hidden agenda of the novel, colored and controlled Mann's critical perspective for a protracted period.

The Visual Element

There is, according to Bergsten (1963), a strong visual component in *Doctor Faustus*, especially when one thinks in terms of Dürer's significance for the novel. His *Melencolia 1*, of course, portraying the gloomy female figure surrounded by all the trappings of science as well as by the magic square, comes to mind as one source of implied visualization. This feature and the cycle of drawings entitled *Apocalypsis cum figuris*, in addition to Dürer's many portraits, engravings, and sketches of Renaissance figures who may at one time have served as pictorial models for certain of Mann's characters (especially Jonathan and Elsbeth Leverkühn), make a strong case for a reading of the novel constantly conditioned by visual impressions (Wysling and Schmidlin, 1975). Concurrently with Bergsten, Walter Rehm (1963) undertook a general assessment of Dürer's role in Mann's work, while an article published in the same year and authored jointly by Wilhelm Holthusen and A. Tauber, argued on behalf of fictional portrayals based on specific works of the dean of German Renaissance artists. In 1965 Hans Elema contended that Dürer and his art play a far greater role in the *Faustus*-novel than merely that of supplying local color or a Nuremberg ambience: the artist's surroundings (his parental home, his studio), his physical appearance (the *Ecce homo* countenance in the self-portrait of 1498), and even a possible syphilitic infection (Dürer's engraving entitled *The French Disease* or *Die Franzosenkrankheit*) are all cited as factors that could rank the Renaissance genius along with Dr. Faustus and Nietzsche as a mythic forerunner of Leverkühn — a daring hypothesis, but one not to be dismissed out of hand. Jeffrey Meyers's article (1973a) pursues a similar path, augmenting the evidence for a Dürer connection by the claim that in the engraving *Knight, Death and the Devil*, the armored figure symbolizes Nietzsche's (that is, Adrian's) struggle with demonic madness and disease (56). Meyers also notes that Dürer's art links Adrian to the frenzied world of the Reformation and makes patently visible the themes of artistic sterility and apocalyptic destruction. 1973 also was the year in which Ulrich Finke published a very workman-like essay on Mann's Dürer indebtedness, citing most of the above connections but also underscoring the role of the mythical and archetypal in the visual arts and their literary transpositions. Finke feels that the "creative adaptation of 'archetypal mythical forms' is achieved by the artistic method of montage" (125), and therefore Dürer's Nuremberg, Nietzsche's Naumburg, and Mann's Lübeck all stand as mythical models for Leverkühn's Kaisersaschern. Just as Mann came to prefer quotation to independent invention, so, too, his visualizations substantiate in their unique idiom Harry Levin's now legendary dictum, which Mann once applied to his own work in *The Genesis of 'Doctor Faustus'*: "The best writing of our contemporaries is not an act of creation, but an act of evocation, peculiarly saturated with reminiscences."

The intrinsic element of the visual embodied in the verbal artifact (Höhler, 1968; also in this regard, Pache on Blake,1973b and Blomster's pietà,1975) was, in more recent times, augmented by an extrinsic component — the cinematic version of the novel by Franz Seitz in 1982. This was an adaptation for the screen with all the concomitant positive and negative features of fiction transposed to film, and therefore one that reaped both critical acclaim and blame, as will be documented in the next chapter. Of course, the precursor to this cinematic adventure with a major work by Mann was Luchino Visconti's *Death in Venice* (1971), a film adaptation that took such poetic license with the novella as grafting onto the story of Aschenbach the brothel episode with Hetæra Esmeralda from *Faustus* and transforming the aging protagonist from a writer into a misunderstood composer of modern music. In addition, the visual element in the film *Death in Venice* is further enhanced by the aural dimension of a musical score (excerpts from Mahler's Fifth Symphony and Third Symphony as background music). In 1973 a literal musicalization of the novella was undertaken with the operatic adaptation by Benjamin Britten. It was therefore not entirely fortuitous that Seitz selected excerpts from Britten's compositions as background music (perhaps "foreground" would be more appropriate) for his *Doctor Faustus* film, together with an original musical score by the composer Rolf Wilhelm. Wilhelm sought to capture some of the essence of Leverkühn's constructivist technique, for example, by incorporating the cryptic five-note Hetæra Esmeralda cipher H-E-A-E-ES or HEtÆra ESmeralda (in German notation) as a major melodic-harmonic motif (in English music terminology, this sequence of notes would be B-E-A-E-E-flat). There seems to be at least one major flaw in Seitz's overall approach to the work as film, however: one wonders, for example, if the average moviegoer who has not read the novel would ever be able to understand fully what takes place on the screen, to make any of the analogical connections required to piece together the intricate aural-visual montage transpiring before his eyes? Did Seitz simply compound the "felony" of much modernist art, so to speak, by transferring to the viewer the onus usually placed on the reader to forever connect what is apprehended either as word or image, since a work like *Doctor Faustus* will supply no clue to help decode the ultimate meaning or message of what has been depicted? When all the evidence has been weighed in the balance, one cannot in best conscience put forth the claim that the filmed versions of Mann's novellas and novels — including *Doctor Faustus* — rival the feat of that man (in the parabolic passage serving as the motto of this chapter) who carries a light on his back at night, "which does not light him, but lights up the path for those coming after."

3: Illumination by Biographical and Autobiographical Revelations (1975–1992)

> *"But that tone ... to which only the spirit hearkens ... abides as a light in the night"*
> (Doctor Faustus)

Setting the Scene

THE THIRD AND most recent stage of *Doctor Faustus* research was marked by the appearance of studies that make extensive use of now published autobiographical sources such as the volumes of Mann's diaries edited by Peter de Mendelssohn (1977–1982) and, after his death, by Inge Jens (1986; 1989; 1991; 1993). Mann's correspondence with other German writers and key personages in his life, particularly during the composition of the novel (Dietzel, 1977; Wysling and Sprecher, 1988; Vaget, 1992b), is also of prime interest. One of the most valuable tools for an understanding of the genesis and scope of *Faustus* was the publication of the third volume of the series *Thomas Mann: Dichter über ihre Dichtungen* (Thomas Mann: Writers on their Writings) (Wysling and Fischer, 1981), which contains over two hundred pages of excerpts from the author's letters with direct and indirect bearing upon *Doctor Faustus* — here collected in one single section of this handy volume. The extant notebooks of Mann also appeared in print in a two-volume edition (Wysling and Schmidlin, 1991; 1992; Wysling, 1991) and this was a landmark event. These autobiographical data were supplemented by a volume of Mann's collected commentaries on *Faustus* as well as on the "novel of a novel" gleaned from a variety of additional sources (Wysling and Eich-Fischer, 1992). Into this same category of convenient research tools falls the second volume of Klaus W. Jonas's mammoth 1979 bibliography of criticism on Mann through the year 1975, augmented to some extent by the select bibliography of Kurzke (1985a) and by a recent publication of primary sources (Potempa and Heine, 1992). A candid assessment of the role played by Mann's notes, his correspondence, diaries and other personal documents by Michael Maar (1992) should, in spite of its whimsical title (in translation) "The Flight of the Stuffed Birds," help put this mass of material into clearer perspective and a meaningful context.

From the philological standpoint, mention should be made of Eva Schiffer's study entitled *Zwischen den Zeilen* (Between the Lines, 1982), which examines changes from the manuscript versions of works to the final printed format of a number of Mann's texts (listing, for example, forty-five changes in the first chapter of *Doctor Faustus* and part of the second). By reading between the lines of the published version of the novel and the unexcised original material, Schiffer initially simply registers the alterations in style and diction, and then tries to analyze what has been achieved aesthetically by the author's continual polishing, chiseling, and emendating of his prose.

Of crucial importance to scholars and readers alike in an era when the amount of material written about an author or, in the case of *Faustus*, about a single work, has reached genuinely staggering proportions is the steady flow of summarizing inventories of research. Gert Sautermeister (1977), for instance, tries to assess the reactions to the novel with reference to Germany's manner of coping with the recent past, anticipating the "battle of the historians" and the holocaust controversy that flared up in the decade of the 1980s. These sensitive issues were to have widespread ramifications and persist as volatile topics up to the present day. Not only did Herbert Lehnert continue his levelheaded and concise commentary on *Faustus* criticism (1977, 1992), but several new scholars, some of whom were subsequently to leave their distinctive stamp on Thomas Mann studies, made their debut after 1975. First and foremost in the field of critical accounts of research was Hermann Kurzke with three major publications: 1977, 1985a, 1985b (second revised and enlarged edition 1991). Another rapidly rising force in Mann criticism, Hans Rudolf Vaget, gave penetrating and informative assessments in a survey entitled provocatively "No End to Thomas Mann" ("Thomas Mann und kein Ende," 1980) and in an unbroken string of individual and cumulative book reviews (in this latter category, for instance, falls his 1990 collective assessment of recent works). Rudolf Wolff's book (1983), which bears the promising title *Doktor Faustus und die Wirkung* ('Doctor Faustus' and Its Influence), contains, for the most part, reprinted articles of various scholars plus a select bibliography on the novel, but unfortunately the anthology falls short of delivering what the title implies. Two essays on *Faustus* scholarship, one by Edward Dvoretzky (1979) and the other by Hubert Orlowski (1981), deal retroactively with the harsh critical reactions to *Doctor Faustus* in Germany during the earliest years (from 1947 to approximately 1958), while Volkmar Hansen, in a section of his concise Thomas Mann monograph of 1984 labeled "Faustus-Zeit (1943–1950)" (The Period of Faustus) presents a balanced thumbnail sketch of critical opinion up to 1982 (as does Inta M. Ezergailis in the introduction to her 1988 collection of critical essays). Finally, in 1990 there appeared undoubtedly one of the key contributions to Thomas Mann research tools in recent years and one that, because of the array of first-rate scholars represented in it and the type of wide-sweeping coverage it advocates, will definitely establish itself as a standard reference work: the *Thomas-Mann-Handbuch* (The Thomas Mann Handbook), edited by Helmut Koopmann (1990b). Included among the highly incisive material in this reference work (which covers virtually every phase of investigation touched upon in the present overview and enlists the talents of the major critics and top-notch researchers) are the comprehensive histories of critical studies on Thomas Mann by the editor (1990d) and his colleagues (Wagener and Wißkirchen, in Koopmann 1990b), together with a challenging essay on *Doctor Faustus* (Koopmann, 1990c). It has undoubtedly been said by many reviewers of secondary literature that a given book under scrutiny will be "indispensable to future students and scholars," but this has not always been the case. However, in this instance, we have the proverbial exception that proves the rule, for the *Thomas-Mann-Handbuch* contains such diverse, deftly written, in-depth essays that the information found in any of them together with the appended bibliographical source references should serve into the next millennium as a solid orientation for students, teachers, scholars, and the lay reading public alike. The same cannot be maintained of a work such as Jürgen Jung's effort (1985) to deal with "old and new" material on *Faustus* — including sources and literary models for the novel, problems of myth, psychology, music, theo- and demonolgy, and fascism. This published dissertation, despite its wealth of informative detail, is too diffuse in scope and gives the impression of being a compendium of footnote annotations rather than a coherent discussion. Such an eclectic conglomeration of diverse material, which seeks to be all things to all men, unfortunately results in not being much of anything to anyone. On the other hand, Karlheinz Hasselbach's instructive manual (1978, revised edition, 1988) for the didactic deployment of *Faustus* in educational institutions (from grade school to graduate school), continues a trend which has existed ever since the controversial novel appeared in Germany: the search for the place of this difficult work in the curriculum or canon of the educational establishment of that country. Hasselbach proceeds beyond the stage of coping with the recent historical past in *Faustus* by introducing aesthetic, ethical, and societal issues of broader scope as potential pedagogical tools. His helpful article of 1980 dealing with methods of alerting the literarily less sophisticated reader to the distinctive linguistic and stylistic features of the novel is derived from the earlier didactic study and is also well suited for instructional implementation.

Religious-Theological Approaches

The decline in the number of studies devoted to religious and theological facets of *Faustus* is indicative of either a waning of interest in such issues or the conviction that religion and theology, at least with respect to this novel, have by now been covered adequately. The latter conjecture, however, is belied by the fact that in each of these two areas at least one new and exciting mode of investigation has been launched. With regard to religious implications, for instance, Eitel Timm (1989) omits the conventional questions of sin, grace, and redemption in the novel and treats instead the subject of heresy and its relation to the plight of modern art in general and, as mediated through Kierkegaard, to the status of music in particular. Heresy and music have a common ground in several areas of concern: in their breakthrough to the "numinous;" in the isolation or ostracization of the heretic or composer from the established community; and in the choice both figures must make between suffering in silence or articulating their grief in a medium to be heard. For the composer, music provides a means to voice the inner essence of experiences, something that can be articulated *expressis verbis* only in an unsatisfactory manner through the deficient verbal medium.

If the concept of grace could, by the mid-80s, be classified in the religious-theological context virtually as a conventional topos in *Faustus* research, then Vaget succeeds in infusing new lifeblood into such an atrophied topic with his article bearing the catchy title "Amazing Grace" (1987). In contrast to Holthusen's longstanding negativity with regard to finding any religious transcendence or hope for redemption in Mann's novel, Vaget points to a series of signposts in the work that seem to indicate a conscious effort on the part of the author to suggest a possible salvation for the protagonist, in spite of what appears to be certain damnation (help from above is also well-founded in Michael Beddow's informative article on what he calls "analogies of salvation," 1986). These clues are threefold, manifesting themselves in Adrian's musical compositions; in personal liaison with the femme fatale

(Esmeralda) and through indirect contact with her reputed counterpart, the eternal feminine (von Tolna); and, finally, in echoes of Kierkegaard's paradoxical formulations of hope beyond hopelessness. In each instance, the clues of potential divine intervention are carefully counterbalanced by hints of probable condemnation because of seemingly inextricable demonic entanglement. Leverkühn's ultimate fate thus takes on a Janus-faced aura, which manifests itself in what Vaget calls the contradictoriness of the German spirit; this trait is in keeping with the "pervasive pattern of equivocation" (181) and paradox that permeates every facet of the text.

Possible links of Leverkühn to Christ, a kinship that the novel occasionally fosters through such images as the moribund composer's *Ecce homo* countenance, are pursued by H. S. Gilliam in an examination of Mann's "other holy sinner" (1977). The critic develops the concept of prefiguration, a religious term for the theory that an earlier individual and his fate (in this case, Christ) may serve as the pattern for a later person's life (a kind of religious variant of mythic recurrence). On the other hand, T. E. Apter, in her book on the devil's advocate (1978), pursues a gloom-and-doom line of religious investigation by tracing Mann's unholy alliance with its Romantic legacy of disease, darkness, and death as augmented by a morbid fascination for the demonic and deviltry. The latter, however, is regarded by this critic as a force that is presented in the novel in a "contrived" fashion (recalling Hamburger's view that the entire Faustian symbolism in the work has an anachronistic overtone), a topic that was to arouse renewed interest in succeeding years. Whereas Eberhard Scheiffele proposes three levels of narrative interest in the novel — the German heritage, musical composition, and the religious-theological-mythological complex — it is ultimately the last of these which dominates. This contention is founded on Zeitblom's strong Catholicism that, thematically as well as structurally, controls the reader's perspective on events, even in ex negativo cases (for instance, by stating that he avoids the religiously tinged term "inspiration" when commenting on art, Leverkühn subliminally calls to mind the divine force behind such creativity). Helmuth Kiesel (1990a) questions the ability of a modern writer even to speak of religion or God at all, and he finds in Mann a certain oscillation in religiously tinged utterances between acceptance and rejection. Kiesel's final verdict, however, is that allusions to salvation, grace, and the like near the conclusion of the novel signal not Christian views but rather humanistic values. The subtitle of Irene Kann's 1992 monograph *Schuld und Zeit* (Guilt and Time) reads in translation "Literary Activity in Theological

Perspective," and this concept shares marginal affiliations with studies dealing with strictly theological questions. However, Kann regards guilt as stemming not from infractions against Christian morality and its spiritual credo but rather from man's precarious status with respect to time. The human condition hovers somewhere between states of stagnation, sterility, regression, boredom, and sloth — the cardinal sin of the Catholic Middle Ages — and a contemporary, headlong and heedless flight into the frantic activism of the breakthrough under the auspices of the diabolic. The mediator between these and other complementary forces in operation — archaism and modernity, artistic calculation and spontaneous improvisation, the time-bound and the timeless — is the narrating voice, Zeitblom. His often cumbersome account brings Leverkühn's existential and aesthetic guilt trip into correlation with German culpability for Nazism via Nietzscheism. The charge is leveled not so much at the latter's cult of strength or the superman concept but rather at his indifference to the political and social ramifications of the philosophical tenets he espoused — a kind of existential malingering to which Germany also fell victim.

Historical Perspectives

The relationship of Mann's *Faustus* to the history of Germany has always been treated in manifold fashion because of the novel's tripartite chronological overlay: the actual life-span of the hero (1885–1940); the cultural heritage of Germany as the "land of the middle" from medieval to modern times; and the events in that country and much of Europe during the closing years of the Second World War (1943-1945). The latter aspect is conveyed primarily via Zeitblom's asides interspersed periodically throughout the narrative. With regard to the rise of National Socialism, one school of thought maintains that the twentieth-century German people and their demonic characteristics can be represented and appreciated only by re-presenting their past — the genesis of Nazism stemming, as it were, from a venerable German tradition. In order to undergird this theory, it became necessary to trace the roots of Nazism back in time to epochs and events that precede the actual advent of National Socialism (1933–1945) by centuries.

An innovative approach to the general historical dimensions in the novel is taken by Hans Rudolf Vaget (1977) who focuses on the fictitious city of Kaisersaschern with the grave of Emperor Otto III and makes this site the basis for an analysis of the conflict between German chauvinism and European universalism. These competing forces are correlated with Leverkühn's career, which likewise fluctuates between an original intellectual openness to the world and a subsequent restriction to the confines of a narrowly circumscribed sphere of aesthetic activity (Kreutzer, 1989, has an interesting variant perspective on this development). The upshot of this situation, however, involves the inevitable ambivalence factor, which, in the historicopolitical arena, manifests itself in the clash of diverse opinions: were there actually two Germanies, the one good and the other evil (according to the leftist-leaning critics such as the Austrian Ernst Fischer); or, as Mann seems to have eventually advocated — to the dismay of some of his countrymen in exile including Bert Brecht — were the good and bad components so inextricably and homogeneously mixed in the German character and historical evolution that National Socialism appears inborn and integral to the Teutonic temperament (the view of English diplomat and Germanophobe Robert G. Vansittart)? In abbreviated form, these opposing positions might be summarized as the theory of two Germanies versus the one-Germany view.

For the socialist camp in the tradition of Lukács, clarity rather than ambivalence in the historical message of *Faustus* remains the order of the day: thus the novel, according to Thomas Metscher (1976), clearly sounds the swan song of the bourgeois age, and it offers at the same time a pathogenesis of German fascism. But this latter phenomenon is not, according to Metscher, representative of the entire Germany or of all Germans — both the antifascist faction and the workers are excluded (echoes of Fischer), and they are presumably to be reckoned with the contingent of the "good" German people.

In the wake of the "battle of the historians" during the decade of the 1980s, the issues of historicism, historiography, and historicity dominated many a *Faustus* discussion. Arnold Busch (1984) confronts a question posed already in the late 1940s: how could writers like Döblin and Mann, having been exiled from their homeland, ever hope to render an accurate account of the origins and evolution of Nazism? Busch's seriousness of purpose causes him to underplay the role of narrative irony in Mann's case — a shortcoming that, as has been shown before, is not a rarity among critics, especially of the German school. Helmut Wiegand (1982) finds it easier to distill Mann's historicopolitical stance from the author's essays and expository prose than from the *Faustus* novel, because of that very ironic presence in the latter. Wiegand wisely argues that the Lukácsian view of Mann as evolving from the nonpolitical man to the democrat and finally to an advocate of socialist thought must be taken with many grains of salt, especially following the publication of the diaries, in which the unvarnished truth of the writer's oscillating stance toward political causes comes to the fore in less oblique fashion.

In the *Faustus* section of her study, *The Uncompleted Past* (1983), which examines the relationship of the post-war German novel to the Third Reich, Judith Ryan regards Mann's consciously equivocal account (because of the double-focus approach in narration, the coincidence of regressive and progressive elements, and the simultaneous use of mythic and ironic literary forms) as a pacesetter for diagnoses found in other contemporary works, literary as well as historical. Adrian's mature music, composed with the dialectic of freedom in mind (as self-imposed restraint), is "the ultimate flower of evil, which is at once a harbinger of Nazism and a protest against it.... Such ambiguities are only to be expected in a novel whose basic form depends upon equivocality... the mesh of equivocality that constitutes the terms in which the novel is couched" (55). Donna Reed's study of the Nazi past and the novel (1985) focuses on Zeitblom's woefully inadequate initial perception of the magnitude of the atrocities perpetrated by Hitler's cohorts. But she also stresses Serenus's gradual comprehension of the fact that the irrational and demonic may indeed be fascinating and even disturbing in art, but in the social and political realms, they can be lethal. Hence there follow in her investigation chapters such as "Indicted Aesthetics," in which the aloof, introverted, and socially irresponsible artist is chided for either indulging in mere parodic play or plunging into the primitive and archaic for the sake of achieving sovereign mastery over sterile formalism. The irrationalism of Nazism in its "rationalized" form of fascist ideology is seen as analogous to the irrational quality of music's tonal idiom in spite of its logically conceived superstructures.

The most comprehensive study of contemporary history as reflected in *Doctor Faustus* was undertaken by Hans Wißkirchen (1986), whose analysis makes copious use of the material in the Zurich archive. He judiciously points out Mann's double life with regard to his public persona (as the quasi-democrat of the Weimar years and later the avowed opponent of Hitler) and his private self, which clung to the German Romantic tradition in spite of the Nazi distortions of that tradition. If *The Magic Mountain* reflects the author's coming to terms with a historical situation observed firsthand in pre-First World War Germany, then *Faustus* illustrates Mann's coping with the pre-fascist and Nazified German plight from the vantage (or disadvantage) point of an American exile. Accustomed to viewing history as a function of his own fate, in terms of its effects on his life and work, Mann hoped by clarifying the historical implications of these cataclysmic twentieth-century events, to experience personal enlightenment. He found that, as a cumulative effect of both conflicts, his faith in the German Romantic tradition, to which he had staunchly clung all his life, had been severely shaken but could not be entirely broken. The question whether or not *Faustus* and its attendant myths were indeed the proper vehicle to fashion a parallelism between Mann's aesthetic-ethical credo and the jagged path of German history — a hypothesis to which Wißkirchen seems to subscribe — is still open for debate after almost half a century of conjecture. The *Faustus* chapter in Dominick LaCapra's book *History, Politics, and the Novel* (1987) does not really address the historical dimension head-on but rather in a more peripheral fashion, and it is consequently of limited use for Mann studies. Although nationalism — German or otherwise — was, as Peter Michelsen shows (1989), not endemic to the Faust legend, the Faustian figure did, in the course of the nineteenth century, become more and more entangled with the ideology of German nationhood. Especially after 1871 there evolved a double-barreled concept: an ideological upgrading of Faust was accompanied by a critical devaluation of him on other grounds, an affirmation of the demonic accompanied by a rendering innocuous of that same demonic factor. In this novel, however, Mann turns the tables and reactivates the diabolic nucleus in full force for both the central figure and the national spirit he embodies.

Scholars of the 1990s have not slackened in their zeal to tackle the slippery issue of Mann's stance toward recent German history, especially with respect to the impetus for, and impact of, the Nazi era, based on both the author's "factual" texts (expository prose accounts) and his fictional contexts. Koopmann (1990a), for instance, citing the diaries and expository prose writings from the war years, points to Mann's genuine lack of knowledge of the actual events that were taking place in Europe. Koopmann is convinced that the atrocities committed by the Nazis were beyond the limits of language to express or even to approximate. The result of this double handicap was that Mann had recourse to a visual frame of reference derived from Michelangelo — Nazi rule as hell, the war as a plunge into the depths of that hellish abyss, and the end of the war as a Last Judgment — in order to communicate in some way what was beyond the ability of words to convey ("Transverbales," "that which transcends the verbal;" "ins Metasprachliche," 28; "into that which goes beyond language"). Was it, however, wise of Mann, the critic Martin Travers muses in a survey of 1991, to persist in operating within the confines of German intellectual and cultural history (music, for instance) when seeking an aesthetic objective correlative for the Nazi period or to make the mythic background (for example, the Nietzschean prototype) the vehicle with which to come to terms with contemporary historical events? With respect to the "battle of the historians," Travers resuscitates Käte Hamburger's earlier concept of "anachronistic symbolism" whenever the Faustian framework and its magical trappings are applied to a twentieth-century historical dilemma. The compact with the devil and the contributions of the latter to the rise of an innovative musical aesthetic seem to be hardly compatible with the momentous human tragedy of a Hitlerian Germany in the throes of nascent fascism. Yet, Travers argues, by reading Faustus historiographically (with full awareness that one is always regarding the past through the prism of the present), one can qualify, at least with respect to the German psyche of the Nazi era, the claim that Mann's symbolic correlation was inappropriate or inadequate to represent recent historical developments. Under the Hitler dictatorship, for instance, contemporaneous and remote ideological configurations such as the medieval concept of the thousand-year empire in its modernized garb could indeed coexist symbiotically. This contemporaneity makes it evident why the so-called anachronistic symbolism does have qualified validity after all. In addition, Leverkühn's final composition fuses baroque devices such as the Monteverdian echo effect with twentieth-century, twelve-tone serial techniques as essential features of the breakthrough to a kind of "reactionary modernism." On the other hand, a reaffirmation of the Hamburger thesis of 1969 that the Faustian framework actually constituted "symbolic anachronism" is undertaken by Dieter W. Adolphs (1991), who subscribes to his predecessor's view that the Faust-devil myth is merely grafted onto the novel rather than being tightly interwoven into the fabric of the text (echoes of Apter, 1978). Dagmar Barnouw (1992) compares the fusion of fascism and forms of artistry in *Mario and the Magician* with those of *Doctor Faustus* in a wide-ranging essay which invokes such theoretical treatises as the Adorno-Horkheimer *Dialectic of Enlightenment* of 1944. Her contention is that in the novella of 1930 the linkage of the political and the aesthetic obscures the anti-fascist message, while in the novel of 1947 the aestheticizing tendency helps contain or curb disturbing political phenomena. What Barnouw rejects are interpretations that dote on extra-textual politics or that resolve too facilely intra-textual contradictions.

In 1992 two studies appeared that deal with one of the major complaints of critics immediately following the debut of *Faustus* on the

German scene and often reiterated over the years: how reliable is an account of life in Nazi Germany written by someone who was not even there? Walter Huder (1992) gives an assessment of *Faustus* as a novel of German national guilt, but the work is categorized as a j'accuse document conceived in exile and thus subject to considerable qualification (a view akin to that of Koopmann, 1990a, cited above). Paul L. Sauer (1992) broaches the subject of "being there" from a central structural principle in the novel — the tension between the narrator, Zeitblom, a fictitious "inner emigrant" and a humanistically trained intellectual, who had to relate to the regime and its policies in a variety of subtly nuanced ways, and Mann himself, a member of the "outer" emigration of exiles, who could experience these adverse forces only vicariously.

Of course, with the collapse of the German Democratic Republic in 1989 and the inauguration and implementation of the official unification process in 1990, one of the longstanding historically tinged ideological dichotomies in *Faustus* research — the familiar clash of East bloc critics flaunting their more or less standardized Marxist views of literature before Western critics, who have their own ideological axe to grind — seems, at least on the surface, to have abated. But this historically conditioned, forty-year-long dichotomy has not disappeared entirely from the scene and could yet assume new disguises, paralleling Germany's difficult process of achieving true unity despite its official (re)unification. With reference to *Faustus* and Mann's other wartime writings, Vaget (1992a) ponders how the author might have reacted to the advent of the unification of the two German states. At first glance it would appear that Mann could never forget or forgive the horrors of the holocaust as well as the ill-gained hegemony of the scum of the earth in his native land, however transitory this might have been. He would, so it seems, even today harbor resentment against Germany, united or otherwise, for its betrayal of its best traditions. But then Vaget weighs the following contingency: given Mann's conception of Germany as a "Kulturnation," a country with a rich cultural heritage, that might someday even be integrated into a larger European context should it manifest signs of that humanism with a Christian stamp that mark the end of *Faustus,* would the author be totally condemnatory? In spite of all his equivocating tactics, Mann left the reader of *Faustus* — as Vaget has argued elsewhere — with at least a remnant of hope for redeeming grace for his native land, so that this newly constituted German state might just find qualified acceptance, even though not wholehearted endorsement, in Mann's eyes, were he alive to witness this albeit fragile phenomenon of unity which seemed so utopian just a few short years ago and certainly quite remote during the last decade of Mann's life (1945–1955).

Themes, Genre Studies, Problems

In view of the fact that comprehensive life-work analyses of Mann were, in a sense, put on hold pending public access to and eventual publication of the material in the Zurich archive after 1975, there was a marked decline — almost an embargo — on such wide-ranging studies in favor of monographs that trace a specific thematic complex through various stages in the author's career. One marked exception to the above contention, however, was Hans Mayer's comprehensive analysis of the major works and their evolution (1980). The section on *Faustus* is characteristic of Mayer's overall approach: replete with cleverly formulated and incisive original observations, judiciously cautioning against any one-dimensional interpretation of the multi-dimensional work, his text is interwoven with key phrases from a host of authors — primarily Goethe (even though Mayer contends that the direction taken by Mann's protagonist deviates significantly from the path followed by Goethe's *Faust*). Mayer's commentary is still tinged by socialist thought, even though he does not appear to be an advocate of the unadulterated ideology of socialism in its dogmatic forms, and he not infrequently takes to task staunch adherents of that credo whenever he feels they overstate their case (for instance, Ernst Fischer).

One of the prominent and persistent themes that surfaced particularly after the Second World War involves the nature of Mann's humanism: was this admirable stance merely rhetorical or was it real, as Frank Trommler had once asked? Whereas one Western critic (Apter,1975) responds with that trademark ambivalence concerning any genuine commitment on Mann's part, and posing, with particular reference to *Faustus*, the alternatives of nihilism or humanism, the response from the leftist camp was delivered with typical clarity of conviction. The Hungarian Germanist Antal Mádl (1980), for instance, in a major investigation derived from his numerous earlier essays, presents a systematic account of the different stages in the evolution of Mann's concept of humanism. These levels extend from the initial manifestation of "humanitarian individualism" through such intermittent modes as Mann's "new humanism" (his breakthrough in the Weimar era from a conservative bourgeois writer to a defender of the Republic and democracy) and "militant humanism" (during the exile period), to a culminating final form, labeled appropriately enough for a Marxist critic of the Lukácsian stamp, "social humanism." It is difficult to see, however, how this last stage of humanistic thought, which fosters such positive values as love, nature, and morality, could apply to *Faustus* (especially with regard to the ban on love or the inept performance in that very work of the humanist par excellence, Serenus Zeitblom), even though elements of a "cosmic humanism" (grace, supraconfessional religiosity) do find some slight resonance in the plight of Leverkühn. In Steven P. Dowden's study of the German novel of modernism, *Sympathy for the Abyss* (1986), the problem with humanism is said to stem from its faulty basis in anthropomorphic subjectivity, and this shortcoming emerges as the "unexpected root of the crisis of modernity" (136). Mann's fictional solution is an art form that reconciles ethics and aesthetics, a holistic theory of composition originating not in personal "interiority" but rather in the "exteriority" of the world as a whole. Art's mission is to articulate an ecology of man caught between the natural poles of good and evil; this would constitute the restored "humanistic" function of art, presently absent, according to the worst scenario or, following a more propitious script, humanism temporarily held in abeyance.

What Mádl had sought in his anthology of 1980 and in his earlier essay of 1979 — the clear line of demarcation between diverse, carefully delineated stages of humanism progressing to a socialist apex or even a cosmic climax — was something that not even other Marxist critics with a finer-honed critical acumen could accept unequivocally in Mann's case (for instance, Eike Middell's review of Mádl's work, 1982). Western scholars, on the other hand, perhaps went overboard in the opposite direction, avoiding clear-cut distinctions as a matter of principle and discovering a host of designations for Mann's perpetual ambivalence, ambiguity, and equivocation. Some of the other designations for the author's elusive stance include "double optic," "dialectic," "aporia," "paradox," "duality of perception," "dynamic counterpoise," "doubleness," "doubt" (the latter is etymologically linked to "duo" or twoness), and, of course, the ubiquitous "irony," just to name a few options in English. Oskar Seidlin examines the theme of ambivalence in *Faustus* in terms of the "open wound" as a symbol of this vulnerable condition (1982), while Gert Sautermeister finds yet another impasse in the novel between the contrary forces of edification and mystification (1979). A fundamental residue of unresolved ambivalence seems to persist even in those studies not specifically devoted to this topic, as evidenced by Erhard Friedrichsmeyer's analysis (1984) of Leverkühn's laughter, which functions as a two-edged sword: the smile of reason and the smirk of the rascal or rogue ("Schelm") operate in dialectical fashion, revealing the tragedy underlying the human condition. Bernard Schubert's exposé of the demise of bourgeois reason and the rise of prefascist barbarism in *Faustus* (1986) proceeds from the premise of both a departure from the bourgeois way of life as well as its complementary antipode — adherence to this outmoded modus vivendi. Both patterns are tightly intertwined in the novel, and this results in neurotic entanglements and in the unredeemed state of the bourgeoisie, for which condition Nietzsche, Lukács, and Adorno offer differing remedies. Even the "taking back" of Beethoven's Ninth Symphony with its commitment ode to joy by the gloomy prognosis of the *Dr. Fausti Weheklag'* is qualified by Helmuth Kiesel (1990b) when he diagnoses how attributes of "serenity" and cheerfulness counterbalance the otherwise morose side of the ledger. But the argument that this reinstatement of a brighter note can be ascribed to the introduction of comic relief (in figures such as Fitelberg) or to the "vacillating" (often bungling) narrative style of Zeitblom is far from persuasive. A thematic study such as that of Karen Drabek Vogt (1987) treating the importance of female inspiration in Mann's novels (but relying too heavily on the principle of the eternal feminine) paints a portrait of an artist who engages in a two-pronged creative process, one that entails the interplay of inspiration and critique, of self-abandonment and self-control. Ulrich Kinzel (1988) devotes an entire book to a comprehensive analysis of Mann's "system of ambiguity," which in *Doctor Faustus* proceeds from the interrelationship of reason and the "other." But considering the nature of *Faustus* criticism from the very outset (Holthusen's annoyance at the lack of clear-cut alternatives) and extending to the widespread advocacy of the ambivalent stance assumed by both the author and his interpreters, it would seem that this topic, like no other, persists in virtually every facet of critical investigation and may never be exhausted nor examined to the complete satisfaction of inquisitive intellect. On the other hand, Thomas Steinfeld emphatically cautioned in 1985 against any pseudo-resolution of the host of antinomies (the divine and the demonic, individual freedom and the ordered structures of society, reflection and inspiration in the creative process) which permeate the *Faustus* novel.

Helmut Jendreiek's comprehensive 1977 investigation of Mann's "democratic" novels seems, on the surface at least, to fuse both thematic concepts and generic concerns — provided one can accept the premise of a genre dubbed the democratic novel. Once again a critic falls victim to his own gullibility, accepting in blind faith Mann's apodictic statements about his novels and his intentions in those works.

One is reminded of Mádl's credulity (a trend sometimes referred to tongue-in-cheek as "first-hand secondary literature") concerning the author's random pronouncements about his path to an enlightened humanism, disregarding in the process some glaring contradictions in expository prose texts as well as conflicting evidence that comes to light via the diaries, notebooks, and correspondence. In *Faustus*, according to Jendreiek, the protagonist's extreme inwardness and aloofness make him immune from any sense of democratic spirit, and this flaw can be considered the root cause of his eventual apocalyptic downfall. As a remedy against the consequences of such radical aestheticism, Mann is said to advocate social humanism; in place of barbarism he proposes the humanity of reason; and to offset the constrictions of a doctrinaire political system, he champions a social democracy. Admirable sentiments that indeed may apply to certain novels and essays, but difficult to substantiate with respect to *Doctor Faustus*.

The late 1980s brought several attempts to place *Doctor Faustus* into an ever larger thematic-generic framework, such as Russell A. Berman's assessment of the work in the context of the rise of the modern German novel (1986). Heavily laden with the sometimes cryptic vocabulary of critical theory, Berman's study ultimately draws upon familiar gambits such as ambivalence and ambiguity to pinpoint the modernism of the work. Noting that "ambivalence of serial permanence and developmental progress persist" in the paradoxical antinomies of Leverkühn and Zeitblom, Berman speculates that it is the oscillation of such tensions between order and change, historical development and mythic permanence, or synchronic and diachronic aspects of culture that dictate the contours of Mann's modernist strategy (280). In fact, ambivalence is credited with being a modernist technique par excellence, which, aside from evading closure, provides a kind of "Socratic education," emancipating the reader or "recipient" from the straitjacket of the "fascist spectacle" and the "illusions of the culture industry" (283). David Kiremidjian (1985) also operates within the familiar confines — those of modern parody — in comparing Mann's *Faustus* with Joyce's *Ulysses*. Whereas the "primary work of art" (a much disputed concept, since virtually all literature can be shown to be, in a sense, derivative, replete with inherent intertextuality) will reveal what is *in* the world, parody reveals what is *wrong with* the world (4). Several of the modalities of parody distilled by Kiremidjian such as those involving unmitigated appropriation of subject matter, the juxtaposition of self-reflexivity and referentiality, emulation of one part of the novel by another, certainly conform to themes and techniques in *Faustus*. If Kiremidjian's assertion is valid that Leverkühn's late works could be considered a parody of Schönberg's style, then this leads to the suspicion that, by having his composer follow this path, Mann might also be implying that something is indeed *wrong* with Schönberg's mathematically crafted music. This hypothesis may not be totally amiss, considering the author's inherently Romantic and Wagnerian preferences in the tonal art in spite of his literary lip service to more modern manifestations of music. *Faustus* as the influential catalyst for the contemporary generation of writers (Grass, Böll, Lenz), inducing them to produce a form of social criticism correlated with the critique of art found in Mann's novel, is the subject of Hannelore Mundt's monograph of 1989. This study covers much familiar territory (for the *Faustus* symposium of 1988 discussed below, Mundt prepared a condensed version of her investigation: Mundt, *Thomas-Mann-Jahrbuch*, 1989; English translation in Lehnert and Pfeiffer, 1991), delving into such paradoxes as Mann's discomfort with the amoral, asocial, apolitical aspects of his art and yet, concomitant with this spiritual malaise, his unabashed affirmation of that art.

A major event in the evolution of *Faustus* studies as well as in Mann research took place in 1988 at the Irvine Campus of the University of California, when a symposium of scholars was convened to discuss this single work, ostensibly from a single perspective: *Doctor Faustus* as a novel at the "margin of modernism." Selected lectures from this conference were published in German in the *Thomas-Mann-Jahrbuch* (1989), while the majority of the essays, including all of those in the Mann yearbook and the rejoinders to them, appeared in a separate volume in English (1991) edited by Herbert Lehnert and Peter C. Pfeiffer. The dust cover of the latter anthology suggests yet another refinement of the concept of literary ambivalence, for on the book jacket we read that this novel reveals itself as "both . . . a signifier of change in our awareness of modernism, and . . . a historical document that — for some critical tastes especially — betrays traces of datedness." Put another way, however, one might pose the problem as follows: is perhaps modernity not dated, especially now that critics are coming to terms with the phenomenon of postmodernism? In the incisive introductory section of this book Lehnert speaks of "contradictory fictional messages which make a novel indeterminate" (1). As is often the case with symposia papers, not all those contained in the collection deal with the announced topic of the conference; but in this instance, the vast majority of them do so. Nearly all make reference to the ambivalence or multivalence factor to greater or lesser degree, adhering to the view that a modern novel, in Lehnert's well chosen words "does not advocate one set of ideological orientations, but leaves the reader with different, even contradictory valuations," thereby defying closure (2). With a few succinct phrases, Lehnert succeeds in delineating in capsule form a majority of the themes and problems that have surfaced in the course of recent *Faustus* research. For instance, he notes how music deploys "ambiguity as a system," is morally indifferent and functions as the paradigmatic objective correlative for modern art, the essential mode of expression of which is ambiguity and which remains open-ended with regard to definitive moral judgments. If André von Gronicka's article of 1948 could serve — with Mann's blessing — as a suitable prolegomenon to *Faustus* for the following decades, then Lehnert's introduction to this volume should be accorded a similar accolade for the 1990s and beyond.

The following overview will cover those articles from the Lehnert-Pfeiffer anthology that touch in some way upon the marginality theme announced in the title and then developed in the introduction under the rubrics of ambivalence, ambiguity, and poly- or multivalence. The remaining essays will be dealt with in the subsections on love, myth, and psychology, to which they are better suited. Helmut Koopmann (in *Thomas-Mann-Jahrbuch*, 1989; English version in Lehnert and Pfeiffer, 1991), by analyzing the history of German introspection and inwardness in the novel chronologically rather than phenomenologically or psychoanalytically, attempts to visualize something — the German spirit — that is actually invisible. For instance, in order to adhere to the one-Germany "both good and bad" theory rather than the two Germanies "one good, the other bad" position, Mann deliberately internalizes or interiorizes the disputation with the devil so that the arguments are conducted within the mind of a single individual. The polyperspectivism and polyvalence that dominate the novel make it impossible for the critic either to fix chronologically the precise moment when unadulterated intellectualism slipped into evil or to offer an exegesis of what the "bad" really is. But the reader, in decoding the text, keenly senses that evil is endemic to the work and to the world it depicts.

Two essays from the volume, one dealing with the women in the novel (Prutti, *Thomas-Mann-Jahrbuch*, 1989; English version in Lehnert and Pfeiffer, 1991) and the other with Jewish characters and character (Schwarz, *Thomas-Mann-Jahrbuch* , 1989; English version in Lehnert and Pfeiffer, 1991), can both be said to reflect some of the conventional and antimodern elements inherent in the work. The first by Brigitte Prutti, depicts the sexism and prejudice against females prevalent in Mann's social class during his early life. Women's roles are those of real or surrogate mothers, seducers, potential wives, devoted admirers of great men — all subservient relationships enlisted to foster Adrian's creativity and all linked to the "'male fantasy' of redemption" (112). Yet the status of these women is also marked by that ubiquitous ambiguity latent in Mann's eroticism: "the ambivalent experience of love, encompassing both pleasure and pain" (108). The second study examines the kind of traditional German anti-Semitism that regards Jews as outsiders. When Egon Schwarz weighs the author's public pronouncements against comments in his private papers and fictional portrayals, the upshot is a deep and "insurmountable ambivalence towards Jews and Judaism" (123). Whereas Mann, for the most part, could be classified neither as a strict philo-Semite nor as anti-Semitic, he does exhibit an awareness of Jewish otherness, and the overall negative characterization of Jewish figures in *Faustus* reveals that even they, perhaps because of their very subservience to German culture, were not immune to the virus that catapulted the Nazis to power yet proved so inimical to the ethnic kith and kin of the Jews.

Ehrhard Bahr (in *Thomas-Mann-Jahrbuch*, 1989; English version in Lehnert and Pfeiffer, 1991) broaches the subject of the "deconstruction of the (Nietzschean) binary opposition" in art, which prevailed in Mann's early works (145). Bahr counters this dualism with a dialectical concept of the aesthetic medium in *Faustus* stressing "the identity of the non-identical" (a precept derived from Adorno's posthumously published work *Aesthetic Theory*). Thus we discover art striving to become non-art and, in the sphere of ethics, the protagonist as both a good and bad Christian. Such identity of the nonidentical entails a mediation which, to be sure, transcends Nietzsche's binary dilemma and remains ever under the aegis of "the ambiguity of modernist art" (146).

If *Faustus* stands at the "margin of modernism," at the threshold of a new age but not yet fully ensconced in it, then this novel must likewise partake of the traditions and conventions of the premodernist period, as critics such as Victor Lange (in Bludau, Heftrich, and Koopmann, 1977) and Karol Sauerland (1979) have previously argued. Vaget (*Thomas-Mann-Jahrbuch*, 1989; English version in Lehnert and Pfeiffer, 1991) addresses the question of the modernism of *Faustus* by comparing its status as a "mythical cliché" of the chapbook with Joyce's daring innovations or "eccentric avantgardism" (168) and, somewhat surprisingly, ultimately with Wagner's "principles of narrative" (171) as transposed to prose fiction. This procedure which looks back rather than ahead, is undergirded thematically by the highly antimodernist subtext of grace (illustrated not only by considerable evidence from the work itself, but also by Mann's incisive comment of March 17, 1948, to Agnes Meyer: "How could I not believe in grace since it allowed me to write this book in old age?" 185). By showing how Mann in a sense has his cake and eats it too by "modernizing tradition without breaking with it" (173), Vaget feels justified in refuting the widely held view that the novel in its design and structure seeks to emulate Schönbergian twelve-tone methods of serial or row composition. He argues convincingly that instead of engaging in an *imitatio* of Schönberg's methods in his narrative strategies, Mann opts for a continuation and refinement of Wagnerian techniques involving leitmotif, linearity of exposition, and even closure. The result is a "contradictory configuration" of a text advocating avant garde music and a textual structure derived from an older, less modern compositional model — all of which conforms to the novel's "pervasive pattern of equivocation" (181). This brings us full circle back to the parameters of ambivalence and ambiguity that seem to constitute the hallmark of this work, as its interpreters never tire of telling us. One wonders also what the reactions of Holthusen, who in 1949 categorically denounced the text for its inherent equivocation and for portraying a "world without transcendence," might have been to Vaget's theses of a "pervasive pattern of ambivalence" and "subtext of grace."

The above conjecture involving a kind of "elective affinity" (albeit one entailing negative and positive polarities) between attitudes toward the novel on the heels of its appearance in 1947 and *Faustus* research some forty years later confirms the commonly heard cliché: what goes around comes around. In a similar vein, Siegfried Jäkel (1983) pits the conventional diction of the "heroic" but outmoded Zeitblom idiom against the innovative linguistic experimentation of the "genius" Leverkühn, and leaves it up to the ingenuity of the "third party" in this alliance — the reader — to "think creatively" (136), to transcend Serenus's limitations and attain Adrian's visionary heights. In this process of reader response and responsibility, however, the question of the conventionality and originality of Mann's language somehow gets lost. The use of archaisms in Mann's German (Orton, 1950) and the potential corruption of his native language through his exile in an English-speaking environment (Suhl, 1948), were further diagnosed in the decade of the 1990s and found to be disruptive, but certainly not destructive stylistic factors. Henry F. Fullenwider (1991) sees the novel's verbal infractions as deliberate distortions of the canon of classical rhetoric, exemplified by Leverkühn's overly ingenious, laconically witty style; his inappropriate use of maxims; the barbaric mutilation of expressions; and the interlarding of German diction with foreign imports, persiflage, parody, and archaisms. The "ambivalence of Leverkühn's archaistic diction" (587) becomes yet another manifestation of the virtually unavoidable equivocating factor in Mann scholarship. Through Leverkühn's abuse of language by incorporating the above devices, Mann may be suggesting that the style of the moderns is threatened by those same infractions against which the ancient rhetoricians such as Cicero ranted. The Ciceronian purity of diction, however, is preserved in the work — not without irony — by Zeitblom, thus creating a further ambivalent premise: linguistic abuse versus rhetorical polish. Perhaps it has been the manifold layers of discourse or the interlaced levels of articulation that have rendered deeper forays into the language and style of Mann's *Faustus* the stepchild of criticism. This Herculean task remains a desideratum that in this day of computer-generated searches and statistical surveys should come to fruition in the foreseeable future.

Source Studies

The pursuit of sources for major and minor aspects of *Faustus*, fostered so auspiciously by Bergsten and furthered so capably by Voss and an array of other scholars, continued unabated after the centenary celebrations and still constitutes a major factor in present day research. Even though it is still the more speculative quests for elucidation of all or parts of the novel that prove most intriguing, those based on solid factual evidence garnered from textual, intertextual, archival, or other documentary holdings will most likely better stand the test of time. For instance, 1982 saw the reprinting of Peter de Mendelssohn's erudite postscript to his edition of *Doctor Faustus* (1980), in which the critic, using the diaries and other biographical sources in a judicious and economical fashion, presents a chapter-by chapter account of the origins and import of key aspects in the design and structure of each segment of the work. Mendelssohn embodies the positivistic approach at its best; his work is a gold mine of meticulously organized and clearly presented factual knowledge with few, if any, speculative gambits or unbridled guessing games. It is a more informative than inflammatory expedition into sources, especially for those somewhat familiar with Mann or with the extant critical literature on his work.

After first touching briefly upon several of the more provocative conjectural source studies (such as the fictionalization of actual or imaginary geographical locations), the following discussion will turn to attempts of scholars to identify from among Mann's circle of friends and acquaintances those who may have served as prototypes for certain characters in *Faustus*. This phase of the investigation is followed by a glance at a group of thinkers and philosophers whose ideas manifest themselves in the novel, not so much as part of Adrian's biography (as, for instance, had been demonstrably the case with Nietzsche), but rather for their views or their stylistic features. Next, this section will treat literary and aesthetic source studies, some focusing on small details that may or may not have larger implications. Finally, the discussion returns to the now well established patrimony of the Volksbuch in determining the course of Mann's narrative; but it also considers the extent to which Goethe's *Faust* may still be a potent factor in the evolution of the novel, despite the author's assertions to the contrary.

An unpublished letter from Mann actually becomes an important "nonsource" for the novel because, in the final printed version of the work, the fictionalized adaptation of the material derived from this bit of correspondence (involving a definition of God and the question of grace) was eventually deleted. However, E. Bond Johnson's anecdotal account of Mann's criteria for inclusion or exclusion (1979) of these passages whets the reader's appetite for further probings into the fascinating topic of the whys and wherefores of a definitive text (akin to Schiffer, 1982). The dean of scholar-sleuths who can find in the minutest atom of a literary matter a magnitude of relevance — Oskar Seidlin — identifies the Lübeck printer of error-ridden texts, Johann Balhorn, as the culprit who outfits Sammael, the angel of poison, with the deceptively sanitized costume of Samiel from the *Freischütz* episode during the bordello scene (1983a).

Using a similar technique — proceeding inductively from minor detail to major deductions and thereby deriving maximum interpretive profit from Mann's minimalist investments — scholars have continued to trace the source and significance of fictional locales or actual geographical locations in *Faustus*, a field of inquiry onto which Bergsten and Voss embarked and that was expanded by critics such as Klaus R. Goll (1975) and intensified by Vaget (1977). The latter probes the deeper layers of significance embedded in the city of Kaisersaschern and its demonic ambience — past and present. Seidlin investigates a "Hungarian connection" in the novel (1983b, c) and makes the striking observation that it was in this remote milieu that Adrian's breakthrough in both the sexual and musical senses of the term initially took place and that during his second visit to the country (this time with Schwerdtfeger) similar forces are in operation. Thus the Hungarian syndrome, consisting of three components — sex, the stimulation to musical creativity, and the inexorably baneful bondage to the devil — is elevated from an ostensible bit of trivia to the spotlight of interest. Seidlin plays his trump card, however, when he alludes to hints of a Hungarian affiliation already in Tonio Kröger's reference to "Gypsies in the green wagon," a force that the earlier artist successfully resisted but one to which his ancestor some forty years later succumbed. Thus in their interpretations of one geographical designation and one journey destination, Kaisersaschern and Hungary respectively, these perceptive scholars have been able to evoke a larger and more coherent picture of Mann's novel as a whole than many other critics have done in treating themes that, by the very nature of their premises, involve much broader perspectives.

The major emphasis with regard to sources for individual portrayals in the novel and their real life counterparts falls on the role played by Mann's coterie of acquaintances or on his intellectual predecessors in the world of thought and letters together with their respective metamorphoses into fictional contexts. Just how the much-discussed principle of montage functions in this operation (for which technique Mann once coined the intriguing phrase "higher copying") is analyzed on a general basis by Eckhard Heftrich (1991). Kaisersaschern's master of archaic fascism, the rabid rabbi Chaim Breisacher, who had previously been linked by Bergsten with Oskar Goldberg, is again subjected to close scrutiny by Stéphane Moses as a Goldberg incarnate (1976), with no startlingly new revelations. Among other figures previously cited, the antifascist theologian Paul Tillich returns for an encore appearance because of his contributions to the novel above and beyond his direct influence on the discussions of the Winfried group (Wirth, in Brandt, 1978). However, much more interesting reminiscences of influential individuals come to the fore with the publication of new documentary materials. Vaget (1987b), for example, proposes that Agnes E. Meyer, the wife of the owner of the *Washington Post*, an avowed Germanophile and devout adherent of Mann's work who played a major part in his coming to the United States and establishing affiliations with both Princeton and the Library of Congress, ultimately served as the model for Leverkühn's unseen benefactress, Frau von Tolna. Vaget's essay is derived from evidence found in his subsequent edition (1992) of the protracted Mann-Meyer correspondence (some 330 letters, in which the author often addressed Mrs. Meyer as the "Princess," "die Fürstin"). The exchange of letters contains a plethora of examples revealing her contributions to Mann's career in general as well as further support for the von Tolna connection. Another of Vaget's masterstrokes (1991) involves both a real person and a work of fiction as impetus for Mann's advocacy of a single Germany, with both good and bad components inextricably intermingled, rather than the Brechtian two-Germanies concept. According to Vaget, Sebastian Haffner's book *Germany: Jekyll and Hyde* (1940) maintained that the Germans, like the protagonist in Stevenson's novel, were "commingled out of good and evil" (252). What is impressive about Vaget's arguments as well as those of Seidlin is the ability of the critic to tie microcosmic findings to a macrocosmic interpretation of the entire work. Here, for instance, the good-evil Germany amalgam is allied not only with the sin-grace dialectic but also with the narrative strategy of juxtaposing an Apollonian narrator with a Dionysian protagonist.

Among the interesting theories about sources for specific figures in the novel are Osman Durrani's conjectures concerning the lineage of the child Echo (1983). He extends Echo's ancestral roots from figures in Greek mythology to a character in a Hermann Hesse novel as well as to real personages (Fridolin, the youngest child of Mann's youngest son, Michael). Such analyses, however, only hover on the periphery of genuine depth perception. More substantial are the efforts of critics to trace in *Faustus* Nietzschean, Kierkegaardian, and even Spenglerian elements (not in the sense of biographical details, but rather with respect to attitudinal, ideational or stylistic features). Claude Gandelman (1978) notes that Nietzsche cites the sand configurations of the German physicist Ernst Chladny (or Chladni) as an analogy to illustrate the interconnection between physiological and artistic activity and to express, on a metaphorical level, the discrepancy between language and the things it designates (signifier and signified). Adrian's stance toward his father's demonstrations of "visible music" thus anticipates his own dodecaphonic compositional technique, which becomes a structural demetaphorization of Chladny's discovery. The image of Nietzsche, as refracted through the lens of his biographer Ernst Bertram (the latter one of Mann's acquaintances who, unfortunately, gravitated toward the Nazi camp), leads Bernhard Böschenstein (1978) to compare the views of the philosopher and Leverkühn on music and composition and to postulate a stylistic link between their respective aphoristic and montage styles of writing. Leverkühn's laughter (Friedrichsmeyer,1984), which undercuts the stability of serious, established truths and, not infrequently, unmasks humanist positions as "necessary errors," is compared by Mark W. Roche (1986) with that of Nietzsche. In his novel Mann uses laughter to ironicize both positions: Serenus's firm convictions as well as Adrian's qualifications of those inflexible standpoints, thus leading to the labeling of the work as one of "self-cancellations." In 1989, Jürgen Hillesheim, writing on the "world as artifact" (whereby the "making" of art and the "make-up" of Schopenhauer's irrational Will are compared and contrasted), analyzes the impact of Nietzsche's essay "The Case of Wagner" (a "rich quarry" for quotations) on Mann's entire œuvre, including *Faustus*.

Mann's original triadic constellation of intellectual luminaries — the triumvirate Schopenhauer, Wagner, and Nietzsche — has remained basically intact over the years, even though there have been occasional shifts in apperception and assessment. However, in more recent times this "Dreigestirn" has been expanded to a virtual "Viergestirn" (a quadratic constellation) since the name of Kierkegaard must be added to the list, especially in conjunction with *Faustus* research (Mann only casually mentioned reading *Either / Or* in The *Story of a Novel*). Hans-Joachim Sandberg stands in the forefront of this development, with essays on the Kierkegaard complex in the novel (1978), showing how Mann was alerted to the Danish philosopher by Tillich's initial allusion, by Georg Brandes's biography, and by Adorno's doctoral dissertation. The latter dealt with such Kierkegaardian topics as the theme of despair, the interdependence of language and music, concepts of irony and humor, the *Don-Juan* analysis, the artist between aesthetics and morality, and the dialectic of hope beyond hopelessness. Leverkühn's existential status, enmeshed as it is in "despair," can be compared with the plight of Kierkegaard according to Sandberg's close reading of *Faustus* (1979). A similar tack is pursued by Thomas A. Kamla (1979), who demonstrates how the Kierkegaardian theory of the infusion of sensuality into music, in spite of Christianity's efforts to preclude this very development, peppers the devil's account in the famous encounter in Palestrina which some critics regard as a dialogue, others as a monologue. Finally, Heinz Gockel (1980; 1981) properly links the sensuality-spirituality dialectic endemic to both music and Christianity with Kierkegaard's essayistic exposé of the musical erotic and Mozart's opera *Don Juan*.

Sporadic attempts to tie other philosophical thinkers such as Oswald Spengler to the ideology of *Faustus* by André Dabezies (1979) and Helmut Koopmann (the novel as a chronicle of the "decline of the West," 1980) pale in comparison to the Kierkegaardian onslaught. However, the star of Wagner, a member of the original cosmic configuration, has continued to rise and may now have entered an even higher orbit. In 1984, James Northcote-Bade traced the central role that the "Liebestod" pattern, derived primarily from *Tristan und Isolde*, plays in Mann's works — including *Faustus* — and he speculates that Wagner "represents possibly the greatest single influence on Thomas Mann's work" (12). George W. Reinhardt (1985) outlines Mann's covert strategies with regard to Wagnerian influences on *Faustus*. In a sense, the author would both eliminate and elevate Wagner (who, to Mann's chagrin, became so much adored by the Nazis). This attitude reflects his lifelong ambivalence toward this man and his music, an ambivalence that tilted the scales in favor of Wagner's compositions over his aesthetic and ethical theories, all the while retaining an abiding affinity for the composer's late Romantic musical idiom. Mann found such music (especially *Parsifal*) much more amenable to his tastes than the modern atonal style or the constructivist techniques of the Schönbergian serial school in Vienna. Wagner's "rhetoric of recurrence" (Reinhardt, 118) in the form of leitmotifs and reiterated scenic tableaus are also part of the arsenal of Zeitblom's techniques of narratology, and it is because of this structural parallelism that the novel becomes a truly Wagnerian experience. Perhaps it was mere coincidence, but shortly after Reinhardt's analysis appeared in 1985, Maria Hülle-Keeding, a student of the musicologist Hermann Fähnrich, collected and edited the material on which her late mentor had been working before his death (see Fähnrich, 1986). The subject of these posthumously published writings was Mann's epic musicalization of Wagnerian techniques entailing the double focus of both parody of, and competition with, the master. In spite of his estrangement from the Wagnerian mystique of the Nazis during the time when he was writing *Doctor Faustus* and the fact that Adorno tried to foster an anti-Wagner attitude in the author with his harsh critiques of the style of the music dramas, Mann staunchly maintained his customary ambivalent admiration-admonition stance toward the composer. According to Fähnrich, Mann alternated between criticism of Wagner's pathos and an undeniable proclivity for certain musical moments in the composer's vast œuvre. But aside from a promising start, the bulk of Fähnrich's notes for his Wagner exposé does not prove particularly edifying or enlightening, especially when Hülle-Keeding arrives at what is ostensibly the meat of the matter: the influence of the music on the specific form and structure of *Faustus*. Fähnrich's transpositions of musical concepts to literature do not go beyond the awkward and sometimes embarrassing attempts of literary scholars to find in the media of prose or poetry correspondences for sonata form, rondo structure, polyphony, harmony, and a host of other compositional devices. Perhaps death prevented Fähnrich from treating Mann's late novel in a fashion which would have better suited its complex nature. Mary A. Cicora (1988) explores Wagnerian parody in *Faustus* and also finds that the novel bears many traces of *Parsifal* (for example, themes of sin and salvation, questor figures, and the like). She concludes that Esmeralda undergoes a metamorphosis (to Frau von Tolna), akin to that of Kundry, whose tormenting duality as both an *instrumentum diaboli* and a redemption-seeking penitent also captivated Mann's imagination — a modern manifestation of the Eva-Ave (Maria) polar duality, with the woman as both the path to sin as well as salvation, as seductress and savior in one. In 1989 Cicora went on to claim that the extensive sections on Beethoven in the novel are derived not so much from Adorno's accounts as was previously believed, but rather from Wagner's theoretical writings that Mann treated ironically because of his lingering ambivalent attitude toward that composer's art in general. In fact, she conjectures that in his late works Leverkühn "undoes Wagner via Beethoven" (276) and that in the *Weheklag'* he actually reverses the Wagnerian schematic teleology of music history by regressing to barbarism. It should be remembered in this connection that Vaget's examination (in *Thomas-Mann-Jahrbuch*, 1989; English version in Lehnert and Pfeiffer, 1991) of the Joyce-Wagner connection and the extent of the modernism of *Faustus* takes up the question posed earlier by Reinhardt: is *Faustus* a Wagnerian novel or not? Vaget's answer, as indicated previously, is emphatically affirmative.

In his major study of Faustian figures, Alfred Hoelzel (1988b) presents a spirited, but relatively modest case for Beethoven's significance in the novel. But this composer, along with other familiar figures including such luminaries from the pantheon of music as Schumann, Hugo Wolf and Alban Berg (Schwarz, 1987), together with the idiosyncratic Pennsylvania teacher-preacher Beissel, have all but faded from contention for prime reader interest. They have been supplanted by Gustav Mahler and Anton Webern who will be considered later in the section of this study that deals specifically with musicians and musicology, since their functions in the novel involve this facet of the investigation more than those of source or biographical background.

The palette of literary and artistic figures who, in varying degrees, helped paint the panoramic canvas of the novel and populate its pages with a cast of characters has grown exponentially over the years. Works treating the pantheon of poets who may have contributed to the ambience of Mann's novel either intentionally and subliminally include both sweeping accounts (for instance, that of John K. Newman, 1980, dealing with the novel's classical background) and finely honed vignettes. An example of the latter is Hermann J. Weigand's delightful 1984 exposé of the actual circumstances of the dead-mouse subterfuge perpetrated by Schiller's great-grandson, the Baron von Gleichen-Rußwurm, an infraction illustrative of the moral confusion of the present age when compared with the rigors of Schiller's idealism. Between the extremes of wide-ranging comparisons and source studies of minutiae lies a host of comparative investigations such as Henrik Birnbaum's attempt (1976) to show in *Faustus* and *Doctor Zhivago* the influence on two mature writers of a specific exile experience: Mann living in actual banishment from his homeland but publishing elsewhere; Pasternak banned from publication while still living in his native country. Moving in the opposite chronological direction with regard to comparative study, Dagmar von Gersdorff (1979) traces the function of art and the figure of the artist in *Faustus* back to similar facets of the Romantic work that Mann greatly admired and acknowledged reading sporadically during the course of his novel's gestation period: E. T. A. Hoffmann's *Lebensansichten des Katers Murr* (The Philosophy of Life of Murr the Cat, 1822). This investigation not only uncovers thematic or stylistic correspondences and divergences between the two works, ranging from basic attitudes toward music to the use of specific metaphors, but also subsumes the ambivalent relationship of Mann, as a "late modernist," to Romanticism in general (finding more contra than pro evidence to bolster the claim of a Romanticist *redivivus*).

Before turning to the two sources for *Faustus* touted at different times as either seminal (the chapbook) or peripheral (Goethe's *Faust*) one should mention the results of more limited searches for literary backgrounds in conjunction with Mann's often much maligned montage procedure and the matter or manner of intertextuality. For instance, in 1980 I examined the significance of Clemens Brentano and this problematic Romantic writer's poetry and lifestyle for such phases of the novel as Adrian's relations with the good-evil prostitute and for his proclivity to ally music intimately with the verbal sphere (1980a, b). This analysis was followed by my account of how one of the grandes dames of German letters in the twentieth century, the Franco-German essayist Annette Kolb, came to assume (as Jeanette Scheuerl) such a pivotal role in Adrian's later life as a member of the entourage of self-effacing females who devote so much time and effort to the cause of the composer and his music (1982). Dostoyevsky and *The Brothers Karamazov* had been and remained a prime source for assessing the role of the devil as advocate in the novel — even, somewhat surprisingly, for the ultimate purpose of destroying evil, according to one recent critic (Del Caro, 1988). Shakespeare still stands out (Cerf, 1981) as a paradigm for both facts of Leverkühn's life (triangular love affairs with a tragic potential such as that between Ines Institoris, Schwerdtfeger and Marie Godeau; the links of the latter to the "dark lady" of the sonnets; the Echo-Ariel-Prospero complex) and facets of his creative life, with special emphasis on the opera *Love's Labour's Lost* and on the violin concerto (Szudra, 1979; Cerf, 1985).

Under the justifiable assumption that in a novel extolling total control of aesthetic means and ostensibly written in conformity with this principle of strict composition, not even the most casual aside can be serendipitous but rather must be carefully orchestrated, Ulla Hofstaetter (1991) compiles a massive, evaluative compendium of virtually all the inter- and extratextual "demonic writers" cited directly or indirectly in *Doctor Faustus*. She also examines the criteria that may have led the author to select a particular work, a specific edition of the text, or an unidentified passage (the source of which must sometimes be ferreted out of Mann's often obfuscating prose by dint of educated guessing or of an encyclopedic storehouse of literary knowledge, which Hofstaetter seems to possess).

Hardly has one gained the impression that with such thorough detective work as that conducted by Hofstaetter, the hunt for literary sources should have reached a kind of happy hiatus, when new venues present themselves. One such approach was taken earlier by Nina Pelikan Straus (1987), who treats *Faustus* from the standpoint of a rhetorical question posed in the novel itself: "Why must everything seem like its own parody?" Her response is that the work contains a large dosage of deliberate and deconstructive parody of Freud and Freudian theories. Predictably, this investigation relies on a duality that leaves the reader in the familiar limbo of ambivalence: the acknowledgment of the scope of Freud's revolutionary truths is counterbalanced by the uncovering of his limitations. An interesting conjecture by Straus, however, fueled by the Freudian background, centers on Zeitblom, who, although clearly predisposed to favor the ego over the id, is said to long in secret for a homosexual liaison with Adrian, his adored friend and highly admired artist. Challenging too is the observation that the novel maintains basically a homosexual-heterosexual dialectic, in which the female element is subordinated to the male (the perspective is thus homocentric) and reduced to shadowy imagery or, in one major instance (65), restricted to a few "musical notes" (H-E-A-E-Es, the cryptic code for Hetæra Esmeralda). On a less speculative level, Harry G. Haile (1992) points to Mann's acquaintance as early as 1941 with the film adaptation of Stephen Vincent Benét's story "The Devil and Daniel Webster," published in 1936. Haile's surmise is that it was this latter work with its historicopolitical implications for the United States (America's pangs of conscience over the institution of slavery) that provided Mann the impetus to incorporate similar features into his rendition of the Faust myth involving the German nation and the question of national culpability.

A step in the reverse chronological direction — not an earlier literary text as a source for *Faustus* , but rather Mann's novel as a springboard for a later, highly profiled work — is taken by Evelyn Cobley (1989) when she traces elements of Umberto Eco's *The Name of the Rose* (1983) directly back to *Faustus*. There is little mystery to this assertion, since Eco himself stated openly in the postscript to his novel that he was captivated by the "enunciative duplicity" of Zeitblom (341) and thus modeled his own narrator, Adso, on Mann's humanist schoolmaster. Cobley's evidence that *Faustus* served as an intertext for the *Rose* is intriguing, even though the proofs are couched in such familiar terms as "the deconstruction of oppositions" (Adrian's father, for instance, achieves this in his experiments when the inorganic "cheats" in order to assume the guise of the organic), leading to a network of ambiguities and paradoxes (342). The "slippery or duplicitous nature of all signs" (344), the sense that "opposites implicate each other" (346), the struggle for semiotic closure undermined by the incursion of infinite semiosis, the logic of a systematic subversion of everything systematic, and finally, the reciprocity of good and evil — each constituting as well as contesting its opposite — are just some of the tantalizing formulations of reciprocity in the two works. Cobley's argument runs that any effort to close off an "inside" (one of the above oppositions) from the "outside" (the opposing partner in the dichotomy) is doomed to reproduce exactly what it intends to exclude. This articulates *in nuce* an axiomatic principle leading to a better understanding of Mann, Eco, and a host of contemporary writers. Imitation as the sincerest form of flattery seems also to be in operation in Jens Rieckmann's 1992 analysis of Steven Millhauser's mock-biography *Edwin Mullhouse: The Life and Death of an American Writer (1943–1954), by Jeffrey Cartwright* (1992), the very complex title of which calls to mind the *Faustus* forerunner that it, in turn, mocks. Rieckmann shows how, by means of scrupulous distortion, the respective narrators Zeitblom and Cartwright deliberately draw attention to things that otherwise would have remained unnoticed because of the reader's routine familiarity with them.

Because Vaget in his 1991 essay (in Lehnert and Pfeiffer) on *Faustus* could demonstrate effectively how some of the Wagnerian features he adduces from the text also support his earlier thesis — that "grace is the hidden agenda" underlying Adrian's thinking and composing (1987a: 182) — this critic finds himself arguing for an ultimately more affirmative, Goethean-tinged resolution of the Faustian dilemma than the complete negativity of the Volksbuch denouement would otherwise dictate. The critical tug of war to decide whether the roots of *Doctor Faustus* are firmly and forever planted in the soil of the original, condemnatory verdict of 1587 or whether Goethe's lifelong project, culminating in Faust's redemption through a striving that is aided and abetted by love "from above," had a greater impact on Mann's novel, still constitutes a hotly disputed topic among source searchers. Whereas advocates of the dominance of the chapbook still make by far the stronger case (Frank Baron, 1982, draws some fine distinctions — for instance, music replaces magic — but he still considers Mann's version as falling within the historical framework of chapbook), the arguments of the Goethean contingent are not entirely without merit or increasing momentum, in spite of the vehemence and eloquence of those who, like Mann himself, strongly contest the Goethean connection.

Two major works from the mid-1980s seem to establish the chapbook's hegemony once and for all. Marguerite de Huszar Allen (1983, 1985) finds the Faust chapbook of 1587 to be a model for what has been termed formulaic fiction, a literary device which also determines the course of the medieval saint's legend. In practice, however, the chapbook actually reverses the stereotyped pattern of the sacred vita because of the advent of Lutheranism and the Reformation (these forces making the veneration of saints and the ultimate salvation of Dr. Faustus impossible). Allen develops the theory of the hagiographic potential in *Faustus* proposed earlier by Hubert Orlowski in 1966, but she goes on to show how Zeitblom (with Mann's help) succeeds in producing only an antihagiography. By parodying and undercutting essential hagiological components, Mann is able to capture some of the complexity and confusion of the modern life as opposed to the schematically structured universe in medieval formulaic fiction. By the same token, the manifestly definitive title of David G. Ball's 1986 investigation, *Thomas Mann's Recantation of 'Faust,'* leaves little doubt in the reader's mind about the thrust of argument, and the critic proceeds relentlessly to divest *Doctor Faustus* of any Goethean affiliations of consequence. Leverkühn, for instance, is actually the anti-Faust (or antithesis to him), for whom an anti-Gretchen has to provide artificial stimulation for a diabolically controlled creativity, a breakthrough, which, in the artistic medium, leads to no daringly new genres, but rather to a puppet-like state. There is not even a proper devil in this work: at best the great tempter becomes a projection of the protagonist's alter ego. Hinrich Siefken's penetrating diagnosis (1981) of Mann's ties to Goethe (the latter embodying the "ideal Germanness"), is based on the image of "repeated mirrorings," a Goethean concept that could even be considered a metaphor for Mann's artistic practice as a whole. Siefken settles the Faustus-Faust issue more markedly by omission than by commission. His thorough investigation of the signs and sources of Mann's reputed Goethe *imitatio* concentrates on fictional and political writings of the author only up to 1939 (especially *The Beloved Returns*), and therefore *Faustus* is treated only peripherally. On the other hand, Helmut Koopmann (in *Internationales Thomas Mann Kolloquium 1986 in Lübeck*, International Thomas Mann Colloquium in Lübeck, 1987), is even more openly radical than Ball and Siefken, denying any affinity to, or validity of, Weimar classical ideals in this novel with its tragic outbreak of irrationalism. Koopmann labels Zeitblom a "caricature of humanism" who simply spouts classical ideals; Mann's entire novel becomes a contrafacture of Goethe (121), in essence a work that can "get along quite well without the Goethean *Faust*." (120). *Doctor Faustus* is ultimately unmasked as "a document of a renunciation of Goethe, one which contains many elements of a Goethe-critique" (120). In much less emphatic terms, Alfred Hoelzel, in his comparative analysis *The Paradoxical Quest. A Study of Faustian Vicissitudes* (1988b), also cuts any Gordian knot that may have bound Mann's Leverkühn to Goethe's Faust. Hoelzel again pinpoints ambivalence (and related concepts such as equivocation) as a (if not, *the)* fundamental dimension with regard to the final disposition of the hero of the Faust legend, from its biblical roots in Eden over the chapbook, Christopher Marlowe, and on to Goethe's "re-conception" of the myth. But for Hoelzel Leverkühn's fate remains "unambiguously beyond debate" (168); the composer's career ends in pain, suffering, insanity, and humiliation. This critic does not even touch upon that hint of grace from above on which others have staked their claim to a more charitable denouement. On the other hand, 1988 also marked the appearance of Heinz Gockel's paper "Faust im Faustus" (Faust in Faustus) which by its challenging title also takes to task Mann's assertion of 1953 that his novel had nothing in common with Goethe's epic except for their mutual roots in the chapbook. Gockel realizes that Mann's blanket pronouncements often contain half-truths or are meant to provoke the reader to probe deeper behind the façade of the bland statement. By isolating hidden *Faust* quotations smuggled intertextually into Mann's novel and then establishing correspondences between figures from Goethe's drama and those in the novel (for instance, Echo-Euphorion and especially the entire Mephistophelian progeny), Gockel makes a convincing case for a close kinship between the two works. Two years after having denied any meaningful Weimar classical heritage in *Faustus*, Koopmann reinforced his position (1989), citing in his title the same dictum of the author that Gockel and many others have quoted: "Mit Goethes *Faust*... hat mein Roman nichts gemein" (132: "My novel has nothing in common with Goethe's *Faust*"). According to Koopmann, *Doctor Faustus* actually makes a conscious detour around Goethe's *Faust* because of Mann's growing estrangement from everything that was German, for he had once considered Faust to be proto-German to the core. A modern Faust figure, on the other hand, could no longer be equated with Faustian striving, but rather would be bound to the non-intellectual and demonic. Tragedy was unavoidable. Germany itself had become a synonym for evil and could never hope for salvation; there was only the fall. Zeitblom's allusion to some sort of light in the night, to hope beyond hopelessness, was only wishful thinking. Goethe's protagonist was thus so thoroughly disenfranchised through Mann's conception that the only possible response to a Faust drama ending in salvation had to be an indirect, ironic one, a tantalizing game played with Goethean formulae. The question as to why Mann assumed this stance at a time (the years immediately after the Second World War) when an avowed allegiance to Goethe might have had beneficial effects on a war-torn and divided Germany can only be answered obliquely. Perhaps Goethe's status as the embodiment of "ideal Germanness" had become too tarnished an image for even the Germans to accept in the wake of the war's devastation and inhumanity. After Auschwitz no more Goethean Fausts either, to paraphrase the famous Adornoism: "After Auschwitz, no more poems."

This overview of source studies, which began with a glance at a non-source for *Faustus* because the deletion of a passage in the final manuscript led to the disappearance of that very segment of the text, has concluded with the most emphatic denial to date of Goethe and his *Faust* as a prototype for the figure or fate of Mann's Adrian Leverkühn. And yet, in the light of Vaget's investigation of "amazing grace" as a potential counterpart to Goethe's salvation of Faust through unending activity reinforced by the power of terrestrial and transcendental love, one is hesitant to conclude that the final verdict has been rendered. After all, Goethe had resorted to the ambiguity of the hypothetical subjunctive when extricating his Faust from the full implications of the pact (*"dürft'* ich zum Augenblicke sagen," "I *might* say to that moment," italics mine). So perhaps Mann was justified in taking recourse to his favorite intellectual gambit — ambivalence, to "systematic ambiguity" or equivocation — in order to suggest that a faint glimmer of hope, a ray of redeeming light, might yet shine down upon this protagonist who, in his hour of not so quiet desperation, consummated a pact with the forces of darkest destiny.

Biographical and Autobiographical Backgrounds

By 1975 the figure of the historical Nietzsche had become so firmly entrenched as a biographical model for Leverkühn that little research of consequence dealing with this topic has been published since that date. The extent to which Mann incorporates biographical data from the lives of other historical personages, however, continues to provide considerable food for thought, and some of the major figures introduced earlier — Luther, first and foremost — still stand in the limelight. Herbert Lehnert, who did pioneering work with regard to the reformer and *Faustus*, judiciously admonishes the critic in a general article on the biographical roots of the novel (1989) that factual sources never render satisfactory causal explanations for the unique fictionality of a work but rather only set parameters for a general understanding of the text. The question of level or type of discourse must be taken into account in interpreting the bland words on the printed page. With great sensitivity Lehnert draws attention to some fine distinctions which should be made in citing excerpts from such sources as the diaries, and he delineates subtle manner in which ideas expressed in the modality of the "real" world transfer to a fictional context. In the case of Mann one should always take into account such factors as his hypersensitivity to the role he ascribed to himself as curator of the German cultural tradition, especially during his American exile; his pronounced narcissistic tendencies are also a coloring or conditioning factor. Perceptive observations abound in this essay, above all Lehnert's axiom (in translation) "Whereas the open structure of a modern novel not only permits, but also demands play with unresolved contradictions, it was much more difficult for Thomas Mann, the representative figure of the German-speaking, antifascist contingent in exile, to explain to his new countrymen the behavior of those in his native land" (237).

The year 1983 marked the five hundredth anniversary of Luther's birth, so it is not surprising that the figure of the reformer and his affiliations with Leverkühn's world were revived, reviewed, and revised, with Herbert Lehnert leading the way as he had previously done

(1965). In an essay published in 1984, Lehnert finds that the clash between nihilistic skepticism and humanistic sympathy in man's neverending struggle for meaning in life permeates Mann's works. Luther and Erasmus become personifications of the respective sides of this dualism (143). Leverkühn assumes the Luther role of an inwardly directed, stubborn demolisher of society's conventions, while Zeitblom, the cautious and pliant humanist, tends toward the enlightened Erasmean pole. Gerhard Kluge (1984), at an international, interdisciplinary Luther symposium at the University of Amsterdam in 1983, argued that Luther's Romantically tinged "inwardness" was a dangerous disease that could readily metastasize into the kind of irrationality found in Adrian and ultimately result in the criminality of a Hitler and the Nazis. Whereas Kumpf is fundamentally a Luther caricature based on Lukas Cranach portraits and the nineteenth-century trivialized lore with its various misapprehensions of the reformer, this comic figure, fusing elements of reaction and progress, embodies characteristics of a "conservative revolution." In the same volume with Kluge's assessment is Ferdinand van Ingen's article (1984), that contrasts Stephen Zweig's affirmative attitude toward the Luther-Erasmus dichotomy with Mann's perspective of the reformer in *Faustus,* in whom Mann acknowledged an "embarrassing kinship" with himself (104), an affinity encompassing, first and foremost, that precarious Romantic inwardness mentioned above. The Luther element kindles a fermentation process that stands at the center of the novel, but it also subsumes the concept of "grace" that comes to sinful man "from above," revealing his total depravity and complete dependence on the beneficence of God as opposed to any effort on the part of the individual to intervene on his own behalf (a truly Lutheran stance).

Lehnert's dichotomy of nihilism-humanism and the distribution of the Luther and Erasmus roles to Leverkühn and Zeitblom respectively, again calls to mind Mann's now legendary idea of a secret or hidden identity between the protagonist and his narrator (and the theory of some critics that the two reflected complementary sides of the author's own psychic disposition). E. Bond Johnson (1976) broaches this autobiographical dichotomy via an analysis of the point of view in the novel. He distinguishes between a controlling intelligence — the author, Mann, shaping the fiction with a logic of clearly discernible patterns and guiding the reader's comprehension of the work, and a narrating consciousness — the implied author, the author's "second self," Zeitblom, who is often inaccurate or unreliable in his account (137). By carefully playing off the controlling intelligence against the narrating consciousness, Mann is able to sustain the impression that there could still be a meaningful pattern to existence, however obscure that schematic design may seem. It was one of the most venerable of Mann scholars, Hermann J. Weigand (1977), who enumerated several Zeitblomian infractions against the limits of narratology — instances in which what is reported lies beyond Zeitblom's purview and thus must stem from another source (Mann himself). This intrusion factor is extended to a breach of anonymity with regard to a "real" person portrayed in the book, as demonstrated by the aforementioned mouse scandal surrounding Baron von Gleichen-Rußwurm. By implicating in a mail fraud a living individual for whom Mann had little respect and with whom he had crossed swords on several occasions, the author actively intervenes, so to speak, and removes the reins of narration from Serenus's hands and takes them into his own in order to inflict vengeance on this foe for personal affronts. Jens Rieckmann (1979a) develops the identity premise (Serenus = Adrian) by showing that the contrast between traditional and avant-garde musical views is not attributable — as the reader might assume — to Zeitblom's and Leverkühn's respective discourse levels. Adrian's pronouncements on music as well as his compositions often reveal a conservative component worthy of both Serenus and the author himself. Mann felt at home in the tonic, triadic world of the *Ring* and declared that, as far as music was concerned, he was head over heels in love with "Romantic kitsch" (58). There is an element of unconscious irony implicit in such sentiments as well as in comparable remarks on Wagner's *Tristan und Isolde*, for in such works as these, the composer not only preserved much of the Romantic, emotional component of music but also prepared the way for the advent of modernism by undermining the very harmonic system that had held sway in the musical domain for more than two centuries. Koopmann (in Wolff, 1983) dubs the novel a "double autobiography" (20) insofar as characteristics of the author are embodied in Zeitblom as well as in Leverkühn. The unique ingredient, however, is the passionate concern of Zeitblom-Mann for the fate of someone (Leverkühn-Nietzsche) or something (Germany) that is both foreign and yet familiar. *Faustus* represents a kind of anomaly when compared with Mann's earlier works, which had also presented contrasting pairs; now the author no longer identifies completely with the artist type but rather paints his self-portrait in both figures, perhaps as a result of a divided ego stemming from his dichotomous situation as a German in American exile. An entire monograph on *Faustus* by Michael Schäfermeyer (1983) is devoted to proving that Zeitblom, the conventional humanist, has outlived his function and is hopelessly overmatched by the task he assumes. Serenus has no access to the essential core of Leverkühn's being and thus embarks on an enterprise that is doomed to failure from the outset. Although Zeitblom, characterized by Osman Durrani as "the tearful teacher" (1985), is reputed to have many autobiographical connections with Mann, he also is said to share much in common with Adrian. Durrani also draws an interesting parallel between Zeitblom's chronicling what he has not personally experienced and Mann's writing about Germany while in absentia from his homeland.

Dietrich Assmann (1987), lamenting the lack of studies dealing with narrative technique (an odd complaint stemming, perhaps, from his sole concentration on German criticism), refurbishes the Orlowski-Allen thesis about the close resemblance of Zeitblom's account to the medieval hagiographic tradition of saints' legends (a genre that in the eighteenth century was superseded by the artist novel). He catalogues common features of both in support of this contention — such as the trait cited in his title: "Herzpochendes Mitteilungsbedürfnis und tiefe Scheu vor dem Unzukömmlichen" ("heartthrobbing need to communicate and deep aversion to the unseemly"). Zeitblom's viola d'amore becomes the focal point of an analysis by Ford B. Parkes-Perret (1989), who seeks to reveal a homosexual inclination on the part of the narrator for Adrian (as in Straus, 1987) based analogically on this antiquated instrument with its amorous designation and double set of strings. Namely, when the prime seven strings are bowed (the moving force — Leverkühn — setting the tone, so to speak), the second group resonates "sympathetically" (as does Zeitblom), even though these latter strings are never touched physically. This situation is regarded as a metaphor for Serenus's unique mode of attachment to Adrian and, by extension, for Paul Ehrenberg's relationship to the author.

A great boon to the biographical-autobiographical branch of Mann research was inaugurated with Eckhard Heftrich's lecture (1975) on *Faustus* as a "radical autobiography" (in Klussmann and Fechner, 1978), a theme that was then expanded and incorporated into Heftrich's second volume of Mann studies *Vom Verfall zur Apokalypse* (From the Decline to the Apocalypse, 1982) under the slightly altered rubric: "Radikale Autobiographie und Allegorie der Epoche" (Radical Autobiography and Allegory of the Epoch). In his initial article Heftrich seeks to uncover indirect autobiographical elements embodied in the text, the radical nature of the personal disclosures precluding straightforward recording and requiring instead an encoding process as cabalistic in nature as the cryptology of modern musical composition.

"Radical" (from the Latin "radix" or "root") does not necessarily imply that shocking or scandalous private secrets are divulged but rather merely indicates the uncovering of the "roots" of Mann's intellectual and personal experiences in spite of his acknowledged "reticence in the face of direct autobiographical revelations" (180). Because one of these roots is extremely pertinent to Mann scholarship as a whole, the passage describing this process will be translated in its entirety: "The ambiguous and ambivalent is not an ingredient of which Thomas Mann makes occasional use. Rather his entire art is fundamentally ambivalent, its stages of development reveal themselves to be a deepening and refining of ambiguity. The much heralded irony and the 'pathos of the middle' that is part of it are the result of this ambiguity, not its cause. Perhaps it would be less disturbing to speak of ambivalence instead of ambiguity — that is, of that double validity with which psychology operates and which one recognizes as belonging to the essence of the mythic" (146). Since Nietzsche analyzed the ambivalence of the modern soul and Mann assimilated this concept into his highly developed artistic consciousness, *Faustus* embodies this component in such forms as the secret identity of narrator and narrative subject or as a radical autobiography, both features preventing the work from becoming merely a forced allegory of the modern artist. Heftrich closes with the keen observation that since the appearance of *The Story of a Novel*, critics have spent endless hours in search of sources but have accomplished precious little with regard to the real roots of the work itself, even though Mann's novel concerning a novel offered an open invitation — almost a direct challenge — to decipher the message cleverly incorporated into the text by the author.

Heftrich's book version of this early essay builds on the above premises in greater depth and detail (perhaps too much so) but also adds several new dimensions. The novel now becomes an encoded history of Mann's work, an artistic cabala concealing radically esoteric autobiographical components that need to be rendered exoteric. It is an artifact that, within the confines of the work of art itself (and in conjunction with *The Story of a Novel*) justifies the work of the artist; finally, it becomes an allegory of the epoch in which Mann passed unrelenting judgment on himself. In this expanded version of his earlier text, Heftrich offers concrete examples of how the elements of a radical autobiography are subsumed into the finished product. Thus, for instance, Adrian's mysterious trip to Graz in 1906 to attend the premiere of *Salomé* in that city, stands in relationship to Hitler's journey in the same year to the same place for the same reason. Biographical as well as autobiographical and daring confessional elements that Mann, because of his usual reluctance to commit personal details to paper, relegated to indirect and intricately concealed portrayal, are systematically revealed by Heftrich in this exposé because of his tremendous fund of intimate knowledge of the subject.

Heftrich had made abundant use of the biographical and autobiographical data contained in Mann's diaries and certain previously inaccessible sources, but his research into this domain was modest in comparison with Rolf Günter Renner's investigation (1985) of the life-work connections on a subtle, psychoanalytical level. Renner also employs the techniques of discourse analysis for the major writings of Mann while at the same time revealing the inner connectedness of texts from the early to late periods in the author's life. The prime psychological focus is on Mann's narcissism (Freud's concept of the narcissistic as amplified by Lacan and Kohut) and the process by which the writer is able to both cunningly conceal yet cleverly reveal the ramifications of his neuroses in fiction as well as in essays and other expository prose writings — especially with regard to sexual and homosexual penchants. Thus Mann's total output reflects the process of a cultural socialization of a psychic state, and Renner enumerates the levels of discourse involved in articulating this transmutation. For *Faustus* this entails the continuity of conflicts and tensions stemming from the interplay of a host of disparate forces including the concrete and abstract; the ego and the "other;" original diction and acquired idioms of speech; music as a mode of social discourse and as a personalized document of the self; and, with reference to *The Story of a Novel*, fictitious versus authentic autobiography. Unfortunately, the diaries for the years after 1944 were not yet published when Renner completed his monograph (Jens, 1986; 1989; 1991), so the *Faustus* section suffers from certain deficiencies that should be remedied in future editions.

One area of biographical-autobiographical concentration that has pervaded and literally invaded Thomas Mann studies since 1975 (as evidenced by the work of Heftrich, Renner and almost every other critic to some degree) is the author's attitude toward the realm of the erotic. Mann's treatment of the subject of love ranges in scope from crass sexual aberrations to the more standard modes of human bonding. Undoubtedly, the author's disclosures pertaining to his own sexual orientation and to his now openly acknowledged homosexual proclivities, which came fully to light only after the twenty-year restriction on opening the sealed packet of diaries following his death had expired, have given added impetus to this field of interest. Up to 1975 love and eroticism in Mann's work had been explored only superficially and in predominantly fictional contexts (during the two decades from Hirschbach's monograph of 1955 to Ezergailis's study of 1975). On the other hand, there is presently good reason to believe that since 1975 so much ink has been spilled on Mann's sexual fantasies, hang-ups, and perversions — those he overtly disclosed as well as the covert tendencies that critics have assiduously discovered — that the moment may have arrived to place an injunction on some of the more uninhibited erotological speculations altogether (Koopmann,1992: 218). Indeed, when one critiques certain studies in this area that lay claim to the status of scholarly research, the proposal to curb unfounded excursions into Mann's erotica does not seem completely amiss. In several of the following investigations, one has the impression of learning more about the critic's sexual preferences and erotological practices than those of the author.

Leslie Adelson (1980) inaugurates the general inquiry into the realm of Eros with a straightforward investigation of heterosexuality among the bourgeoisie in *Doctor Faustus*, and this objective approach is continued by Susanne Kimball (1989), who treats the problem of love and Mann's solipsistic, narcissistic male protagonists in matter-of-fact fashion. However, other scholars and critics eagerly venture into areas of sex or erotology that range beyond the pale of standard amorous fare. For example, Laurence M. Porter (1980) considers "syphilis as muse" and indicates that even today the theory still persists that brain lesions caused by neurosyphilitic incursions might inspire original thought and creativity. Winfried Schleiner (1985) analyzes Schleppfuß's "revolting" tale of Barbara and Heinz Klöpfgeißel (the "devil's martyr") as a paradigmatic Renaissance account of witchcraft and male impotence stemming from the use of magical potions. Schleiner regards this anecdote as a precursor of what will ultimately happen to Leverkühn. But he does note that Schleppfuß's report of the incident is actually conveyed by Zeitblom, who is uncomfortable in matters of the flesh and therefore may give a tainted account because of his own latent homoeroticism, not to mention that of the author. Alfred Hoelzel (1988a) discusses Echo as a manifestation of Adrian's imaginary incestuous relation with his sister Ursula, and traces other instances of the brother-sister incest in Mann's work as well as in actual medical records, revealing the significant fact that the incidence of meningitis in children of syphilitic parents is particularly high. Schoolfield had already hinted at potential (repressed in Adrian) and actual (in the Gregorius legend) mother-son incest as early as 1956, arguing that the liaison with the prostitute "answers the secret love for the mother" (184).

One of the pioneers in probing Mann's sexual orientation even before the diaries and other autobiographical sources had been made available was Ignace Feuerlicht. The chapters entitled "Love" and "Homoeroticism" in his 1966 study that treated the means of expanding the boundaries of the ego constituted pioneering work. In 1982 Feuerlicht published a kind of chronological account of Mann's loves and erotic longings, primarily those involving members of the male sex, and on this occasion the critic specifically cited the diaries as a prime source. The "usual confusion and unreliability of his sex life" (91) where young men are concerned leads Mann to feelings of indifference toward his wife, Katia, and even to marital impotence. Unfortunately, Feuerlicht's rather mechanical registration of cases, though factually informative, tends to dull the edges of an otherwise provocative subject. This flaw persists in his 1988 German adaptation of the same topic. Documenting the sheer number of instances in which Mann found adolescent boys appealing or athletically imposing men attractive is not as significant as an examination in depth of the emotions the writer experienced in his relationship with a particular individual — as witnessed, for instance, by the now well-documented Paul Ehrenberg or the Williram Timpe and Armin Martens scenarios.

Analysis of the autobiographical bases for Mann's sexual attitude has recently become a virtual cottage industry in the hands of a cluster of critics — the names of Claus Sommerhage, Mechthild Curtius, Frederick A. Lublich, Gerhard Härle, and Klaus Werner Böhm come to mind in this connection. Sommerhage's early study entitled *Eros und Poesis* (Eros and Poetry, 1983) is built on the presumed link between the erotic substratum of the psyche and the artistic sphere of creativity. The critic maintains that such central literary concepts as ironic predisposition or the entire Spirit-Life thematic complex can be adequately understood only with reference to Eros. The public format of the literary work provides the means to give qualified expression to what the author must otherwise repress or sublimate for the sake of what is considered proper social decorum. But in fictional contexts, an author exposes himself publicly to the same scrutiny as when one subjects oneself in private to a lover. The almost pathological habit of Mann to transform autobiographical details into literary fictions is no longer ascribed to a lack of imagination but rather to the need to sublimate suppressed erotic drives. The roots of narcissism and homoeroticism, together with their respective literary projections, are investigated in detail by Sommerhage, and his *Doctor Faustus* analysis — unfortunately more descriptive than interpretive — serves as a summarizing discussion for the entire monograph. To what extent does erotology function as a background of, and basis for, poetology (in the broader sense of aesthetic creativity as such)? That is the question. However, at least one key query in this regard still remains unanswered: if the novel deals with a crisis situation in the artistic sphere, does that not entail a corresponding crisis in the domain of the erotic?

The flurry of investigations of Mann's stance toward love and sex burgeoned during the course of the 1980s, but *Doctor Faustus* only hovers on the periphery of many of these studies, ceding precedence to such other novels as *The Magic Mountain* and *Felix Krull*. This is the case with Mechthild Curtius (1984), who isolates sexual fantasies in Mann's works as well as erotic fringe areas and border zones such as incest, androgyny, and idealized utopian reveries. These constitute literary escalations of, or compensations for, life's shortfall with regard to Eros. Some of these subjects do find resonance in *Faustus*. However, Curtius comes up with certain theories which cannot be equally embraced by all readers, such as the view that the mother's womb represents humanity's wish-dream. But one must concede that certain modes of unusual sexual orientation may lurk in the psychic depths of Mann's modern Faust. Androgyny, hermaphroditism, and bisexuality stand in the forefront of Barbara Wedekind-Schwertner's study (1984), which cites in the title Mann's revealing confession "'Daß ich eins und doppelt bin" ("That I am both single and double"). An androgynous being such as Echo is assigned the role of intermediary and mediator, which the critic parallels with Brentano's "Büblein" (the "little lad") from one of the Romanticst's fairy tales. Like Mignon in Goethe's *Wilhelm Meister*, Echo is of dubious sexual provenience and also shares features with the nymph Echo from Ovid's *Metamorphosis* . But if the androgynous being also embodies the cosmic coincidence of the diabolic and the divine as well as the masculine and feminine, could this unique individual also be said to subsume that fatal linkage in Leverkühn's mature art between culture and barbarism, modernism and archaism?

One striking phenomenon with regard to the entire corpus of books and monographs devoted to the role of erotic love and sexuality in Mann's work is the fact that in virtually every case, except Sommerhage, *Faustus* is touched upon only marginally if at all. This is markedly so in Frederick Alfred Lublich's investigation of the dialectic of Logos (the logic of language) and Eros (the emotion of love) in Mann's œuvre (1986). As in many of the interpretations dealing with Eros and its sensual components, Lublich founds his study on what he terms "new readings" of the works (stressing even such features as acoustical properties of the text or subsidiary narrative elements catapulted into prominence), with the result that even the informed and impartial reader is suspended in a limbo region somewhere between the "intention of the text" and a "reinvention of the texture." The interplay of Logos and Eros, the art of writing and the act of lovemaking, is regarded by Lublich as a fundamental structural principle in the author's creative efforts (akin to Sommerhage's Eros-Poesis thesis), evolving from a primarily antagonistic form in the early works to a harmonious amalgam in the late writings. But if this premise is valid, then why is *Faustus* so conscientiously circumvented in the discussion? Was Lublich, like his fellow advocates of erotology, deflected from pursuing his topic in all its ramifications by a work in which the central premise is the prohibition of love? Gerhard Härle, in his 1986 study of the "form of the beautiful" concentrates on the theme of homosexuality in Mann (focusing on *The Magic Mountain)*; while in his later book *Männerweiblichkeit. Zur Homosexualität bei Klaus und Thomas Mann* (Male Femininity. Concerning Homosexuality in Klaus and Thomas Mann, 1988), he mentions *Faustus* only in passing (the "secret identity" of Mann and Zeitblom now clearly derives from their mutual homosexual inclinations; Leverkühn's love for Echo is regarded as pederastic). One glaring example of how the search for sexual inferences can easily deteriorate and descend from the sublime to the ridiculous is Härle's admonition against overindulgence in marzipan. He notes the "Zwittrigkeit" (androgyny) and "Zweideutigkeit" (ambiguity) of almond paste when it is used as an ingredient for edible male figurines ("Markusbrot"). Concomitant with this theory, Härle recalls the almond-shaped eyes ("Mandelaugen") of both Hetæra Esmeralda and Saul Fitelberg. In an anthology of essays edited by Härle (1992) with the intriguing title "'Affliction and Sweet Poison:' Erotics and Poetics in Thomas Mann" (*"Heimsuchung und süßes Gift." Erotik und Poetik bei Thomas Mann*) *Faustus* is again conspicuously absent, even though the editor, in the introduction to this collection, sounds a familiar theme concerning Mann's works: "The discourse on Eros, or better: erotic discourse — erotology — seems . . . to be the soul . . . of this very author's writing, at the same time, its poetic basis" (11). Finally, Karl Werner Böhm, who in 1984 had probed the homosexual (or to use Mann's preferred term, homoerotic) elements in *The Magic Mountain*, produced in 1991 an in-depth study of the "stigma of homosexuality" in Mann bearing the title *Zwischen Selbstsucht und Verlangen* (Between Egoism and Yearning), which argues that the more Mann feared the scandal that would probably result if he revealed his true sexuality, the more cryptic and convoluted his fictional strategies for concealment became. But this analysis, too, is restricted to the early works, and its ultimate conclusion is rather banal: because he could not *live* as he wanted to, Mann devised a way of writing that cautiously clarified yet shrewdly clouded his homoerotic predisposition.

Helmut Koopmann may not be entirely off the mark with his admonition at the close of a trenchant review (1992) of several of the above investigations: "There should be an end to the erotic fantasies about Thomas Mann" (218). Note that the reviewer is calling for a moratorium not on the study of Mann's erotic predilections per se but rather on the highly speculative and idiosyncratic erotica of critics writing about Mann and his work.

Falling somewhere between a cut-and-dried catalogue of erotic encounters as they are found in *Doctor Faustus* and the possible projection of the personal sexual phantasmagoria of the critic into Mann's texts are several studies that I published from 1989-1991. The first is an essay for the 1988 symposium at the University of California, Irvine (*Thomas-Mann-Jahrbuch*, 1989; English version in Lehnert and Pfeiffer, 1991) in which I attempt to trace the close alliance between music, love, and death in the novel. Then, on a more speculative level, I isolate twelve modalities of the erotic temperament in the work, which, because of their differing emotional or physical constitution, might be correlated with the twelve tones comprising the tempered scale, thus providing raw material for the serial or row technique in Leverkühn's compositions. This latter hypothesis, however, was not incorporated into my comprehensive 1990 study *Music, Love, Death and Mann's 'Doctor Faustus,'* in which I traced, on the basis of a close reading of the text, instances of a triadic constellation that I termed the "Melos-Eros-Thanatos" configuration. My aim is to show how the three components mutually interact in theme and variation fashion and on micro- and macro-levels from the outset to the conclusion of *Faustus*. This is achieved without recourse to the specifically Freudian interpretations of "Eros" and "Thanatos" as adumbrated by Lacan, Kohut, Dierks (1972, 1989) and others or by combing through Mann's diaries, notebooks, or correspondence. This approach, remaining strictly within the confines of the fiction — overlooking the results of recent erotological criticism and not looking over autobiographical commentary — might be regarded as a form of the methodologically passé New Criticism but it does achieve two goals: the study concentrates exclusively on the erotic components of the *Faustus* novel, an area treated in stepchild fashion by the majority of critics, and it seeks to sidestep some of the more fanciful sexual extravaganzas (such as the marzipan man) in which the critics of the psychoanalytic persuasion are wont to overindulge.

Music, Musicians, Musicology, Musicalization, and Musical Magic

This section on music must begin with a word of caution pertaining to an undated work (though known to be 1989) by Helmut Lorenz with the ungainly title *Die Musik Thomas Manns in Erzählungen, Buddenbrooks, Essays, Betrachtungen eines Unpolitischen, Zauberberg, Doktor Faustus, Tagebücher* (Music in Thomas Mann's Narrative Tales, Buddenbrooks, Essays, Observations of a Non-Political Man, The Magic Mountain, Doctor Faustus, the Diaries). The awkward title is only an external indication of the internal problems to follow: there is little publication data in this confusing monograph, apparently printed in a Berlin copy shop; its analysis of *Faustus* consists of content summaries of each of the forty-seven chapters, followed by a one-page postscript containing irrelevant information. It is publications of this calibre that have given comparative studies of music and literature, admittedly a difficult field of interdisciplinary analysis, a bad name and an even worse reputation than they might otherwise deserve.

Those interested in recent research on the role of music in *Faustus* in more meaningful terms can profit from Rowland Cotterill's perceptive paper on "hesitant allegory" (1977), which argues sensibly that the interpreter must free himself from the "constraints of allegorical exactitude" (for example, the facile allegorical equations Nietzsche = Leverkühn = Germany, and Leverkühn + Zeitblom = Thomas Mann) in order to appreciate the subtle interplay and the hesitation of the many texts and subtexts that stride across the surface of this stubbornly new novel (86). The musical depictions in *Faustus* are then marshaled to illustrate how one should and could avoid such one-dimensional interpretations. A similar path is pursued by Joachim Kaiser (1988 and 1989) in an impressionistically written essay replete with personal recollections of the acrid, cold-shoulder reception that the novel was accorded in Germany in the late 1940s, such as Brecht's curt and cutting assessment "seniles Altersgeschwätz" ("the senile prattling of old age," 31). Kaiser and other members of the younger student population at the time were better attuned to the border zones and boundary situations in which Mann was operating. They understood that interpreting the text from the vantage point of a rigid, smug self-righteousness tends to miss the many tension-filled aporias and antinomies (including those of the musical dimension) in the work, in a novel that is steeped in allusions and cannot be conveniently encapsulated into a monolithic, catch-all categorization.

In a major study of music and the novel in the twentieth century, Alex Aronson (1980) demonstrates how music and its accoutrements (concerts, composers' lives, various genres of program music) can provide access to unconscious experiences, to erotic and morally ambiguous situations, and even to the possibility of spiritual transcendence. However, the title of the *Faustus* chapter, "The Devil's Disciple," is a sufficient warning that for this modern musician there is an inversion of the upward-bound pattern, dashing all hope for redemption or transcendence (could Aronson be a direct descendent of Holthusen or a disciple of Apter?). The discord in this work becomes a barometer of spiritual and intellectual bankruptcy in a disastrous age. An equally gloomy prognosis for Leverkühn's music obtains in the religiously tinged 1990 essay by George Pattison alliteratively linking "Music, Madness and Mephistopheles," so that this unholy alliance of the three components in concert, so to speak, produces nothing but the "systematic dismantling of the hopes of German music" (2). In consequence of music's failure to fulfill the promise vested in its breakthrough, the novel may also be said to reflect the political failure of Germany to break through its geographical and provincial confines to the freedom of a cosmopolitan power. This essay bears some of the earmarks of those facile allegorizations that Cotterill was hesitant to endorse. On a more pragmatic level, but unfortunately in an obscure publication that is extremely difficult to access, Carla Henius (1990) probes the challenging issue of the relationship between real and invented musical compositions in the novel.

Among the musicians — factual as well as fictitious — who appear in some capacity in the work, many have already been mentioned under other rubrics such as "sources" and "biography" and could have been treated in conjunction with these topics. In this section, however, it is the status of these figures as fictional creative artists which dominates the discussion. For instance, vom Hofe's 1977 comparative analysis of the accounts of Wackenroder's Berglinger (from 1796) and Leverkühn as composers with a "disturbed conscience" lays bare striking parallels in narrative procedure, form, and content in the tales of the two musicians separated in time by more than 150 years (Schoolfield had inaugurated this comparison already in 1956). There is, however, no evidence that Mann ever read the work of his Romantic predecessor

(Hasselbach, 1992, pursuing a similar comparative venue, maintains that Mann did know Wackenroder's work). Berglinger's spiritual malaise stems from the historical situation of music in an age of transition from the baroque doctrine of the affections to a more personalized expression of feeling. Leverkühn's dilemma signals the lamentable state of music in the twentieth century and the need to purge this art form of the ballast of outworn convention, to convert it into an idiom amenable to modern aesthetic tastes and ethical needs. The Romantic dream of metaphysical redemption through music finds its twentieth-century corrective in a nightmare, in a radical debunking of that Romantic illusion: *Dr. Fausti Weheklag'* certainly does not end with a bang, but rather with a whimper of uncertainty.

In contrast to most scholars, who now accept Hans Mayer's thesis of 1950 that the figure or phantom in Palestrina who appears with horn-rimmed glasses and speaks so knowledgeably about modern music and its current plight is Theodor Wiesengrund Adorno, Michael Maar (1989), following a lead of Hans-Peter Brode (1973), marshals musical, visual, and ideational evidence to argue for Gustav Mahler. This hypothesis adds fuel to the fire of those who, like Terence J. Reed (1974), advocate close ties between Gustav Aschenbach (whose facial features were clearly those of Mahler) and Leverkühn, between other aspects of *Death in Venice* (published in 1911, the year of Mahler's death and of Adrian's ominous sojourn in Italy) and the novel of 1947. Even the alternative apparitions of a redheaded, snub-nosed, insolent vagrant from the Munich-Venice milieus in the early novella have reverberations in the late novel. With information gleaned from the diaries, Maar traces Mann's personal acquaintance with Mahler's music (especially the ties of the *Lied von der Erde* or of the *Kindertotenlieder* to Echo) as well as with the composer's career (particularly Mann's reading of a book on Mahler by the great interpreter of his music, Bruno Walter). But the question of how much Mahler there might be in Leverkühn himself remains a moot point, even though the critic tries valiantly to reveal the extent to which the *Weheklag'* reflects Mahleresque features from his later years. But if this work does mark the breakthrough, as Maar claims, then Mahler must be the paragon of a new music, one that proclaims not the transcendence of longing, as Adorno postulated, but rather "transcendence of despair," as Mann declared (246). But who, one must ask, would ever consider Mahler's music the product of a mathematically engendered, constructivist technique of composition?

Tamara S. Evans (1992), wisely regarding Mann's references to a specific composer by name (even to Schönberg in the postscript) as a "playfully ironic diversionary tactic" (159), tries to unravel the author's hide-and-seek tactics in the arcane world of Leverkühnian identity in favor of Anton Webern (following the lead of Heimann, 1964; Dörr, 1970; and Puschmann, 1983). She adduces as one bit of evidence the device known as the Sator or magic square, which Webern admitted using as a structural framework for certain compositions (especially for his *Concerto for Nine Instruments*, Opus 24). Although Mann is quite tight-lipped about Webern in all available sources, he was familiar with the composer through the writings of Adorno and Ernst Krenek. Evans also indulges in some speculative number symbolism (such as Opus 24 = 24 years of creativity) and postulates that Mann's silence on the subject might be the ultimate tribute to Webern. After all, the author underlined the following sentence in Adorno's typescript of the *Philosophy of Modern Music*: "In Webern the musical subject grows silent and abdicates." (167). But the idea that one pays homage to an artist by an act of omission (silence) rather then commission (a tribute articulated in words) does strike the reader as a bit far-fetched. Judging by such a premise, the musical and artistic world might just consider itself overrepresented in the novel by the number of musicians and artists passed over in silence.

With regard to musicology as the study of music history and theory, the Polish scholar Lech Kolago (1980) traces stages of music's entire historical evolution in the course of *Faustus*. Arranging textual evidence that appears sporadically throughout the novel into a clear, closely knit chronological sequence, Kolago demonstrates how one can portray the major developments and key turning points in Western music, from precultural to postmodern times, by simply using whatever information the author provides. The reader is, however, left with the fallacious impression that the novel can be read as a convenient repository for factual data, because this article makes what is ancillary in the work a matter of primary concern.

Attempts to assess Schönberg's proper role in the novel, especially with regard to the form and function of the twelve-tone serial technique, are still a favorite preoccupation of musicologists. Eberhard Kneipel (in Brandt and Kaufmann, 1978), an East bloc critic who manages to evade some but not all of the standard pitfalls of that school (such as paying lip-service to the inevitable decay of late bourgeois society), regards Schönberg's melodrama *A Survivor of Warsaw* (completed in 1947, and thus coincidental with Mann's novel) as a composition that actually succeeds in fusing strict musical construction with genuinely moving expression of human emotion. Even though the subject matter of the *Survivor* evinces thematic ties to Leverkühn's *Weheklag'*, Kneipel enumerates the differences between Schönberg's gradually evolving twelve-tone technique and Mann's ad-hoc version of that theory, including Adorno's sometimes deflecting influence on the author's comprehension of what Schönberg had in mind. But Kneipel's conclusion — that the *Weheklag'* signals the end of the bourgeois era because new music must not stem from an aesthetic revolution nor from a revolution in the material means of composition but rather from the changed social role and relevance of music — is vividly reminiscent of the Lukács tradition. Less tailored along party-line dogma is Mathias Hansen's (1976) assessment of the close links between literary and musical creativity with regard to Mann and Schönberg respectively.

Much more subtle, on the other hand, in its interpretation of both the literary and musical components is the analysis of the fictitious twelve-tone music by the music historian Carl Dahlhaus (1982). His formulation regarding the essence of ambivalence in the novel is the epitome of clear and precise thought — even in English translation: "The most difficult hermeneutic problem is not to discover everywhere paradoxes and ironic refractions, but rather to decide impartially which ambiguities are essential for the structure of the novel and which are not" (246). One of these paradoxes that would be hampered rather than helped by an arbitrarily achieved resolution or full-fledged elucidation centers on the Schönberg controversy and Adorno's role in fanning the flames of that feud (Karol Sauerland, 1979, had argued that Adorno's influence and interference are actually responsible for a break in conceptualization of *Faustus*). Adrian's compositions are not to be considered products of the twelve-tone technique, Dahlhaus maintains, even though many conceptual configurations of the novel are indebted to this musical device for their full realization. Dahlhaus presents five axiomatic reasons Mann might have been drawn to the twelve-tone row system, including the view that it combines the archaic and modern, the highest and lowest echelons of human endeavor, and rational thought and magic. In short, such music is the signature of a dialectic of freedom in compulsion, emotion amid rational constraint; yet Dahlhaus feels that Adrian's path is not compatible with Schönberg's own dialectical progression from free atonality to dodecaphony. The upshot of all this intellectual maneuvering is that Mann deviates from Schönberg's system as well as from Adorno's interpretation of that system and therefore fails to achieve the unbroken ambience of religiosity manifest in the composer's later compositions — in spite of the numerous allusions to grace and Zeitblom's open-ended, yet quasi-optimistic light-in-the-night interpretation of the concluding measures of the *Weheklag'* with its ethereal high G (not a grace note, to be sure, but perhaps a note of Grace?) in the cellos.

Throughout the preceding discussion the name of Adorno and his contributions to the final form of *Faustus* have cropped up consistently and yet somewhat confusingly since the exact extent of the role of this eminent philosopher, avid social critic, and sometime composer is still hotly debated. Rolf Tiedemann (the editor of Adorno's complete works), in a 1992 article on "Mitdichtende Einfühlung" ("literarily coproductive empathy") tries to settle the dispute once and for all, and to some extent he succeeds. Arguing sensibly and akin to Lehnert that the mere knowledge of the borrowings that a writer incorporates into his creation constitutes only "schoolmaster" scholarship (falling prey to the belief of the now out-moded positivistic method that facts were the end-all of interpretation rather than the means to the interpretative end), he endeavors to probe deeper into the nature of Mann's montage technique or the "art of higher copying" ("Vom höheren Abschreiben," Heftrich, 1991), especially with regard to the author's indebtedness to Adorno's writings on music. An interesting dynamic develops when Adorno's eagerness to contribute to the enterprise is contravened by Erika Mann's antipathy toward the philosopher and by her behind-the-scenes machinations to eliminate his contributions entirely or at least reduce them to the absolute minimum (especially with respect to the frank acknowledgment of Adorno's help that her father originally intended for The *Story of a Novel*). Adorno's decisive intervention begins with the description of the oratorio *Apocalypsis cum figuris* and extends from the violin concerto and the chamber music to the *Dr. Fausti Weheklag'*. Often Mann appropriated only key words from his unofficial musical adviser, gleaned from their conversations or from notes dictated by Adorno that the author reworked and transposed into his own idiom. The wealth of previously unknown or unused evidence that Tiedemann amasses is persuasive and does justice to his title but can do little to justify the aloof stance that Mann assumed toward Adorno after 1945 in spite of his previous dependency on this intellectually generous musical mentor.

Two literary critics, Jens Rieckmann and Helmut Koopmann, take on the musical dimensions of the breakthrough and the strict style respectively, and their investigations come to negative conclusions in both instances. Rieckmann (1979b) contends that the crisis in art cannot be overcome until the crisis in our world is resolved once and for all — a crisis consisting of dilemmas in life and in art, both of which are entangled in an all-embracing web of relativity and ambiguity, plagued by hollow conventions, by the paralyzing consciousness of the past, and, in the aesthetic realm, by the glaring discrepancy between a work of art as play or appearance and the reality of human suffering. Koopmann (1988), in contrast to many critics who naively accept Mann's extrinsic statement about the novel's actually embodying what it purports to convey — the impact of constructivist music — deflates this position by denying any correlation between the concept of the "strenger Satz" and the narrative style or the fictional strategies of the work. Strict composition requires that there be no free note, that all facets of a work appear related and interrelated, yet the montage technique and the principle of polyvalence preclude the attainment of such a tightly knit structure. In the course of this analysis Koopmann recapitulates most of his views on the novel expressed in other contexts, a trait which tends to make the article more tedious and works to the detriment of the overall focus. The attempt to recapitulate at length or to pack an inordinate number of divergent perspectives into an interpretation which ostensibly targets a single theme can result in an out-of-focus interpretation. Perhaps some interpreters do so because they concur with the Mannian principle "Relationship is everything" which they correctly interpret to mean that everything is related to something else. But unless the critic demonstrates how the excursion into an area not directly germane to the central topic adumbrates that prime concern, the extraneous portions of the text prove more annoying than edifying.

Aside from music, musicians, and musicology as factors in interpreting *Faustus*, there is a related subject which has attracted a staunch clique of adherents. This approach has been termed here the musicalization of literature and it is practiced by a sinecure of scholars guided by Oskar Walzel's concept of "the reciprocal illumination of the arts." However, this exclusive domain of interdisciplinary correlations has long been observed with a wary eye by the critical community at large, and not infrequently it has borne the brunt of scathing reviews — some justified (when "reciprocal illumination" deteriorates into mutual obfuscation), some less so (on those occasions when the musical correlative actually sheds light on literary form and content). Two major studies from the 1980s attempt to wrestle with this subject. The title of Agnes Schlee's 1981 monograph, *Wandlungen musikalischer Strukturen im Werke Thomas Manns. Vom Leitmotiv zur Zwölftonreihe* (Changing Musical Structures in Thomas Mann's Work. From the Leitmotif to the Twelve-Tone Row), indicates the direction of her inquiry. Whereas the Wagnerian device of leitmotif, with its almost myth-forming pattern of recurrence, determines the basic structure of a work such as *The Magic Mountain*, the dominant force in *Doctor Faustus* is the constructivist music of the Schönbergian twelve-tone row or series, together with the related concept of strict composition permitting no free note. Of course, Schlee accepts at face value Mann's statement that the structure of *Faustus* corresponds to constructivist music, but the theory that Mann's prose is in any way a literary manifestation of music's serial technique has been under attack almost since its promulgation (most recently by Koopmann, 1988). Schlee also interprets Mann's remark concerning the secret identity of the narrator and protagonist as pertaining to the identity of the former's mode of narration and the latter's method of composition. The fundamental row, according to Schlee, is established by Father Jonathan Leverkühn's experiments involving twelve subjects (truly a mixed bag of components, encompassing natural phenomena of visual deception such as the "heavenly blue" of the sky; the creatures inhabiting our world — the translucent butterfly; and purely abstract concepts — mimicry as a principle of survival), each of which she traces throughout the novel (using the Adorno-generated dialectic of proximity to — or remoteness from — nature as a common thread for the disparate elements). Schlee's aim is to prove that these literary themes and images (as tunes or tones?) function in much the same way as do the twelve notes in a musical row. Variety and variation are achieved by inversion of the row, the crab form (performing the row backward), and the inverted crab (in which the intervals in the series are turned upside down as the row is performed in reverse order). Other musical techniques utilized by Mann include, according to Schlee, parallelisms, the polyphony of time levels (more than one chronology superimposed upon others — recalling Vogel's theory of "polyphonic structure,"1973), number symbolism, and play with numerical configurations.

Schlee's numbers' game also figures very prominently in Harald Wehrmann's interpretation of *Faustus* (1988) from a dual perspective: the nature of the fictitious works of the composer and the "musical" structure of the novel. The first topic subsumes such questions as what the real models were for certain Leverkühn compositions? what is the exact chronology of his twenty-six works? and is it feasible for a composer to outdo himself in each successive piece? But when Wehrmann addresses the musical *structure* of the novel, beginning with speculations about mathematical symmetry, and then divides the novel into four sections by chapters, each cluster of which is said to correspond to a specific row of a serial composition, reservations crop up. For instance, chapters 1–12 are supposed to comprise the basic figure of the serial row; 13–24, the inversion of that figure; 25–36, the crab; and 37–48, the inverted crab. One has to wonder who is actually being ingeniously clever here: the author or the critic? For instance, the appearance of the diabolical docent Schleppfuß in chapter 13 (a not insignificant numeral in demonology, to be sure) inaugurates the inversion of the original row (Schleppfuß might be considered the inverse of the Luther-paraphrasing, devil-cursing Professor Kumpf of chapter 12). Exactly twelve (that seminal digit for dodecaphonic music) chapters after the introduction of Schleppfuß into the composition of the text, namely in chapter 25, the precise middle or heart and soul of the work, we have the document telling of Leverkühn's encounter with the diabolical apparition in Palestrina — the crab form of the basic figure. This is followed in chapter 37 (likewise removed from the center by a factor of twelve), by the scene in which Saul Fitelberg, a devilish tempter to the great world, makes his debut. This figure inaugurates the final variation of the basic row — its inverted crab. No matter how startling such deductions and revelations may seem at first glance, one must ponder the extent to which purely numerical calculations of this sort — as central as these may be to serial composition — contribute to the "musicality" or "musicalization" of Mann's prose. Also, given the fact that Mann was by no means enamored of Schönberg's serial music and was not very well acquainted with theory of the dodecaphonic technique before Adorno indoctrinated him into these mysteries long after much of the novel had been completed, can one really hazard the opinion that chapters 1–12, for example, were conceived in conformity with a principle of modern dodecaphonic musical composition that Mann neither knew nor appreciated?

Two shorter studies claim to make musical components the paradigm for Mann's prose style. H. Wald (1983) compares Dostoyevsky's polyphonic principle of narration with Mann's "double encoding" of the epochal essence. Various voices in Dostoyevsky's text express their opinions on an idea that is socially relevant for the epoch, with the "truth" emerging from the totality of the intersecting opinions in a contrapuntal texture that involves both the author and reader in the deliberation process and the decodification procedure. Mann's dual encoding practice characterizes the end of the bourgeois era, with music representing the intellect and the intellect representing the epoch, whereby Schönberg's techniques are enlisted to serve as a means of foreshortening the sociopolitical process. The skeptical reader might ask: how does this happen, and why is this particular music enlisted?

The answer: because it signals the end of the humanistic age, the bourgeois epoch — as Wald, citing Hanns Eisler (1973), never tires of informing his reader in good Marxist fashion. Adrian's narrating friend alone cannot, in the medium of words, proclaim the truth of his age; rather Zeitblom reflects the capitulation of the bourgeois intellectual when confronted with the onslaught of a force such as fascism. But what does all this have to do with the principles of musical structure as applied to modern prose? Precious little, and that is symptomatic of many of the attempts to equate musical forms with literary formulations. Critics become hopelessly bogged down in analyses of the content, the play of ideas or viewpoints expressed in the work, which are then loosely approximated with themes or motifs manipulated by the writer as a composer in prose.

A similar shadow hangs over Susan von Rohr Scaff's investigation of the "crisis of musical narrative" in the novel (1990). Scaff's basic premise is a sound one and derives from the concept of the spatializing influence of Schönberg's music (possibly the simultaneous sounding of all the notes in the space of a tonal row) as opposed to the temporalizing sequence (unfolding of a melody in time) of traditional music. The latter engages the audience's attention by a succession of prescribed intervals or traditionally structured melodies and harmonies. What emerges as a result of the serial technique, however, is a sense of suspension in a spatial zone. This spatial suspension coincides with the central concern of Leverkühn: an unending apocalypse (an example of the modern myth of man in "perpetual crisis," impending doom seems to lurk around every corner for the eschatological mind, 30). Dodecaphonic music locks the listener into a cacophony of simultaneous sound and reconfirms modern man's anxiety in the face of the demise that perpetually threatens him but never seems to arrive. It is only in the *Weheklag'* that the true breakthrough occurs, when this composition, written with a keen sense of both love and loss, transcends its spatial format to free the world from an apocalyptic state of mind and usher in a new era. But there is little of substance here which deals with the "musical narrative" indicated by the title of the essay, and even the writer eventually questions the practice of ransacking the novel "for the precise feature of a musical form like dodecaphony" in a work that "in a loose sense at least, shares some of the serial attributes" (37). This kind of qualified retraction is not unusual in musicoliterary studies, which can more readily identify and interpret the "literarization of music" (when a poetic text serves as the framework for a musical composition, as in a tone poem) than the "musicalization of literature" (the extent to which prose or poetry acquires the nonmimetic, self-referential structural features of the nonverbal art of music, which communicates with the listener via sui generis channels).

A final phase of the different roles that music, musicians, musicology, and musicalization play in the novel deals with a subject already touched upon in various contexts: the links between music and magic (the latter usually affiliated with some form of numerical calculation). Wehrmann (1988), it will be recalled, dealt with this problem by isolating the number twelve and postulating its real or assumed role in structuring the chapter sequences of the novel. In past research and in the context of other works, Mann scholars have pointed to his fetish for the integer seven, including also 3 + 4 and 34 combinations, to mention one example of the numerological games critics play (Hatfield, 1968, 1979a and b; Pritzlaff, 1972). In the 1980s this field was dominated by one scholar and a single work: Rosemarie Puschmann (1983) and her monograph on the nexus of the magic square, melancholy, and serial music. The magic square, pictured in Dürer's engraving *Melencolia I* and introduced in chapter 12 of the novel, represents both the connection between the Faust legend, imbued as it is with magic, and the musical component, infused as it is with mathematics. Since in the dodecaphonic system the basic figure (the fundamental sequence of tones utilizing all twelve notes of the tempered scale) can appear horizontally in the melody as well as vertically in the "harmony," this situation is regarded by Puschmann as analogous to the vertical and horizontal sum totals in the magic square, each of which must add up to 34 (3 + 4). Puschmann, perhaps a victim of her own superabundant ingenuity, considers the magic square the key to the organization of the entire novel with all its attendant ambiguities. This critic is also on the hunt for squares and circles as geometric figures in the work. Thus the Kridwiß Circle and its corresponding "round table" and the district doctor ("Kreisphysikus") all take on unexpected dimensions of significance. Some of Puschmann's arguments, however, impinge upon the credulity of the reader: the two farms, Buchel and Pfeiffering, for instance, are laid out in square form but have a round bench or a wreath of trees at the center; the four movements of a symphony and even the swastika are said to embody the secret structure of the magic quadrant. At such a juncture Puschmann might have recalled her own warning about overinterpreting evidence, lest a fruitful idea become an unfruitful idée fixe. On the other hand, regarding enharmonic change or modulation as the tonal objective correlative for that tangential nexus of interaction between the dichotomous forces of salvation and damnation, upper and lower worlds, or celestial order (cosmos) and terrestrial disorder (chaos) is a persuasive musicoliterary analogy. At such points of intersection, opposites may become identities in a grandiose ensemble of interrelationships. When Hetæra Esmeralda, for example, "becomes" Frau von Tolna, this seems to confirm Puschmann's interpretive strategy (provided, of course, the reader also accepts the identity theory postulated by Oswald in 1948). But there is also much chaff to be separated from the wheat in this study, and after one has done so, the nagging question remains: was this highly sophisticated exercise — sometimes bordering on sophistry and occasionally on the sophomoric — worth the effort? Similar thoughts surround the work of Puschmann's successors such as Rainer Baasner in his investigation of number symbolism in *Faustus* (1986), which begins with a disclaimer that the structures of music and those of the prose text can even be compared with one another. But then the critic isolates chapters significant for their content by virtue of their respective numbers (7, 8, 9). In fact, these integers, either in their own right, as sum totals (3 + 4 = 7), as products of multiples (3 x 3), or even as components of larger numbers (16 = 1 + 6 = 7; 25 = 2 + 5 = 7 and so forth), gain additional symbolic import — until the danger point is reached where a hidden meaning is sought for virtually any digit whatsoever. Perhaps the most telling observation made by Baasner is that the modern author does not operate with preassigned values or meanings for individual integers as was the case in the secret symbolism of numbers in ancient or medieval literature. On the contrary, the proper inferences for any numbers above and beyond their mere numerical value should evolve from their function in the text itself and its fictional network of allusions and associations.

Myth and Psychology

As previously indicated, the publication of Mann's diaries and the increasing availability of personal documents following the death of the author and the twenty-year moratorium imposed by him on such materials, opened the floodgates after 1975 to both myth-hunters and those applying psychological, psychoanalytical, and even psychopathological theories to the interpretation of his literary works. Although it impinges only indirectly on *Faustus*, the study by Hans Wysling (1982) on narcissism in Mann (with special reference to *Felix Krull*, a work which spans virtually the entire productive lifetime of the author, from 1905 to 1955, and thus "frames" his major productions), had much wider ramifications than its title and subtitle would suggest *Narzissmus und illusionäre Existenzform. Zu den Bekenntnissen des Hochstaplers Felix Krull* (Narcissism and the Illusory Form of Existence. Concerning the Confessions of Felix Krull. Confidence Man). Wysling demonstrates the tension in Mann's work between a narcissistic preoccupation with the self and the conscious effort to assimilate external reality into pure fiction (which the critic presumably means by the phrase in his title "the illusory form of existence"). Wysling's lead was followed up by another pioneer and major player in the field of psychology and, to some extent, of myth, Manfred Dierks. For the 1988 symposium at the University of California, Irvine (in the *Thomas-Mann-Jahrbuch*, 1989; English version in Lehnert and Pfeiffer, 1991), Dierks expanded his previous research (1972) and also presented new perspectives on recent theories of narcissism, incorporating the findings of Wysling, Heinz Kohut, and Jacques Lacan. Dierks postulates an analogy between Adrian's psychological constitution and the formative principles of his art, especially with regard to relativism and the system of ambiguity. Leverkühn seeks in theology an integrity to combat disintegration, coherence to counter dissolution. Whereas Freud had assumed a primary narcissism in the developmental stage of the child, Kohut sees the child in a tension-free symbiosis with the mother, the two forming a symbiotic unit narcissistically linked through the libido. An interesting conjecture of Dierks is that Adrian, surrounded by a "narcissistic wall" in his youth (part of which is formed by his own pride and arrogance), will spend his life in an effort to break through this psychic barrier. This lends a refreshingly new aura to the much ballyhooed concept of the breakthrough (Germany's breakthrough to world power and the breakthrough in music to a new, modern idiom). Even Leverkühn's early refusal to compose in any mode resembling traditional music constitutes an aspect of the narcissistic sense of the grandiose self. Those who minister to Leverkühn's needs later in his life are simply continuing the postnatal symbiosis with the mother. Adrian's conflicting emotions as an artist — depression and elation — are also traced to narcissistic roots, as is his artistry itself, for which purpose Schopenhauer's "Will" and "Representation" are both reduced to narcissistic factors. Adrian's extreme ordering principle in art is a defense mechanism of the self threatened by fragmentation, and by achieving an identity of the most manifold musical forces, he renders the world as Will and Representation in musical semantics. To Dierks's mind, Adrian's music does achieve the final breakthrough to order in his gigantic fantasy of lamentation, a cosmic order overcoming the fear of fragmentation and disintegration, or, in mythopsychological terms, the crumbling self (the myth of Orpheus torn apart by the Maenads; for Lacan the "decentered subject"). Adrian's music, with its imposition of a rigid order of utmost precision, offers a unified and coherent image with which to combat potential disintegration.

Other critics have greatly expanded the parameters of the concept of myth. Klaus Thoenelt (1979), for instance, discusses self-alienation as a German mythic phenomenon reflected in *Faustus* as well as in another more ominous source: Alfred Rosenberg's *Mythus des 20. Jahrhunderts*. A broad and idiosyncratic concept of myth derived from a variety of fields — literature, psychoanalysis, and religion — is offered by Uwe Wolff in a study partially subtitled in Dantesque terms *The First Circle of Hell* (1979). Wolff operates with a concept of existence regarded as a nautical adventure and threatened by the danger of shipwreck; he postulates that Adrian ultimately takes hell into himself in order to secure the future of mankind, while Zeitblom, likewise a principal actor in the grandiose scheme of things, shows the way to a new humanism. A similarly positive view toward myth in *Doctor Faustus* is taken by Manfred Frank when he tackles the old and the new mythology in the work (1980, 1982). Frank's initial complaint, in the Romantic vein of Schelling and Friedrich Schlegel, is that the old mythology — an essential feature of which was an affirmation of intersubjectivity, since all shared its tenets and teachings communally — has been lost. It is now incumbent upon the poets to create a new mythology. The breakthrough to this unifying force of myth was certainly apparent to the Nazis, and they used mythologies eclectically to their political advantage. Music, in spite of its "ambiguity as system" and its "systematic ambiguity," can, according to Frank, through a fusion of harmonic subjectivity and polyphonic objectivity, express a sense of functional human interaction and intersubjectivity. Adrian addresses this issue in his *Weheklag'* by developing the theme of suffering, which is something common to all humankind. This music overcomes the coldness of the heart, the frigid atmosphere of the age — those blatant signs of a ruptured bond between people — through warmth, even of that bovine variety that the young composer had emphatically eschewed. This late music, then, might be the new mythology which addresses a sanctified community of hearts instead of trying to appeal to the atomized and uncomprehending, monadic minds of the disenfranchised bourgeois world. Christa Bürger (1986), in a clearly written and intellectually stimulating analysis tracing Mann's design in the biographical format of the novel away from any Lukácsian realism toward Adorno's aesthetic modernity (the interplay of competing these forces eliciting ambiguity in the mind of the reader), focuses on the extent to which the author was indebted to Ernst Bertram's attempt to construct a mythology of Nietzsche in his book on the philosopher of 1918. A central component of the Nietzschean mythologizing practice was a conscious fostering of ambivalence, something which accords well with Mann's own style in general and with the musical compositions of Leverkühn in particular, especially in their ultimate fusion of primitive and avant-garde components.

With regard to the second component of the "myth and psychology" or "myth plus psychology" constellations, there have been advances, but nothing as spectacular as the rapid developments of the mid-1970s. Ursula Mahlendorf (1978) examines the interweaving of depth psychology with aesthetic creativity (Leverkühn) and political activity — or inactivity (Zeitblom) — and their reciprocal interaction. In the case of both Adrian and Serenus, the desire for omnipotence is said to serve as the springboard for the basic drive. But there are key differences. Adrian's play for power involves overcoming the musical limitations imposed by the past. Serenus, as Adrian's social alter ego, seeks gratification of his less obtrusive power trip through a seemingly selfless but actually selfish, vicarious participation in the life of his genius friend and that of his country, with the "dynamics of denial" (2) playing a dominant role. Psychoanalytic forces such as the Oedipal conflict, sublimation, and regression all factor into Adrian's psyche. In this context, Mahlendorf touches upon such interesting topics as the artist as God's competitor in creativity and Adrian, the "second son," as a "disinherited" latecomer who compensates for this alienation from the parental hearth and home through his art. The latter provides a sublimation outlet for his human problems; in this domain of fantasy he can act in an uninhibited fashion (the restrictions at Buchel versus free rein at Pfeiffering). Most impressive is Mahlendorf's psychological unmasking of Zeitblom, whose self-abnegation and claims of artistic ineptitude are shown to be bogus, advocated as a means of shirking responsibility and even of concealing hidden aggression.

If Mahlendorf deliberately avoided the pathological in her psychological study, Christiane Walter made psychopathology, the science of diseases of the mind, the prime target of a comprehensive *Doctor Faustus* investigation (1991). Forms of abnormal or "diseased" mental conditions (insanity and dementia), together with their causes and symptoms, are weighed against so-called normal standards of behavior, especially with regard to the psychically and physically diseased genius.

Walter aims at avoiding too literal an interpretation and the impression of a medical record. But the subsequent analyses of the mental states and aberrations of Leverkühn and his family, teachers, friends, acquaintances, admirers, and his wider social circles, are presented in almost casebook fashion. Thus we have diagnoses of such abnormalities as schizothymia (an emotional state out of keeping with the ideational content of the mind). The ambivalences in Leverkühn mark him as the schizoid type, especially the conflict between his narcissistic, arrogant isolation and his evolving need for human companionship. In the erotic arena, Leverkühn's bisexuality is juxtaposed with Mann's unconscious rejection of his own homosexuality. The presentation of these mind-sets justifies the designation of *Doctor Faustus.* as a psychiatric novel in the eyes of this critic and in those of the myriad number of authorities in the field of psychology and psychiatry whom she cites and quotes voluminously.

The Visual Element

As indicated previously, Mann's novels and shorter prose fiction were strongly influenced by the author's visual experiences — the physical appearance of people whom he knew or whose quixotic personalities and quirks he sought to recapture in fictional characters. In the context of this study of *Faustus*, the figure of Gustav Mahler as the proven model for Gustav von Aschenbach in *Death in Venice* and as a possible candidate for Leverkühn's double has already been mentioned. It is a well-known fact that Mann depended heavily upon the pictorial arts (especially Dürer's portraits and drawings) for his depiction of a host of figures in the novel (Wysling and Schmidlin, 1975). He also used works of that same universally gifted German Renaissance master — etchings, woodcuts, sketches and paintings — as a backdrop for geographic locations and topographic features, not to mention as inspiration for Adrian's compositions (the *Apocalypsis cum figuris* derived from Dürer's series of woodcuts of the same name). As a result, Dürer has long stood in the limelight of investigations of the visual component in the novel, and he continues to do so. Michael Palencia-Roth's article (1980) regards both Dürer and Faustus as polymaths whose lives mark the transition from medieval mind-set to the mentality of the Renaissance. Building on Erwin Panofsky's Dürer study, Palencia-Roth sees the state of melancholy as the precondition for the Faustian compact with the devil; the various implements and instruments lying unused in the proximity of Melancholy herself testify to a lack of inspiration. The magic square, however, affords Melancholy the opportunity to dispel her cares, just as its musical counterpart, the twelve-tone technique, provides the solution for Adrian's creative dilemma. But if, as mathematicians have argued, the magic square is merely an interesting intellectual exercise leading nowhere and producing inconsequential results, does the same hold true, by extension, for music and culture in general? The question of whether the novel ends on an upbeat or downbeat note seems to be resolved in terms of the latter. The tragedy of war and destruction, so inextricably linked with the crisis of culture in the twentieth century, is visually and vividly captured in Dürer's famous etching of 1514.

Claude Gandelman embarks on a semiotic venture stressing the visual component in his study of *Faustus* as a "drama of iconicity" (1984). The principal objectives of investigation are signs and their significance in the form of mimicry (including mythical imitation) in both thematic and stylistic capacities, but with a twist: there is here a dramatic reversal — leading to tragic results — of the usual sequence, in which the icon stands in "bondage" to its model (28). Gandelman documents how, conversely, the model is now indebted to the icon for its essence and existence. Father Leverkühn's experiments in chapter 3 serve as the fulcrum point for this reversal procedure, and the most important question raised involves the temporal sequence of the process: namely, is a given icon an imitation of an extant model (true mimicry) or the prefiguration of a model that is yet to evolve (a pseudomimectic situation, a semiotic inversion). To interpret signs in the latter fashion is a kind of temptation with demonic implications, "speculating in the elements," as, for instance, with the sand arabesques that mimic music. Adrian later inverts this mimetic process and writes new music with mineral character, making his composition the icon of the crystalline structure of sand. Individual tones are organized into patterns (put into place by a "tone setter" — "Tonsetzer" — who "fabricates" an abstract form) akin to grains of sand revealing the silicate beauty of a pure configuration. Adrian's music is the product of a veritable deiconization of Chladny's sand music; what the icon was in the experiment of his father, the sand has now become in his own system: the model. Art as mimicry of nonorganic crystals is a concept which has its roots in Nietzsche and extends as far back as Hegel and the German Romantics. Such crystalline beauty, however, is devoid of warmth and even a harbinger of death, to the extent that the warmth of the living organism has been extracted from it. This concept may apply to what Leverkühn had postulated theoretically for the strict style, but how can his last two compositions, both of which are replete with human emotions (albeit fear and despair) be relegated to the sphere of lifeless crystallography? If the visual element implicit in Gandelman's approach becomes blurred in the course of his analysis, the same cannot be said of Elisabeth Frenzel's study (1986) of Leverkühn's double countenance or two-sided perception and the relationship of these concepts to the intertwining of motifs in the novel, which hopes to shed further light on the concept of perspectivism and our manner of seeing.

The medium in which one can ostensibly best demonstrate the role of the visual element inherent in a literary work would seem to be film, but this has usually proven an unsuccessful vehicle for the transposition of Mann's novellas and novels. Most of the cinematic adaptations of his prose works have been accorded a fairly cool critical reception (Renner, in Koopmann, 1990b). Franz Seitz's 1982 version of *Doctor Faustus* proves to be no exception to this rule, though critics stress such redeeming features as the effort of the director to capture the thematic and structural essence of the novel without slavish adherence to the text. Michael Schwarze, for instance, in an 1982 article that summarizes the subject of the film rather simplistically as "the sinful life of an artist," attributes much of the success of Visconti's earlier screen adaptation of *Death in Venice* (1971) to the fact that this movie is not overly faithful to the literary text but rather takes liberties and makes ample use of cinematic devices in adapting the story for the screen. Seitz, however, exercises less artistic freedom in the case of *Doctor Faustus*, though he takes full advantage of the montage principle that dominates in Mann's fiction. Yet in spite of greater fidelity to the literary text, the cinema must still operate within its own realm of possibilities. What the camera shows via its various angle shots, its myriad vantage points, light and shadow effects (as well as color, the interplay of color with contrasting black and white footage), flashbacks, slow motion, and a multitude of lens foci (magnification, distortion, blurring) may, in the total sum of impressions and images it conveys, be very different from the intentions of the corresponding passages in the original prose. One of Seitz's more successful gambits is the magically surrealistic portrayal of ice flowers throughout the film. However, because the narrator's role has been for the most part usurped by the camera, such valuable dimensions of the novel as the humor engendered by Zeitblom's stylized diction and the ironic distance between his observations and the essential truth of the situation he recounts tend to be lost. But this loss is a necessary evil attendant upon any attempt to capture in the simultaneity of the visual medium something that was originally apprehended only through the temporal sequentiality of the printed word. Operatic renditions of literary works (à la Benjamin Britten) are another case in point; profits in one medium may incur losses in another.

The wife of the film director, Gabriele Seitz, edited a collection of essays in 1982 to which she contributed an incisive and readable overview of *Faustus* issues and problems without the usual trappings of scholarly jargon (Gabriele Seitz, 1982a in Seitz, 1982). Various other individuals involved with the film (the cameraman, the film editor, the script girl, an actress, and an extra) present evidence which documents what they contributed to achieve a successful transformation of Mann's prose to Franz Seitz's movie (Blahacek; Klimitschek; Schick; Uslar-Gleichen, all in Seitz, 1982). Included in the volume are the entire script and numerous photographs from the film (Franz Seitz, 1982a, in Seitz, 1982). In another essay from the book, the director explains his use of an ice cave and glacial background for Adrian's debate with the satanic apparition, culminating in the latter's outburst of diabolic laughter that causes an avalanche (Franz Seitz, 1982b, in Seitz 1982). In this account, Director Seitz also justifies the use of Britten's music in the film to enhance aurally what the screen depicts visually. Britten was selected because of the contention of Ernest Ansermet (the conductor's name is mentioned at one point in the novel), that the English composer was one of the few original musical geniuses of the day (119). Mann himself had unofficially sanctioned this choice when he heard a recording of a recent Britten work in 1948 and commented that Leverkühn would have been proud had this been his composition (139). Britten's *War Requiem* thus became the film score for the *Apocalypsis cum figuris*. This development puts an interesting perspective on the composer Rolf Wilhelm's account of his own contributions to the film as "music of Kaisersaschern" (Wilhelm, 1982, in Seitz, 1982). Wilhelm's compositions make liberal use of the tritone interval that medieval musicians called the "devil in music," as well as more restricted use of the haunting signature tonal cipher of the prostitute Hetæra Esmeralda: H-E-A-E-Es.

The title alone of Rudi Kost's assessment of Seitz's production, "Dr. Fäustchen oder die (De-)Montage der Attraktionen" ("Little Dr. Faustus or the (De-) Montage of Attractions" (in Wolff, 1983, Part II) makes it evident what direction his analysis will take. Like Schwarze, Kost chides director-screenwriter Seitz for adhering too strictly to Mann's text; he feels that a successful cinematic adaptation of the novel would have to depart significantly from the original and assert itself as an independent art form rather than proceed in slavish adherence to the literary work. The process of adaptation to a different medium entails both artistic freedom and a sense of responsibility and integrity toward the original. Kost's pithy maxim (one aphorism among many found in this article) for any such operation is "Literatur läßt offen. Film legt fest," which can be rendered as "Literature leaves things open. Film ties things down," 36). That is to say, when the reader visualizes a scene mentally as a result of comprehending the words on the printed page, he forms a vague eidetic impression of what has been depicted verbally; but when the moviegoer actually sees that scene portrayed on the screen, it remains fixed once and for all in his mind. The devil in Palestrina as presented in the novel might well be an amorphous projection of Adrian's subconscious mind, but in the film he becomes an actual other. Also there is the old Lessing issue concerning the gradual apprehension of a temporal succession of events in a literary text versus the simultaneous impact produced by the pictorial arts. For instance, the use of the same actor to play the role of various diabolic figures in the novel (Schleppfuß, the procurer in Leipzig, the Mephistophelian apparition in Palestrina) concretizes a resemblance that is only suggested by the text and also telescopes into the simultaneity of visual apperception something presented gradually in temporal sequence in the prose narration.

When a tritone interval, "the devil in music," is sounded at the appearance of Schleppfuß, the Leipzig procurer, and the Palestrina apparition, the acoustical dimension of film makes audible what in the context of literature had to be "perceived" by the inner ear and eye of the reader's imagination. This is a technique which, in a novel about music and composing, offers unique possibilities but also poses special problems. This latter topic is addressed in Eitel Timm's study (1987), in which the critic examines the transition from "word music" to "film music." Timm finds that this subject is noticeably absent from the literature dealing with the transposition of works from fiction to film (with the notable exception of the 1982 anthology of Gabriele Seitz). Timm defines four functions that music can fulfill in film: paraphrasing (music corresponding in character to the content of the images onscreen); polarizing (music which evokes a mood or impression not conveyed by the visual images); counterpoint (a tonal idiom contradicting the character or content of what is seen); and background music (creating moods such as dramatic tension). These functions are augmented by two modalities, "on" music and "off" music. "On" music is either played, composed or otherwise visually captured on screen; "off" music is not optically manifest. This schematic system is applied to the central scene in the *Faustus*-film — the confirmation of the pact in Palestrina — and to the sequence immediately following it, which shows Leverkühn actually composing in his new style. The same original music by Rolf Wilhelm is used on both occasions and in both modes: the off-polarization (the glacial background) and an on-paraphrasing (Adrian working on a composition), with the visual and aural elements (ice formations and glacial coldness; the orchestral score on the desk) combining to achieve maximum effect. Yet in the final analysis Timm doubts the viewer's ability to make the crucial musical connection between the two scenes — a valid observation given the complexity of the operation. He also questions the wisdom of using Britten's *War Requiem* as a film score for Leverkühn's music, since it represents the Anglo-Saxon tradition and thus cannot fully capture the German essence of Adrian's compositions — a somewhat more debatable objection.

Whereas Timm's critique of the inadequacies of the film and the audience reception of its musical message have considerable merit, he refrains from offering suggestions for possible improvement, even any recommendations for those who might hazard future film adaptations of Mann's works. Here, perhaps, is one area in which literary critics might want to consider a refurbishing of their metier: after all, to criticize destructively is human, all-too human; to critique constructively, divine. Under such divine and "divining" (in the sense of divination, discovery) critical guidance we, along with Zeitblom, might yet perceive that ethereal tone "to which only the spirit harkens" and which, as the motto of Chapter 3 informs us, "abides as a light in the night." Such a force of lucidity should help to dispel the obscurity of the glass through which the reader of *Doctor Faustus* initially peered "darkly" in Chapter 1. By the same token, it could also fulfill the prophecy of the parable introducing Chapter 2 which told of the man carrying a light on his back, not to illuminate the way for him, but rather for his followers. After all, is it not the task of all criticism, literary or otherwise, to light up the path "for those coming after?"

Conclusions, Contentions, Conjectures

THE PREVIOUS CHAPTERS have treated aspects of Mann's *Doctor Faustus* which critics over the course of the three arbitrarily established chronological periods under review (1947–1955; 1955–1975; 1975–1992) found to be central to an understanding of this complex novel. Throughout the following summarizing assessment of these research results, occasional reference will also be made to studies from the years 1993–1995 (to the extent that these are known and available at this date) that have relevance for the original ten topics serving as the backbone of this survey of criticism of the novel.

Each chapter was introduced by a section entitled "setting the scene," in which primary source information relevant for *Doctor Faustus* was indicated or references to inventories of scholarship dealing with the novel over a specific time period ("Forschungsberichte") were canvassed. In 1993 Mann's diaries from 1951–1952 appeared (Jens) as did an important edition of his correspondence with Erich von Kahler (Assmann). In the following year (1994) Frederick A. Lublich published a report on recent Thomas Mann criticism that incorporates into its title Mann's phrase "'An ocean to be drunk dry'" (a reference by the author to the overwhelming mass of material at his disposal for the *Joseph*-novels). Among the works examined in great detail and quite positively by Lublich are Koopmann's handbook on Mann (1990b) and Vaget's edition of the extensive Mann-Agnes E. Meyer correspondence (1992b). However, Lublich's title closes with the ominous verdict that the books he has just reviewed may constitute "the swan songs of Thomas Mann research." Why is this the case? Lublich's explanation runs that Mann's literary universe, with its thematic complexity and wealth of cosmopolitan allusion (rivaled only by Goethe's), has resulted in a plethora of criticism that is gradually approaching — or may already have attained — a state of exhaustion. This encyclopedic storehouse of information threatens to stifle both the reader and researcher, hence the designation "swan song." Yet writing on the brink of exhaustion, indulging in the "neck-breaking game played by art at the edge of impossibility," to use an image from *Doctor Faustus* (L-P: 218), is in the best Mann tradition. Consequently Lublich trusts that scholarly criticism of quality will still be forthcoming. But for the present, he conjectures, the heyday of the wide-ranging, all-encompassing tome has past; what will take its place are specific, thematically oriented investigations, theoretical discussions, and possibly interdisciplinary, culturally conditioned studies. Such developments postulated by Lublich parallel some of those already outlined in the present account of *Doctor Faustus* criticism.

In accordance with inevitable shifts of emphasis over the almost fifty years since the appearance of the novel, several of the original topics that provided a structural format for this survey of scholarship have receded into the background. For instance, "ideological perspectives" based on East-West tensions stemming from the Cold War have, for the most part, been rendered null and void by the change in world climate and the unification of the two Germanies in 1990. This does not mean, however, that all issues emanating from the postwar division of that country have been resolved as definitively as has, ostensibly, the clash of capitalist versus communist credos. For instance, the dilemma of whether or not there were during the Third Reich and as a result of historical evolution, "two Germanies," one good and the other bad, or whether the Germans comprised a single nation in which the good and the bad were inextricably fused and confused, is still a viable subject for debate. This topic will probably remain a bone of contention on which historians and literary scholars alike (such as Ritchie Robertson in his article of 1993 on *Doctor Faustus* "accounting for history") can ruminate even as we approach the threshold of the twenty-first century.

The theological controversy which initially flared up in Germany between the contingent emphatically denying transcendence for Leverkühn or his country, as opposed to the camp that championed some form of redemption for the bedeviled composer and his homeland — however qualified this salvation might be, however "amazing" such signs of grace would appear — seems to have been resolved in favor of the latter faction (Dieter Borchmeyer, 1994: 152). Nevertheless, there are still those today who would claim that condemnation is the ultimate message of the work (Dieter Beyerle on Thomas Mann and the devil, 1993), while a third group might argue for a theological stalemate, with the familiar appeal to ambivalence, ambiguity, equivocation as the determining factor in controversial matters (Terence James Reed's 1993 analysis of "the last dichotomy," to mention a recent variation on this theme; Borchmeyer, 1994, also deals with the novel's persistent interplay of Saturnian melancholy and serenity with regard to music, but offers no resolution of the polarity).

The days when literary critics found themselves in a position to assess the entire life and work of a major author such as Mann on the basis of complete and competent knowledge of the subject seem to have vanished. The age of generalized, wide-ranging studies (with the exception of general, introductory monographs such as Travers, 1992) has ceded precedence to an era of specialized monographs of more limited purview, to in-depth analyses of a single work or a thematic complex and problem-oriented approaches which tie together several texts by the same writer or by diverse authors. Birgit Schillinger (1993), for example, compares and contrasts the principle of "creative chaos" in *Faustus* and in Hans Henny Jahnn's *Fluß ohne Ufer* (River without Banks), while Heinz-Gerd Schmitz (1994) examines Leverkühn's world view in terms of extremely theoretical semiotic approaches to literary fiction and narration. In an extensive examination of the literary grotesque from Nestroy to Thomas Mann as a prophetic seismograph of misdirected social developments in the twentieth century, Rolf Christian Zimmermann (1995) treats *Faustus* together with its cast of bizarre and sometimes distorted characters in terms of Friedrich Schlegel's paradoxical concept of backwards looking prophecy ("Rückwärtsgekehrte Prophetie," 1993: 124–54).

The death in 1982 of Peter de Mendelssohn, a major representative of that venerable school of painstakingly detailed and comprehensive biography of such literary giants as Thomas Mann, after having completed only the first volume and part of the second (published posthumously in 1992) of his massive critical study of the author, may be of symbolic significance as the last vestige of an era coming to a close. In a sense, Mendelssohn's passing also seems to have sounded the death-knell of those positivistic tomes which were a tribute to the tremendous storehouse of knowledge of the critic and the meticulousness of his reporting. To record the long life and life-long achievements of a complex modern writer such as Mann, taking into account the subtly nuanced shifts of perspective, genre considerations, and narrative strategies that such an undertaking necessarily entails, constitutes the task of a life-time, for which the life-span of a single scholar no longer suffices. This is especially true if the conscientious biographer also attempts to keep abreast of the secondary literature on his subject. In compiling critical material for the present study of *Doctor Faustus*, for example, the collection of data for this novel alone totaled more than 1000 items. This was an often mind-boggling enterprise, but a "labor of love," whose love for the labor was not "lost" in the wealth and welter of detail. Perhaps future literary critics might avoid what philosophers term infinite regress (with regard to the seemingly endless mass of secondary literature) by means of a self-imposed embargo on the duplication of already extant information and interpretation. To be sure, a limited amount of summarizing recapitulation of previous criticism is an integral component of the scholar's repertoire, especially when taking an innovative or combative stance to an established position. On the other hand, critical exegesis that spills inordinate amounts of ink regurgitating earlier research by either tactfully acknowledging or tacitly ignoring the findings of predecessors, can, in both instances, lead to a palling repetition and an appalling explosion of extraneous material. A 1993 case in point is Doris Runge's article on Hetæra Esmeralda and the Little Mermaid, together with the links of these figures to Romanticism and to Brentano. There is virtually nothing here concerning these figures which has not been said before. Perhaps one root cause for such repetition stems from the prevalent habit of some German researchers to disregard already published sources, especially those appearing outside the confines of Germany.

Conversely, it was argued in the foregoing chapters that attention to detail in *Faustus*, even of the most minute dimensions, may, when properly interpreted, open vistas of understanding to larger issues. Hans Rudolf Vaget continues in this analytical vein inaugurated by critics such as Oskar Seidlin, when he probes the musicohistorical significance of the operas *Salomé* and *Palestrina* as secretly coded symbols ("historische Chiffren", 1993: 69) in *Doctor Faustus*. Locating the sources for the vast storehouse of diverse information encoded by the author in this single novel has supplied scholars with an arsenal of ammunition with which to bombard the reading public for years. And the search still goes on relentlessly, so it would appear, not always tempered by the awareness that such minutiae may be of limited audience appeal.

Comparisons of Mann's treatment of his Faustus-figure with earlier versions of the legend are still abundantly in evidence. The subtitle of Bernhard Böschenstein's 1993 investigation "Double Departure from Goethe. *Mon Faust* und *Doctor Faustus* " clearly indicates the direction of the inquiry and this critic's divergent stance from those who claimed that Goethe's Faust was still alive and well and living in Mann's memory. The author of *Faustus* was certainly not a victim of the condition that Harald Bloom once characterized as the "anxiety of influence." Mann probably reveled at each new discovery that led further into the secret chamber of his creative genius, as carefully concealed as this might have been (to a large extent through his deliberate and devious subterfuges). The question which one must ask with regard to the search for sources, however, is this: as intellectually stimulating as the act of uncovering the roots of allusions, references, personages or personalities, literary forerunners, and the like may be, does this information in and of itself enhance our appreciation of the work to any degree? Whereas there might be some personal satisfaction in illuminating areas previously obscured by the dark recesses of Mann's modus operandi — since the author was so adept at camouflaging his intentions, even his intention to camouflage — are the findings of benefit for a better understanding of the novel? Does it enlighten us to know, for instance, that the real life model for Schwerdtfeger was Paul Ehrenberg, for Echo the author's grandchild Frido, or for Schildknapp, Mann's acquaintance Hans Reisiger? Does the reader relish the descriptive accounts of Leverkühn's later compositions any more or less once he learns that Theodor Wiesengrund Adorno helped Mann formulate them?

Both the fictional and non-fictional sources that inspired Mann to creativity, as well as the extent to which his novel serves as a source of creative inspiration for the fiction of other writers, continue to be topics that capture the attention of researchers. In the tradition of Bergsten and Voss, for instance, Ulrike Hermanns's comprehensive study (1994) once again scrutinizes the sources for Faustus by compiling or "reconstructing" the specific texts (from Dante to Nietzsche), historical contexts, scenic backgrounds, characters and ideational concepts which form the backbone of the work. Her aim is to make transparent the major thematic strands of the novel and indicate the degree of significance of the source material. A pioneering investigation in the opposite direction — not the fictional sources for *Doctor Faustus* but rather *Doctor Faustus* as a source for the fiction of others — is the subject of Gabriela Hofmann-Ortega Lleras's book on the "productive reception" of Mann's novel (1995). By tracing in depth elements of *Faustus* found in four works by Brazilian and French authors, Lleras is able to refute — or at least modify — the commonly held opinion that Mann's work was too German to exert any significant influence on writers of the Romance provenience. She even casts a side glance at possible links of the novel to Milos Forman's film *Amadeus*, a topic which again underscores the prominent visual component inherent in the text.

The elation of discovery with regard to sources is particularly applicable to those elements of Mann's fiction which draw their life's blood from real-life facts and figures: the biographical and autobiographical. Even though Walter Windisch-Laube (1994) makes a strong case for the influence of Franz Schrecker, the relatively obscure composer of the 1918 opera *Die Gezeichneten* (The Marked Men), on both the life and works of Leverkühn, the predominant trend in recent *Faustus* research has been for autobiography to supplant biography both in quantity and quality. For instance, the extent to which Serenus Zeitblom, an acknowledged alter-ego of Mann and a fictive "inner émigré" in Germany, should be accorded equal billing with Leverkühn continues to surface, not only because of the humanist's indispensable function as narrating presence, but also because of his status as a fellow creative artist (Hilgers, 1995). Whereas the former hypothesis seems to be a foregone conclusion, the latter thesis is destined to engender strong reservations.

Personal documents of the author coming to light either in spite of — or because of — Mann's avowed intentions, have led to a host of revelations and speculations concerning his attitude toward love and sex. In 1993 Bernd W. Seiler illustrated this trend by tracing the roots of the murder of Rudi Schwerdtfeger by the insanely jealous Ines Institoris in a Munich streetcar to a scandalous affair in Dresden. Some of these revelations in the realm of the erotic do, indeed, enable the reader to throw the entire work into clearer perspective (the devil's frigidity and his embargo on love that warms), to interpret a key scene in a new light (the sojourn of Leverkühn and Schwerdtfeger in Hungary), or to discover dimensions of meaning in an isolated image and passing allusion (Adrian's eagerness to hear Beethoven's String Quartet, Opus 132 with "the Lydian movement, the 'Thanksgiving for Recovery,'" immediately after incurring a syphilitic infection, L-P: 159). For such enlightenment the reader must be grateful. On the other hand, Mann's multifaceted work also provides ample opportunity to "read into" images, scenes or the entire novel some sexual innuendo which may have been the remotest thing from the writer's mind but which lies buried in the subconscious or unconscious recesses of the critic's psyche. In such instances, the third party involved in untangling this network of coordinates, the "implied reader" of the fictional text or the astute critic of literary procedures, will have to judge for himself and draw that fine line of demarcation between authorial intention and critical invention.

A similar caveat holds for aspects of music in this novel, the heart and soul of which is admittedly the tonal art. Of course, there are still the familiar attempts to elucidate further such issues as Mann's ultimate view of Wagner, especially in the wake of the Nazi adulation of this composer (Hans Rudolf Vaget, 1994). Ruprecht Wimmer (1993) catalogues the anti- and pro-Wagner aspects in Leverkühn's attitude toward the creator of the Germanic, heroic music drama and comes to the familiar yet foregone conclusion that the protagonist shared Nietzsche's ambivalent feelings about this man and his music. Whereas it is also a well documented fact that Mann's familiarity with music and musicology was at best that of an educated layman, the extent to which experts in the field — including friends, relatives, composers and musicologists residing in Southern California — helped him acquire a working knowledge of the modern musical idiom has by now been fairly well established, as have their contributions to the depiction of Adrian Leverkühn's musical world and works. Nevertheless, Rainer Schönhaar (1993) continues the quest to clarify the relationship and function of real as opposed to fictitious compositions in the novel. But the ability of the prose text of *Doctor Faustus* to emulate either the constructivist techniques of serial music, musical textures (polyphony, homophony, monody), or specific compositional structures and forms (sonata, fugue, serial technique) still remains an extremely gray area of research, more appealing in its hypothetical formulation than convincing in practical application. In spite of this, Harald Wehrmann (1993) persists in claiming a kinship between the fictional structures and twelve-tone row composition, relying on Mann's statement to the effect that with regard to musical techniques, the novel practices what it preaches.

The note of caution invoked for musico-fictional relations must also be exercised in the case of mathematico-musical correlations. No one will deny that the "numbers game" and certain numerical formulae constitute key facets of tonal relationships (Pythagoras proved that) and compositional strategies (budding serial composers are today still preoccupied with the "magic square" concept as a helpmate for constructivist music). Mann's own dabbling in the symbolism of numbers and numerical configurations is also an established topos in criticism. Volker Dörr (1993) associates "the world of the magic square" with the figures of Dürer and Nietzsche as well as with the composition of the *Apocalypsis cum figuris*. Yet once again, the linking of basic numerical figures such as the integer seven or the number twelve to elaborate literary phenomena and their compositional counterparts, even in a novel devoted to evolution and revolution in modern music, requires a suspension of "disbelief" that not everyone is "willing" to render.

Mann's own terms "myth plus psychology," augmented in succeeding generations by the critics' concept of "myth and psychology," can be considered today as constituting the separate disciplines of "mythology" and "psychology" when applied to *Doctor Faustus*. However, if a particular mythical concept has become an integral component of psychological lore (such as those associated with Oedipus and Narcissus), one might even regard the two fields as coexisting in a symbiotic relationship for both the author and his characters. Myth conveys the idea of a pre-patterned or pre-conditioned form of human response that has persisted over the ages; thus Siegfried Jäkel (1993) can discuss the reception of the figures of Faust and Don Juan in the twentieth century and in *Faustus* under the rubric: European myths of the modern era. Unfortunately, the term "myth" has been invoked by critics so often and has grown to be such common currency in literary studies, that it has lost much of its uniquely Mannian flavor due to what might be termed in the vernacular "overkill." With regard to the "mythical" component (such as the "divine child" concept) in *Faustus*, I examined Goethe's Mignon and Mann's Echo (1993) in terms of the threshold image (the threshold as a site of initiation from one realm into another and of mediation between viable entities). Both figures exude a certain sexual indeterminacy; they hover precariously between childlike innocence and precociousness, and even reside in a kind of spiritual limbo between their native soil and foreign environs, to mention only a few aspects of what could be termed their threshold status. Given the frequency and intensity of the threshold ("Schwelle") as a literal image, metaphorical concept, thematic substructure, and even narratological device in contemporary German fiction, it might be said to have assumed the proportions of a modern myth. Peter Handke's 1983 novel, *Der Chinese des Schmerzes* (translated into English as *Across*), for instance, teems with allusions to literal and figurative thresholds, to threshold situations and threshold seekers, all of which Peter Pütz analyzed in a volume of essays (1990) entitled appropriately *Literature on the Threshold: The German Novel in the 1980s*. In 1992 I attempted to demonstrate some of the threshold potential in both the original text of *Death in Venice* and the cinematic adaptation of the novella. The application of the threshold concept to the entire *Doctor Faustus* novel, on the other hand, is a topic replete with possibilities for present and future scholars. Dieter Borchmeyer, in his aforementioned analysis of music under the sway of Saturn in the novel (1994), notes how Leverkühn's compositions stand poised on an intermediary axis between the polarities of melancholy and serenity, a threshold stance commensurate with the ambivalence which characterizes the acoustical medium and its "message" *ab ovo*.

The psychological aspect of Mann has taken on added dimensions of sexual inference, especially once Freudian psychoanalysis was resurrected by critical theorists, sociologists, semioticians, deconstructionists, and other members of the current academe. Whereas the trained psychologist might run the risk of mistaking a literary work for a casebook history of a particular psychic disturbance, the representative of literature must avoid the danger of amateur psychologizing or, what is perhaps even worse, of projecting into the fictional world aspects of one's own psychic disposition. As previously indicated in this study, Thomas Mann research has not always been immune from this form of the intentional fallacy.

Finally, the concern of critics for the visual element either inherent in *Doctor Faustus*, intrinsic to the author's modus operandi (drawing from iconographic representations, from eidetic images of family members and friends), or implicit in the cinematic adaptation of the work, leads to a problem area which needs to be addressed. Visualizations offered by such media as the film tend to concretize something which, in the realm of fiction, was previously accessible to the insight of the fantasy alone. One might recall in this connection Kafka's refusal to allow the bug from *The Metamorphosis* to be portrayed on the cover of the published edition of the story, for he felt that such a concretization would detract from the mysterious aura that surrounds the creature in its totally non-specific ambience. In the case of the 1982 *Doctor Faustus* film, a dimension of that ambivalence which has become the hallmark of this work and its creator is abrogated by cinematic adaptation. What we have in its stead is a definitive image, a precise pictorial representation with discernible contours (the devil in Palestrina, for instance) of something that we had previously envisioned in our mind's eye alone, guided solely by the printed word on the page. The same holds true in the acoustical realm for Leverkühn's music that emanates from the screen as both compositions of some original genius (Britten) which approximate the style ascribed to Adrian's works or as original works emulating what Adrian's compositional style might have been (Wilhelm). In either case, what was once the provenance of the mind's ear alone now becomes, for better or worse, an actualized aural experience.

Arguing from the opposite end of the spectrum, one might claim that any reduction in the degree of inherent ambivalence and ambiguity in the novel as a result of imagistic or acoustic specificity may, in the final analysis, not be all bad. Any one who has attempted to master *Doctor Faustus* and the secondary literature on Thomas Mann realizes that the "system of ambiguity" invariably serves as the ultimate solution for, or resolution of, most of the problems addressed. Few scholars remain immune from the infectious wave of equivocation that still runs rampant in the critical literature on the author and that seeks confirmation by appealing to the fundamental stance of the "ironic German" with regard to life and its elusive reflection in literature. Certainly I cannot claim exclusion from this clique or exemption from this implicit critique either (Fetzer, 1990). But perhaps the moment may be at hand to place an injunction on the threadbare concepts of equivocality and ambivalence which for so long have performed yeoman service in the cause of Mann criticism, and now need to be relieved of their duty in favor of something resembling a definitive commitment.

Just what that "something" might be, however, will be contingent upon another frustratingly familiar concept that, with Thomas Mann, always has the last word: the ambiguous. The axiomatic claim of young Leverkühn, it will be recalled, reads: "Beziehung ist alles. Und willst du sie näher beim Namen nennen, so ist ihr Name 'Zweideutigkeit'" (Mann: 66); "Relationship is everything. And if you want to give it a more precise name, it is ambiguity" (L-P: 47). But when pondering such statements, one is now alert to the fact that the German word used here, "Zweideutigkeit," does not imply ambiguity as a lack of clarity because of terminological opacity or mental confusion. Rather it signifies a twofold ("ambi-") or double valency that is reminiscent of Mann's "double optic" or, in the case of music, the dual acoustical experience of melody and harmony, monody and polyphony, or the simultaneous engagement of both emotional reaction and intellectual response. When such coequal forces are involved, there is no clear-cut priority for either component; rather a stalemate situation results, one in which the ultimate truth of the matter becomes suspended in limbo, hovering "on the threshold" between viable alternatives of competitive validity. Remember, too, that the budding composer, expanding upon his original premise, subsequently declares "Daß Musik die Zweideutigkeit ist als System" (Mann: 66); "Music turns the equivocal into a system" (L-P: 47). What we have here is a kind of syllogistic argument, ending with the proposition that ambiguity can, under optimal conditions, ultimately lend itself to systematization. Perhaps for the serious student of literature there is even the possibility, as modernism cedes precedence to postmodernist trends in critical thinking, that after approximately a century of Mann studies in general and almost a half century of *Faustus* criticism in particular, we may yet find the key to unlock that elusive system of the equivocal, thereby dispelling some of the mysteries onto which this author, behind the inscrutable mask of Maja and in the guise of the Magician (as he liked to refer to himself and often heard himself referred to) cast his enigmatic spell.

Works Cited (In Chronological Order)

Thomas Mann's Works

1947 *Doktor Faustus. Das Leben des deutschen Tonsetzers Adrian Leverkühn, erzählt von einem Freunde.* Vol. 6 of Thomas *Mann. Gesammelte Werke in zwölf Bänden.* Frankfurt am Main: S. Fischer, 1960. German quotations in the text are from this edition and indicated by: (Mann: + page number.)

1948 *Doctor Faustus. The Life of the German Composer Adrian Leverkühn as Told by a Friend.* Trans. H(elen).T(racy). Lowe-Porter. New York: Knopf. Quotations from this edition are indicated in the text by: (L-P: + page number.)

1949 *Die Entstehung des 'Doktor Faustus:' Roman eines Romans.* Frankfurt am Main: S. Fischer.

1961 *The Story of a Novel. The Genesis of 'Doctor Faustus.'* Trans. Richard and Clara Winston. New York: Knopf.

Critical Works

Abbreviations for frequently cited journals:

    DVLG   *Deutsche Vierteljahrsschrift für Literaturwissenschaft und Geistesgeschichte*
    EG   *Études Germaniques*
    GL&L   *German Life and Letters* (New Series)
    GR   *Germanic Review*
    JEGP   *Journal of English and Germanic Philology*
    OL   *Orbis Litterarum*
    ZDP   *Zeitschrift für deutsche Philologie*

Staiger, Emil. 1947. "Thomas Manns *Doktor Faustus.*" *Neue Schweizer Rundschau* 15: 423–30.

Becher, Hubert. 1948. "Thomas Mann und sein Faust-Buch." *Stimmen der Zeit* 143: 213–22.

Blankenagel, John C. 1948. "A Nietzsche Episode in Thomas Mann's *Doktor Faustus.*" *Modern Language Notes* 63: 387–90.

Boehlich, Walter. 1948. "Thomas Manns *Doktor Faustus*." *Merkur* 2: 588–603.

Colleville, Maurice. 1948. "Nietzsche et le *Doktor Faustus* de Thomas Mann." *EG* 3: 343–54.

Eichner, Hans. 1948. "The Place of *Doktor Faustus* in the Work of Thomas Mann." *GL&L* 1: 289–302.

Fetscher, Iring. 1948. "Der andere Weg. Betrachtungen zum *Doktor Faustus* von Thomas Mann." *Studentische Blätter* 6: 3–6. Reprinted in his *Die Wirksamkeit der Träume. Literarische Skizzen eines Sozialwissenschaftlers*. Frankfurt am Main: Athenäum, 1987. 96–110.

Gronicka, André von. 1948. "Thomas Mann's *Doktor Faustus*. Prolegomena to an Interpretation." *GR* 23: 206–18.

Herz, Gerhard. 1948. "The Music of Mann's *Doktor Faustus*." *Perspectives* 3: 48–64.

Kahler, Erich. 1948. "Die Säkularisierung des Teufels." *Neue Rundschau* 59: 185–202. Translated into English in Kahler, 1969, 20–43.

Maier, Hans A. 1948. "Die Stellung des *Doktor Faustus* im Gesamtwerk Thomas Manns." *Modern Language Quarterly* 9: 343–53.

Mayer, Hans. 1948. Untitled review and discussion of *Doktor Faustus. Ost und West* 2, Issue 6: 23–30.

Mendelssohn, Peter de. 1948. *Der Zauberer. Drei Briefe über Thomas Manns 'Doktor Faustus' an einen Freund in der Schweiz*. Berlin: Ullstein-Kindler.

Milch, Werner. 1948. "Thomas Manns *Doktor Faustus*." *Die Sammlung* 3: 351-60.

Montesi, Gotthard. 1948. "Thomas Mann, der Teufel und die Deutschen." *Wort und Wahrheit* 3: 495–510.

Oswald, Victor A. 1948. "Thomas Mann's *Doktor Faustus* : The Enigma of Frau von Tolna." *GR* 23: 249–53.

Rilla, Paul. 1948. "Notizen zu Thomas Manns *Doktor Faustus*." *Dramaturgische Blätter* 2, Issue 4: 145–55.

Sell, Friedrich. 1948. "Ein Kommentar zu Thomas Manns *Doktor Faustus*." *Monatshefte* 40: 195–203.

Suhl, Abraham. 1948. "Anglizismen in Thomas Manns *Doktor Faustus*." *Monatshefte* 40: 391–95.

Zuckerkandl, Victor. 1948. "Die Musik des *Doktor Faustus*." *Neue Rundschau* 59: 203–14.

Braun, Hanns. 1949. "Die Welt ohne Transzendenz? Zu einer kritischen Studie an Thomas Manns *Doktor Faustus*." *Hochland* 41: 594–601.

Brock, Erich. 1949. "Die ideengeschichtliche Bedeutung von Thomas Manns *Doktor Faustus.*" *Trivium* 7: 114–43.

Butler, Eliza M. 1949. "The Traditional Elements in Thomas Mann's *Doktor Faustus.*" *Publications of the English Goethe Society* 18: 1–33.

Carlsson, Anni. 1949. "Das Faustmotiv bei Thomas Mann." *Deutsche Beiträge* 3:343–62. Reprinted in Wolff, 1983, Part I: 84–123.

Doflein, Erich. 1949. "Leverkühns Inspirator. Eine Philosophie der neuen Musik." *Die Gegenwart* 4, Issue 22: 22–24.

Engel, Hans. 1949. "Musik der Krise, Krise der Musik, oder *Doktor Faustus*. Zu Thomas Manns Roman." *Neue Musikzeitschrift* 3: 336–42.

Fischer, Ernst. 1949. "*Doktor Faustus* und die deutsche Katastrophe. Eine Auseinandersetzung mit Thomas Mann." In his *Kunst und Menschheit. Essays.* Vienna: Globus-Verlag. 35–97.

Frank, Joseph. 1949. "Reaction as Progress, or The Devil's Domain: Notes on *Doctor Faustus.*" *Hudson Review* 2: 38–53.

Goes, Albrecht. 1949. "Tagebuch der Faustus-Lektüre." *Almanach auf das Jahr* 1949, 98–117. Reprinted 1953 in his *Erfüllter Augenblick: Eine Auswahl.* Frankfurt am Main: S. Fischer. 47–69.

Holthusen, Hans Egon. 1949. "Die Welt ohne Transzendenz." *Merkur* 3: 38-58, 161–80. Reprinted 1949 in his *Die Welt ohne Transzendenz. Eine Studie zu Thomas Manns Dr. Faustus und seine Nebenschriften.* Hamburg: Ellermann.

Kaufmann, Fritz. 1949. "Doktor Fausti Weheklag'" *Archiv für Philosophie* 3: 25–48.

Kielmeyer, Otto. 1949. "Thomas Manns *Doktor Faustus* im Deutschunterricht." *Der Deutschunterricht* 2: 23–31.

Knopf, Alfred A., ed. 1949. *A Pocket Guide to Thomas Mann's 'Doctor Faustus.'* New York: Knopf.

Lewalter, Christian E. and Hans Paeschke. 1949. "Thomas Mann und Kierkegaard: Ein Briefwechsel über den *Doktor Faustus* und seine Kritiker." *Merkur* 3: 925–36. For Paeschke's modification of his position here, see his 1975 response to Dolf Sternberger's article of the same year.

Lüders, Eva M. 1949. "Dämonie und Humanismus. Zu Thomas Manns *Doktor Faustus.*" *Stimmen der Zeit* 143: 293–99.

Lukács, Georg. 1949. "Auf der Suche nach dem Bürger. Die Tragödie der modernen Kunst." *Aufbau* 5, Issue 1: 59–79, 154–69. Translated into English by Stanley Mitchel, 1964, in *Essays on Thomas Mann: Georg Lukács.* London: Merlin. 13–97.

Mann, Thomas. 1949. "Thomas Mann's Answer." *Saturday Review of Literature* 32 (January 1,1949): 22–23.

Merrick, Joan Muriel. 1949. "Mann's *Doctor Faustus* and a Passage from Heine." *Modern Language Forum* 34: 127–29.

Müller-Blattau, Joseph. 1949. "Sinn und Sendung der Musik in Thomas Manns *Doktor Faustus* und Hermann Hesses *Glasperlenspiel.*" *Geistige Welt* 4: 29–34.

Oswald, Victor A. 1949. "Full Fathom Five: Notes on Some Devices in Thomas Mann's *Doktor Faustus.*" *GR* 24: 274–78.

Pringsheim, Klaus. 1949a. "The Music of Adrian Leverkühn." *Musicology* 2: 255–68.

———. 1949b. "Der Tonsetzer Adrian Leverkühn." *Der Monat* 1: 84–91

Rice, Philip B. 1949. "The Merging Parallels: Thomas Mann's *Doktor Faustus.*" *Kenyon Review* 11: 199–217.

Rochocz, Hans. 1949. "Thomas Manns *Doktor Faustus* und das Ethos." *Deutsche Beiträge* 3: 182–87.

Schönberg, Arnold. 1949. "Doctor Faustus Schönberg? Letter to the Editor." *Saturday Review of Literature* 32 (January 1, 1949) : 22

Schuh, Willi. 1949. "Thomas Mann und Arnold Schönberg. Zu einer Kontroverse." *Neue Auslese* 4, Issue 3: 71–76.

Seiferth, Wolfgang. 1949. "Das deutsche Schicksal in Thomas Manns *Doktor Faustus.*" *Monatshefte* 41: 187–202.

Sender, Ramón J. 1949. "Faustian Germany and Thomas Mann." *New Mexico Quarterly Review* 19: 193–206.

Times Literary Supplement. 1949, May 6. Anonymous review of *Doctor Faustus.* 49: 293.

Bianquis, Geneviève. 1950. "Thomas Mann et le 'Faustbuch' de 1587." *EG* 5: 54–59.

Blackmur, Richard P. 1950. "Parody and Critique: Notes on Thomas Mann's *Doktor Faustus.*" *Kenyon Review* 12: 20–40.

Bonwit, Marianne. 1950. "Babel in Modern Fiction." *Comparative Literature* 2: 237–47.

Enright, Dennis J. 1950. "The *Doktor Faustus* of Thomas Mann." *Scrutiny* 7: 154–67.

Heintel, Erich. 1950. "Adrian Leverkühn und Friedrich Nietzsche." *Wissenschaft und Weltbild* 3: 297–303.

Kohlschmidt, Werner. 1950. "Musikalität, Reformation und Deutschtum. Eine kritische Studie zu Thomas Manns *Doktor Faustus.*" *Zeitwende* 21: 541–50.

Leonard, Kurt. 1950. "Der Geist und der Teufel. Anmerkungen zu zwei neuen Variationen des Faust-Themas: Thomas Mann und Paul Valéry." *Neue Rundschau* 61: 588–602.

Mayer, Hans. 1950. *Thomas Mann: Werk und Entwicklung.* Berlin: Verlag Volk und Welt.

Orton, G. 1950. "The Archaic Language in Thomas Mann's *Doktor Faustus.*" *Modern Language Review* 45:70–75.

Oswald, Victor A. 1950. "Thomas Mann and the Mermaid: A Note on Constructivistic Music." *Modern Language Notes* 65: 171–75.

Pickard, P. M. 1950. "Thomas Mann's *Doctor Faustus*, a Psychological Approach." *GL&L* 4: 90–100.

Rey, William H. 1950. "Return to Health? 'Disease' in Mann's *Doctor Faustus.*" *Publications of the Modern Language Association* 65: 21–26.

Stein, Jack M. 1950. "Adrian Leverkühn as a Composer." *GR* 25: 257–74.

White, James F. 1950. "Echo's Prayers in Thomas Mann's *Doktor Faustus.*" *Monatshefte* 42: 385–94.

Hatfield, Henry. 1951. *Thomas Mann.* Norfolk, Conn.: New Directions Books.

Klein, Johannes. 1951. "Thomas Manns *Doktor Faustus.*" *Der Deutschunterricht* 3: 55–61.

Mette, Hans J. 1951. "*Doktor Faustus* und Alexander. Zur Geschichte des Decensus- und Ascensus-Motivs." *DVLG* 25: 27–39.

Schulz, H. Stefan. 1951. "Das Menschen-Bild Thomas Manns: eine ideologische Betrachtung." *Monatshefte* 43: 173–86.

Stewart, John L. 1951. "On the Making of *Doctor Faustus.*" *Sewanee Review* 59: 329–42.

White, James Fellows. 1951. "Some Abridged Passages in *Doctor Faustus.*" *Modern Language Notes* 66: 375–378.

Dornheim, Alfredo. 1952. "Goethes 'Mignon' und Thomas Manns 'Echo,' zwei Formen des 'göttlichen Kindes' im deutschen Roman." *Euphorion* 46: 315–47. (Original in Spanish, 1950).

Eichner, Hans. 1952. "Aspects of Parody in the Works of Thomas Mann." *Modern Language Review* 47: 30–48. Reprinted in Ezergailis, 1988: 93-115.

Lesser, Jonas. 1952. *Thomas Mann in der Epoche seiner Vollendung*. Munich: Desch.

Reed, Carroll E. 1952. "Thomas Mann and the Faust Tradition." *JEGP* 51: 17–34.

Eichner, Hans. 1953. *Thomas Mann: Eine Einführung in sein Werk*. Berne: Francke.

Hennings, Elsa. 1953. *Unsterblicher Faust. Eine Genealogie von Simon Magnus bis zum 'Faust'-Roman Thomas Manns*. Hamburg: Veröffentlichung der Universitäts-Gesellschaft Hamburg, Issue 5.

Martin, Alfred von. 1953. "Thomas Mann und Nietzsche. Zur Problematik des deutschen Menschen." *Hochland* 46: 135–52.

Raleigh, John Henry. 1953. "Mann's Double Vision: *Doktor Faustus* and *The Holy Sinner*." *Pacific Spectator* 7: 380–92.

Carlsson, Anni. 1954. "Der Meeresgrund in der neueren Dichtung. Abwandlungen eines symbolischen Motivs von Hans Christian Andersen bis Thomas Mann." *DVLG* 28: 221–33.

Greiner, Martin. 1954. "Thomas Manns Faustus-Roman: Versuch einer Struktur-Analyse." *Sammlung* 9: 539–51.

Hartwig, Thomas. 1954. "Antitheologisches in dem Roman *Doktor Faustus* von Thomas Mann." *Die Befreiung* 2: 57–59.

Heller, Erich. 1954. "Von Hanno Buddenbrook zu Adrian Leverkühn." In his *Enterbter Geist. Essays über modernes Dichten und Denken*. Frankfurt am Main: Suhrkamp. 245–79.

Krey, Johannes. 1954. "Die gesellschaftliche Bedeutung der Musik im Werk von Thomas Mann." *Wissenschaftliche Zeitschrift der Friedrich-Schiller-Universität Jena* 3: 301–32.

Lindsay, James M. 1954. *Thomas Mann*. Oxford: Blackwell.

Sagave, Pierre-Paul. 1954. *Réalité sociale et idéologie religieuse dans les romans de Thomas Mann*. Paris: Belles Lettres.

Taubes, Jacob. 1954. "From Cult to Culture." *Partisan Review* 21: 387–400.

Diersen, Inge. 1955. "Thomas Manns Faust-Konzeption und ihr Verhältnis zur Faust-Tradition." *Weimarer Beiträge* 1: 313–30.

Engelberg, Edward. 1955. "Thomas Mann's Faust and Beethoven." *Monatshefte* 47: 112–16.

Faesi, Robert. 1955. "Roman in Endeszeichen: *Doktor Faustus*." In his *Thomas Mann: Ein Meister der Erzählkunst*. Zurich: Atlantis. 135–61.

Hatfield, Henry. 1955. "Parody and Expressiveness: The Late Works of Thomas Mann." *University of Pennsylvania Bulletin* 65, Issue 3: 47–56.

Hilscher, Eberhard. 1955. "Thomas Mann als Sprachkünstler." *Neue Deutsche Literatur* 3, Issue 8: 56–71.

Hirschbach, Frank D. 1955. *The Arrow and the Lyre: A Study of the Role of Love in the Works of Thomas Mann.* The Hague: Nijhoff. (International Scholars Forum, Vol. 1.)

Jonas, Klaus W. 1955. *Fifty Years of Thomas Mann Studies. A Bibliography of Criticism.* Vol. I Minneapolis: University of Minnesota Press. 174–86. For the second volume, see Jonas, 1967. For the German editions, see Jonas, 1972; 1979).

Birven, Henri. 1956. "Thomas Manns *Doktor Faustus* und das Faustbuch von 1587." *Blätter der Knittlinger Faust-Gedenkstätte und des Faust-Museums* 3: 36–59.

Gronicka, André von. 1956. "'Myth plus Psychology.' A Style Analysis of *Death in Venice.*" *GR* 31: 191–205.

Hatfield, Henry. 1956a. "Can One Sell One's Soul? The Faust Legend." In *Great Moral Dilemmas in Literature. Past and Present*, ed. Robert M. MacIver. New York: Harper. 83–97.

——. 1956b. "Recent Studies of Thomas Mann." *Modern Language Review* 52: 390–403.

Kaufmann, Alfred. 1956. "Gedanken zu Thomas Manns Roman *Doktor Faustus* aus medizinischer Perspektive." In *Thomas Mann zum Gedenken*, ed. Georg Wenzel. Potsdam: VEB Buch- und Offsetdruckerei. 149–64.

Mann, Michael. 1956. "The Musical Symbolism in Thomas Mann's *Doktor Faustus.*" *Music Review* 17: 314–22.

Moses, Stéphane. 1956. "Subjektivität und Dämonie in Jean Pauls *Titan* und in Thomas Manns *Doktor Faustus.*" *Hesperus* 12: 46–48.

Schoolfield, George C. 1956. *The Figure of the Musician in German Literature.* Chapel Hill, N.C.: University of North Carolina Press. 171–90. (University of North Carolina Studies in the Germanic Languages and Literatures, Vol. 19.).

Thomas, R. Hinton. 1956. *Thomas Mann: The Mediation of Art.* Oxford: Clarendon.

Wiemann, H. 1956. "Thomas Mann and *Doktor Faustus.*" *Journal of the Australasian Universities Modern Languages and Literatures Association* 4: 39–45.

Berger, Erich. 1957. "Eine Dantestelle in Thomas Manns *Doktor Faustus.*" *Monatshefte* 49: 212–14.

Buisonjé, J. C. de. 1957. "Bemerkungen über Thomas Manns Werk *Doktor Faustus.*" *Neophilologus* 41: 185–99.

Enright, Denis J. 1957. "The Anti-Diabolic Faith. Thomas Mann's *Doctor Faustus.*" In his *The Apothecary's Shop*. London: Secker and Warburg. 121–44.

Kahler, Erich. 1957. "*Doktor Faustus* from Adam to Sartre." Lecture delivered at Ohio State University. Revised and printed in Kahler, 1969, 86–116.

Kaufmann, Fritz. 1957. *Thomas Mann. The World as Will and Representation*. Boston: Beacon Press. 197–238.

Kaye, Julian. 1957. "Conrad's *Under Western Eyes* and Mann's *Doktor Faustus.*" *Comparative Literature* 9: 60–65.

Söter, István. 1957. "Tagebuch eines Lesers: Zur Struktur des Romans *Doktor Faustus.*" In his *Világtájak*. Budapest: Szépiradalmi Könyvkiadó. Original essay in Hungarian; reprinted in German in Mádl, Antal and Judit Gyóri, 1977: 141–54.

Wolff, Hans M. 1957. *Thomas Mann. Werk und Bekenntnis*. Berne: Francke.

Briner, Andres. 1958. "Wahrheit und Dichtung um J. C. Beissel: Studie um eine Gestalt in Thomas Manns *Doktor Faustus.*" *Schweizerische Musikzeitung* 98: 365–69.

Heller, Erich. 1958a. *The Ironic German. A Study of Thomas Mann*. London: Secker & Warburg.

———. 1958b. "Parody, Tragic and Comic: Mann's *Doktor Faustus* and *Felix Krull.*" *Sewanee Review* 66: 519–46.

Petriconi, Hellmuth. 1958. "'Verfall einer Familie' und Höllensturz eines Reichs." In his *Das Reich des Untergangs. Bemerkungen über ein mythologisches Thema*. Hamburg: Hoffmann & Campe. 151–84.

Simon, Ulrich. 1958. "The Theological Challenge of Mann's *Doctor Faustus.*" *Church Quarterly Review* 159: 547–53.

Sørensen, Bengt Algot. 1958. Thomas Manns *Doktor Faustus:* Mythos und Lebensbeichte." *OL* 13: 81–97.

Bergsten, Gunilla. 1959. "Musical Symbolism in Thomas Mann's *Doktor Faustus.*" *OL* 14: 206–14.

Boeninger, Helmut R. 1959. "Zeitblom, Spiritual Descendent of Goethe's Wagner and Wagner's Beckmesser." *GL&L* 13: 38–43.

Briner, Andres. 1960. "Conrad Beissel and Thomas Mann." *The American-German Review* 26, Issue 2: 24–25, 38.

Bürgin, Hans. Walter A. Reichart and Erich Neumann, eds. 1959. *Das Werk Thomas Manns Eine Bibliographie*. Frankfurt am Main: S. Fischer.

Devoto, Daniel. 1959. "Deux musiciens russes dans le *Doktor Faustus* de Thomas Mann." *Revue de littérature comparée* 33: 104–6.

Diersen, Ingrid. 1959. *Untersuchungen zu Thomas Mann. Die Bedeutung der Künstlerdarstellung für die Entwicklung des Realismus in seinem eräzhlerischen Werk*. Berlin: Rütten & Loening. 229–307.

Heller, Erich. 1959a. "Faust's Damnation: The Morality of Knowledge." In his *The Artist's Journey into the Interior*. New York: Random House. 3–44. Reprinted in Heller, 1962; in German, Heller, 1963.

———. 1959b. "Des Teufels Romancier: Über Thomas Manns *Doktor Faustus*." *Forum* 6: 367–70.

Lyon, James K. 1959. "Words and Music: Thomas Mann's Tone Poem *Doktor Faustus*." *Western Humanities Review* 13: 99–102.

Mayer, Hans. 1959. "Thomas Manns *Doktor Faustus*: Roman einer Endzeit und Endzeit des Romans." In his *Von Lessing bis Thomas Mann: Wandlungen der bürgerlichen Literatur in Deutschland*. Pfullingen: Neske. 383–404. Reprinted in Wolff, 1983. Part I: 106–23.

Politzer, Heinz. 1959. "Of Time and *Doktor Faustus*." *Monatshefte* 51: 145–55.

Wegener, Herbert, ed. 1959. *Thomas Mann. Briefe an Paul Amann. 1915 bis 1952*. Lübeck: Schmidt-Römhild.

Welter, Marianne. 1959. "'The Greatest Dead Novel of our Age.' Some Thoughts on Thomas Mann's *Doktor Faustus*." *Makarere Journal* 3: 61–71.

Williams, William D. 1959. "Thomas Mann's *Doktor Faustus*." *GL&L* 12: 273–81.

Zmegac, Viktor. 1959. *Die Musik im Schaffen Thomas Manns*. Zagreb: Philosophische Fakultät der Universität.

Hellersberg-Wendriner, Anna. 1960. *Mystik der Gottesferne. Eine Interpretation Thomas Manns*. Berne: Francke.

Jens, Inge, ed. 1960. *Thomas Mann an Ernst Bertram. Briefe aus den Jahren 1910–1955*. Pfullingen: Neske.

Krieger, Murray. 1960. *The Tragic Vision. Variations on a Theme in Literary Interpretation*. New York. Holt, Rinehart and Winston. 86–113.

Metzler, Ilse. 1960. *Dämonie und Humanismus: Funktion und Bedeutung der Zeitblomgestalt in Thomas Manns 'Doktor Faustus.'* Essen: Rhoden.

Müller, Joachim. 1960. "Thomas Manns *Doktor Faustus.* Grundthematik und Motivgefüge." *Euphorion* 54: 262–80.

Nemerov, Howard. 1960. "Thomas Mann's Faust Novel." *The Graduate Journal* 3: 205–17. Reprinted 1963 in Nemerov, 1963: 303-25.

Rey, William H. 1960. "Selbstopfer des Geistes. Fluch und Verheißung in Hofmannsthals *Der Turm* und Thomas Manns *Doktor Faustus.*" *Monatshefte* 52: 145–57.

Wilmont, Nikolai. 1960. "Die Tragödie des Komponisten Adrian Leverkühn." *Geist und Zeit* 4: 106–26.

Altenberg, Paul. 1961. *Die Romane Thomas Manns: Versuch einer Deutung.* Bad Homburg: Genter. 207–311.

Borcherdt, Hans Heinrich. 1961. "Das Faust-Problem bei Thomas Mann." *Jahrbuch des Wiener Goethe-Vereins* 65: 5–12.

Meyer, Herman. 1961. *Das Zitat in der Erzählkunst. Zur Geschichte und Poetik des europäischen Romans.* Stuttgart: Metzler.

Müller, Joachim. 1961. "Faustus und Faust. Thomas Manns Roman und Goethes Tragödie." *Universitas* 16: 731-43.

Sontheimer, Kurt. 1961. *Thomas Mann und die Deutschen.* Munich: Nymphenburger. Revised in 1965. Sections reprinted in abridged essay form in Wolff, 1983, Part I: 16–32.

Brown, Calvin S. 1962. "The Entomological Source of Mann's Poisonous Butterfly." *GR* 37: 116–20.

Charney, Hanna, and Maurice Charney. 1962. "*Doktor Faustus* and *Mon Faust.* An Excursus in Dualism." *Symposium* 16: 45–53.

Heller, Erich. 1962. "Faust's Damnation. The Morality of Knowledge." *The Listener* 67, Issue 1713: 59–61; 121–23, 168–70. Reprint of Heller, 1959a. German version in Heller, 1963.

Kerényi, Károly. 1962. "Thomas Mann und der Teufel in Palestrina." *Neue Rundschau* 73: 238–46. Reprinted in Kerényi, 1963.

Koopmann, Helmut. 1962. *Die Entwicklung des 'intellektuellen' Romans bei Thomas Mann.* Bonn: Bouvier.

Mann, Erika, ed. 1962. *Thomas Mann. Briefe.* Vol. 1. 1889–1939 (1962); Vol. 2. 1937–1947 (1963); Vol. 3. 1948–1955 und Nachlese (1965). Frankfurt am Main: S. Fischer.

Mittenzwei, Johannes. 1962. *Das Musikalische in der Literatur. Ein Überblick von Gottfried von Straßburg bis Brecht.* Halle (Saale): Verlag Sprache und Literatur.

Poser, Hans. 1962. "Thomas Mann: *Doktor Faustus.*" *Möglichkeiten des modernen deutschen Romans. Analysen und Interpretationsgrundlagen,* ed. Rolf Geißler. Frankfurt am Main: Diesterweg. 5–44.

Schimansky, Gerd. 1962. "Der Engel des Giftes. Das widergöttliche Angebot in Thomas Manns Roman *Doktor Faustus.*" *Wege zum Menschen* 14: 301–06.

Schwerte, Hans. 1962. "Dürers 'Ritter, Tod und Teufel.' Eine ideologische Parallele zum 'Faustischen.'" In his *Faust und das Faustische. Ein Kapitel deutscher Ideologie.* Stuttgart: Klett. 243–78.

Wenzel, Georg, ed. 1962. *Vollendung und Größe Thomas Manns. Beiträge zu Werk und Persönlichkeit des Dichters.* Halle: Verlag Sprache und Literatur.

Includes:

Dobbek, Wilhelm. "Thomas Manns Weg zu einer humanen Musik." 72–86.

Kirsch, Edgar. "Die Verungleichung des Gleichen. Ein Beitrag zur Analyse des Identitätsproblems im *Doktor Faustus.*" 204–12.

Becker-Frank, Sigrid W. 1963. *Untersuchungen zur Integration des Zitats bei Thomas Manns 'Doktor Faustus.'* Quickborn bei Hamburg: Schnelle.

Bergsten, Gunilla. 1963. *Thomas Manns 'Doktor Faustus': Untersuchungen zu den Quellen und zur Struktur des Romans.* Stockholm: Bonnier. Second edition 1974. Translated into English by Krishna Winston in 1969 as *Thomas Mann's 'Doctor Faustus.' Sources and Structure of the Novel.* Chicago: Chicago University Press.

Engelmann, Hans Ulrich. 1963. "Joseph Berglinger und Adrian Leverkühn oder: über die Wärme und über die Kälte." *Neue Zeitschrift für Musik* 12: 470–72.

Feuerlicht, Ignace. 1963. "Thomas Manns mythische Identifikation." *GQ* 36:141–51.

Frey, Leonhard H. 1963. "Antithetical Balance in the Opening and Close of *Doktor Faustus.*" *Modern Language Quarterly* 24: 350–53.

Heller, Erich. 1963. "Fausts Verdammnis: Die Ethik des Wissens." *Merkur* 17: 32–56. English version "Faust's Damnation: The Morality of Knowledge" in Heller, 1959a. 3–44.

Henning, Hans. 1963. "Faust-Dichtungen des 20. Jahrhunderts." In his *Faust in fünf Jahrhunderten. Ein Überblick zur Geschichte des Faust-Stoffes vom 16. Jahrhundert bis zur Gegenwart.* Halle (Saale): Verlag Sprache und Literatur. 98–116.

Holthusen, Wilhelm, and Adalbert Tauber. 1963. "Dürers 'Philip Melanchton' und 'Bildnis einer jungen Frau' als visuelle Vorbilder für die Eltern Adrian Leverkühns in Thomas Manns *Doktor Faustus*." *Die Waage* 3, Issue 2: 67–79.

Kerényi, Károly. 1963. "Thomas Mann und der Teufel in Palestrina." In his *Tessiner Schreibtisch. Mythologisches, Unmythologisches*. Stuttgart: Steingruber. 86–109.

Kreuzer, Helmut. 1963. "Thomas Mann und Gabriele Reuter. Zu einer Entlehnung für den *Doktor Faustus*." *Neue Deutsche Hefte* 10, Issue 96: 108–19.

Nemerov, Howard. 1963. "Thomas Mann's Faust Novel." In his *Poetry and Fiction: Essays*. New Brunswick, N.J. Rutgers University Press. 303-15.

Pütz, Heinz Peter. 1963a. *Kunst und Künstlerexistenz bei Nietzsche und Thomas Mann. Zum Problem des ästhetischen Perspektivismus in der Moderne*. Bonn: Bouvier. (Bonner Arbeiten zur deutschen Literatur, Vol. 6.).

———. 1963b. "Die teuflische Kunst des *Doktor Faustus* bei Thomas Mann." *ZDP* 82: 500–15.

Rehm, Walter. 1963. "Thomas Mann und Dürer." *Die Wissenschaft von deutscher Sprache und Dichtung. Festschrift für Friedrich Maurer zum 65. Geburtstag am 5. Januar 1963*, ed. Siegfried Gutenbrunner, Hugo Moser, Walter Rehm, and Heinz Rupp. Stuttgart: Klett. 478–97.

Seghers, Anna. 1963. "Woher sie kommen, wohin sie gehen." *Sinn und Form* 15: 11–47.

Stout, Harry L. 1963. "Lessing's Riccaut and Thomas Mann's Fitelberg." *GQ* 36: 24–30.

Stresau, Hermann. 1963. *Thomas Mann und sein Werk*. Frankfurt am Main: S. Fischer.

Willnauer, Franz. 1963. "Der Zeitgenosse Adrian Leverkühn. Fiktion und Faktizität im Musiker-Roman" *Deutsche Rundschau* 89, Issue 8: 56–64.

Bantel, Otto. 1964. "Thomas Manns *Doktor Faustus* und seine Erarbeitung in der Schule." *Der Deutschunterricht* 16, Issue 2: 26–40.

Baumgart, Reinhard. 1964. *Das Ironische und die Ironie in den Werken Thomas Manns*. Munich: Hanser.

Blomster, Wesley V. 1964. "Textual Variations in *Doktor Faustus*." *GR* 39: 183–91.

Carlsson, Anni. 1964. "Der Roman als Anschauungsform der Epoche. Bemerkungen zu Thomas Mann und Günter Grass." *Neue Züricher Zeitung* 185, 21. Nov. 1964.

Heimann, Bodo. 1964. "Thomas Manns *Doktor Faustus* und die Musikphilosophie Adornos." *DVLG* 38: 248–66.

Maatje, Frank C. 1964. "Die Duplikation der Zeit in Thomas Manns Roman *Doktor Faustus*." In his *Der Doppelroman. Eine literatursystematische Studie über duplikative Erzählstrukturen*. Groningen: Wolters. 66–77.

Sachs, Arieh. 1964. "The Religious Despair of *Doktor Faustus*." *JEGP* 63: 625–47.

Schädlich, Michael. 1964. *Thomas Mann und das christliche Denken: Eine Untersuchung über den Zusammenhang von Theologie und Musik in 'Doktor Faustus.'* Berlin-DDR: Kietz. Reprinted 1978 in his *Titelaufnahmen. Studien zu Werken von Thomas Mann . . . und Stefan Heym*. Berlin: Union-Presse Hass. 7–37.

Starzycki, Andrzej. 1964. "Thomas Mann's *Doctor Faustus* — A Contribution to the Studies of Musical Facts in Literature." *Zagadnienia rodzajow literackich* 7, Issue 1: 27–41.

Berendsohn, Walter A. 1965. *Thomas Mann. Künstler und Kämpfer in bewegter Zeit*. Lübeck: Schmidt-Römhild.

Buzga, Jaroslav. 1965. "Leverkühn und die moderne Musik." *Melos* 32, Issue 2: 37–44.

Elema, Hans J. 1965. "Thomas Mann, Dürer und *Doktor Faustus*." *Euphorion* 59: 97–117. Reprinted in Koopmann, 1975: 320–50.

Henze, Eberhard. 1965. "Die Rolle des fiktiven Erzählers bei Thomas Mann." *Neue Rundschau* 76:189–201.

Hilscher, Eberhard. 1965. *Thomas Mann. Leben und Werk*. Berlin: Volk und Wissen. 162–86.

Jørgensen, Aage. 1965. "Thomas Mann's *Doktor Faustus*." *OL* 20: 165–75.

Lehnert, Herbert. 1965. *Thomas Mann. Fiktion, Mythos, Religion*. Stuttgart: Kohlhammer.

Mann, Michael. 1965. "Adrian Leverkühn: Repräsentant oder Antipode?" *Neue Rundschau* 76: 202–06.

Nielsen, Birgit. 1965. "Adrian Leverkühns Leben als bewußte mythologische imitatio des Dr. Faustus." *OL* 20: 128–58.

Oplatka, Andreas. 1965. "Thomas Mann und Richard Wagner." *Schweizer Monatshefte für Politik, Wirtschaft, Kultur* 45: 672–80.

Schaper, Eva. 1965. "A Modern Faust: The Novel in the Ironical Key." *OL* 20: 176–204. Reprinted in Bloom, 1985: 103–22.

Sinn und Form. Sonderheft Thomas Mann. 1965.
Includes:

Barbu, Eugen and Andrei Deleanu. "Serenus Zeitblom." 134–43

Gisselbrecht, André. "Thomas Manns Hinwendung vom Geist der Musikalität zur Bürgerpflicht." 291–334.

Sagave, Pierre-Paul. "Zum Bild des Luthertums in Thomas Manns *Doktor Faustus*." 347–56.

Tillich, Paul. 1965. "Aus den Materialien zum *Doktor Faustus*. Paul Tillichs Brief an Thomas Mann vom 23. Mai 1943." *Blätter der Thomas- Mann-Gesellschaft* 5: 48–52.

Tuska, Jon. 1965. "The Vision of *Doktor Faustus*." *GR* 40: 277–309.

White, Andrew. 1965. *Thomas Mann*. New York: Grove.

Wysling, Hans. 1965. "Thomas Manns Tagebücher. Aus den Notizen zur 'Entstehung des Faustus.'" *Blätter der Thomas-Mann-Gesellschaft*, Zurich 4: 44–47.

Egri, Péter. 1966. "James Joyce and Adrian Leverkühn. Decadence and Modernity in the Joycean Parallels of Thomas Mann's *Doctor Faustus*." *Acta Litteraria Academiae Scientiarium Hungaricae* 8: 195–238.

Feuerlicht, Ignace. 1966. *Thomas Mann und die Grenzen des Ich*. Heidelberg: Winter.

Henning, Margrit. 1966. *Die Ich-Form und ihre Funktion in Thomas Manns 'Doktor Faustus' und in der deutschen Literatur der Gegenwart*. Tübingen: Niemeyer. (Studien zur deutschen Literatur, Vol. 2.)

Lehnert, Herbert. 1966a. "Thomas Manns Lutherbild." In *Betrachtungen und Überblicke. Zum Werk Thomas Manns*, ed. Georg Wenzel. Berlin: Aufbau. 269–381.

———.1966b. "Zur Theologie in Thomas Manns *Doktor Faustus*. Zwei gestrichene Stellen aus der Handschrift." *DVLG* 40: 248–56.

Mayer, Hans. 1966. "Anmerkungen zum *Doktor Faustus* von Thomas Mann." *Sprache im technischen Zeitalter* 5, Issues 17–18: 64–69.

Middell, Eike. 1966. *Thomas Mann. Versuch einer Einführung in Leben und Werk*. Leipzig: Reclam.

Peterson, John. 1966. "The Role of Theological Themes in Thomas Mann's *Doctor Faustus*." *Discourse* 9: 492–515.

Pongs, Hermann. 1966. *Dichtung im gespaltenen Deutschland*. Stuttgart: Union Verlag. 166–83.

Thirlwall, John C. 1966. *In Another Language. A Record of the Thirty-Year Relationship between Thomas Mann and His English Translator, Helen Tracy Lowe-Porter*. New York: Knopf.

Assmann, Dietrich. 1967. "Thomas Manns Faustus-Roman und das Volksbuch von 1587." *Neuphilologische Mitteilungen* 68: 130–39.

Berendsohn, Walter A. 1967. "Thomas Manns Goethe-fernstes Werk: *Doktor Faustus*." *Moderna Språk* 61, Issue 5: 1–16.

Jonas, Klaus W. and Ilsedore B. Jonas. 1967. *Thomas Mann Studies: A Bibliography of Criticism*. Volume II. Philadelphia: University of Pennsylvania Press (for the German edition, see Jonas, 1972;1979)

Kross, Siegfried. 1967. "Musikalische Strukturen als literarische Form." In *Colloquium Amicorum: Joseph Schmidt Görg zum 70. Geburtstag*, ed. Siegfried Kross and Hans Schmidt. Bonn: Beethovenhaus. 217–27.

Plard, Henri. 1967. "Souvenirs d'Andersen chez Thomas Mann." *OL* 22: 129- 39.

Puknat, Siegfried, and E. M. Puknat. 1967. "Mann's *Doktor Faustus* and Shakespeare." *Research Studies* 35: 148–54.

Ruprecht, Erich. 1967. "Thomas Manns *Doktor Faustus* . Ein Dokument der Krise des modernen Romans." *Jahrbuch der Raabe-Gesellschaft*: 7–30.

Scharfschwerdt, Jürgen. 1967. *Thomas Mann und der deutsche Bildungsroman. Eine Untersuchung zu den Problemen einer literarischen Tradition*. Stuttgart: Kohlhammer. (Studien zur Poetik und Geschichte der Literatur, Vol. 5.).

Scher, Steven P. 1967. "Thomas Mann's 'Verbal Score': Adrian Leverkühn's Symbolic Confession." *Modern Language Notes* 82: 403–20. Reprinted in Scher, 1968, *Verbal Music in German Literature*. New Haven: Yale University Press. 106–42.

Scherrer, Paul, and Hans Wysling. 1967. *Quellenkritische Studien zum Werk Thomas Manns*. Berne: Francke. (*Thomas-Mann-Studien*, Vol. I.).

Stern, Joseph P. 1967. *Thomas Mann*. New York. Columbia University Press. (Columbia Essays on Modern Writers, Vol. 24.).

Feuerlicht, Ignace. 1968. *Thomas Mann*. New York: Twayne. 67–84.

Hatfield, Henry. 1968. "The Magic Square: Thomas Mann's *Doktor Faustus*." *Euphorion* 62: 415–20. Reprinted in expanded form in Hatfield, 1969, 166–76.

Hermsdorf, Klaus. 1968. *Thomas Manns Schelme. Figuren und Strukturen des Komischen*. Berlin: Rütten & Loening.

Höhler, Gertrud. 1968. "'Der Verdammte, üppig im Fleisch.' Ein Bildzitat in Thomas Manns *Doktor Faustus*." *Euphorion* 62: 405-14.

Karst. Theodor. 1968. "Johann Conrad Beissel in Thomas Manns Roman *Doktor Faustus*." *Jahrbuch der deutschen Schillergesellschaft* 12: 543–85.

Koopmann, Helmut. 1968. "Thomas Mann. Theorie und Praxis der epischen Ironie." In *Deutsche Romantheorien*, ed. Reinhold Grimm. Frankfurt am Main: Athenäum. 274–96. Reprinted in Koopmann, 1975a: 351–83.

Lehnert, Herbert. 1968. *Thomas Mann. Fiktion , Mythos, Religion*. 2d edition. Stuttgart: Kohlhammer. (Sprache und Literatur, Vol. 27.).

Miller, Leslie L. 1968. "Myth and Morality. Reflections on Thomas Mann's *Doktor Faustus*." In *Essays on German Literature. In Honour of G. Joyce Hallamore*, ed. Michael Batts and Marketa Goetz Stankiewicz. Toronto: University of Toronto Press. 195–217.

Müller-Seidel, Walter. 1968. "Sprache und Humanität in Thomas Manns *Doktor Faustus*." *Acta Germanica* 3: 241–56.

Piana, Theo. 1968. *Thomas Mann. Mit 82 Abbildungen*. Leipzig: VEB Bibliographisches Institut.

Bergsten, Gunilla. 1969. *Thomas Mann's 'Doctor Faustus.' The Sources and Structure of the Novel*. Translated by Krishna Winston. Chicago: University of Chicago Press.

Dittmann, Ulrich. 1969. *Sprachbewußtsein und Redeform im Werk Thomas Manns. Untersuchungen zum Verhältnis des Schriftstellers zur Sprachkrise*. Stuttgart: Kohlhammer. (Studien zur Poetik und Geschichte der Literatur, Vol. 10.).

Hamburger, Käte. 1969. "Anachronistische Symbolik. Fragen an Thomas Manns Faustus-Roman." In *Gestaltungsgeschichte und Gesellschaftsgeschichte. Literatur-, Kunst-, und musikwissenschaftliche Studien: Fritz Martini zum 60. Geburtstag*, ed. Helmut Kreuzer. Stuttgart: Metzler. 529–53. Reprinted in Koopmann, ed.,1975: 384–413; in Wolff, 1983: Part I, 124–50.

Hatfield, Henry.1969. *Crisis and Continuity in Modern German Fiction: Ten Essays*. Ithaca: Cornell University Press.

Hwang, Hyen-Su. 1969. "Die Problematik im *Doktor Faustus*." *Zeitung für Germanistik* 8: 63–81.

Jonas, Ilsedore B. 1969. *Thomas Mann und Italien*. Heidelberg: Winter.

Jung. Ute. 1969. *Die Musikphilosophie Thomas Manns*. Regensburg: Bosse. (Kölner Beiträge zur Musikforschung, Vol. 53.).

Kahler, Erich von. 1969. *The Orbit of Thomas Mann*. Princeton, N. J.: Princeton University Press. 20–43; 86–116.

Kunne-Ibsch, Elrud. 1969. "Die Nietzsche-Gestalt in Thomas Manns *Doktor Faustus*." *Neophilologus* 53: 176–89.

Lehnert, Herbert. 1969. *Thomas-Mann-Forschung. Ein Bericht*. Stuttgart: Metzler.

Myers, David. 1969. "Sexual Love and Caritas in Thomas Mann." *JEGP* 68: 593–604.

Oates, Joyce Carol. 1969. "Art at the Edge of Impossibility: Mann's *Doktor Faustus*." *Southern Review* 5: 375–93.

Orlowski, Hubert. 1969. *Prädestination des Dämonischen. Zur Frage des bürgerlichen Humanismus in Thomas Manns 'Doktor Faustus'*. Dissertation, University of Posen (Pósnán).

Pongs, Hermann. 1969. *Das Bild in der Dichtung*, Vol.3. *Der synthetische Kosmos der Dichtung*. Marburg: Elwert. 463–94.

Reiss, Gunter. 1969. "Sündenfall-Modell und Romanform. Zur Interpretation von Kleists Marionettentheater-Metaphorik im Werk Thomas Manns." *Jahrbuch der deutschen Schillergesellschaft* 13: 426–53.

Wenzel, Georg. 1969. *Thomas Manns Briefwerk. Bibliographie gedruckter Briefe aus den Jahren 1889–1955*. Berlin: Akademischer Verlag.

Wysling, Hans. 1969. *'Mythos und Psychologie' bei Thomas Mann*. Zurich: Polygraphischer Verlag. (Eidgenössische Technische Hochschule. Kultur- und Staatswissenschaftliche Schriften, Issue 130.).

Dörr, Hansjörg. 1970. "Thomas Mann und Adorno. Ein Beitrag zur Entstehung des *Doktor Faustus*." *Literaturwissenschaftliches Jahrbuch* 11: 285–322. Reprinted in Wolff, 1983: Part II, 48–91.

Dück, Hans-Udo. 1970. "Epische Symphonik in Thomas Manns *Doktor Faustus*." In *Vergleichen und verändern. Festschrift für Helmut Motekat*, ed. Albrecht Goetze and Günter Pflaum. Munich: Hueber. 243–58.

Gronicka, André von. 1970. *Thomas Mann: Profiles and Perspectives*. New York: Random House.

Karst, Roman. 1970. *Thomas Mann oder der deutsche Zwiespalt*. Trans. from Polish by Edda Werfel. Vienna: Molden. 258–76.

Kolb, Hans-Ulrich. 1970. "Neue Quellen zu Thomas Manns Roman *Doktor Faustus*." *Archiv für das Studium der neueren Sprachen und Literaturen* 207: 20–29.

Noble, Cecil A. 1970. *Krankheit, Verbrechen und künstlerisches Schaffen bei Thomas Mann*. Berne: Lang. (Europäische Hochschulschriften, Series I, Vol. 30.). 193–219.

Reiss, Gunter. 1970. *'Allegorisierung' und moderne Erzählkunst. Eine Studie zum Werk Thomas Manns*. Munich: Fink.

Sagave, Pierre-Paul. 1970. "Antike Welt und moderner Geist in Thomas Manns *Doktor Faustus*." In *Das Altertum und jedes neue Gute: Für Walter Schadewaldt zum 15. März 1970*, ed. Konrad Gaiser. Stuttgart: Kohlhammer. 229–36.

Schoeps, Hans-Joachim. 1970. "Bemerkungen zu einer Quelle des Romans *Doktor Faustus* von Thomas Mann." *Zeitschrift für Religions- und Geistesgeschichte* 22: 324–55.

Trommler, Frank. 1970. "Epische Rhetorik in Thomas Manns *Doktor Faustus*." *ZDP* 89: 240–58.

Albrecht, Ján. 1971. "Leverkühn oder die Musik als Schicksal." *DVLG* 45: 375–88.

Assmann, Dietrich. 1971. "Faustus junior. Thomas Mann und die mythische Identifikation." *Neuphilologische Mitteilungen* 72: 549–53.

Dill, H. J. 1971. "Zur Erklärung des Namens Pfeiffering in Thomas Manns *Doktor Faustus*." *Germanic Notes* 2: 34–36.

Golik, Iwan. 1971. "Die Kälte der Dekadenz. Zur Kritik des Modernismus im Schaffen Thomas Manns." *Weimarer Beiträge* 17, Issue 3: 151–70.

Hollingdale, Reginald J. 1971. *Thomas Mann: A Critical Study*. London: Rupert Hart-Davis.

Mádl, Antal. 1971. Zwei donauländische Kapitel in Thomas Manns *Doktor Faustus*." *Lenau-Forum* 3, Issue 3/4: 32–46.

Mainzer, Hubert. 1971. "Thomas Manns *Doktor Faustus* — ein Nietzsche-Roman?" *Wirkendes Wort* 21: 24–38.

Pütz, Peter, ed. 1971. *Thomas Mann und die Tradition*. Frankfurt am Main: Athenäum. (Athenäum Paperbacks Germanistik, Issue. 2.).

Rose, Marilyn Gaddis. 1971. "More on the Musical Composition of *Doktor Faustus*." *Modern Fiction Studies* 17: 81–89.

Siefken, Hinrich. 1971. "Romanticism und Chauvinism: Reflections on the Ironic Concept of 'Durchbruch' in Thomas Mann's Novel *Doktor Faustus*." *Trivium* 6: 116–19.

Wenzel, Georg. 1971. "Nachwort" (Postscript) to *Thomas Mann: Doktor Faustus*. Berlin: Aufbau. 684–716.

White, James J. 1971. "Historical Symbolism in Thomas Mann's *Doktor Faustus*." In his *Mythology in the Modern Novel: A Study of Prefigurative Techniques*. Princeton: Princeton University Press. 149–56.

Anton, Herbert. 1972. *Die Romankunst Thomas Manns. Begriffe und hermeneutische Strukturen*. Paderborn: Schöningh.

Dierks, Manfred. 1972. *Studien zum Mythos und Psychologie bei Thomas Mann. An seinem Nachlaß orientierte Untersuchungen zum 'Tod in Venedig', zum 'Zauberberg' und zur 'Joseph'-Tetralogie*. Berne: Francke. (*Thomas-Mann-Studien*, Vol. 2.).

Fass, Barbara. 1972. "The Little Mermaid and the Artist's Quest for a Soul." *Comparative Literature Studies* 9: 291–301.

Floquet, Jean-Marie. 1972. "A propos du *Doktor Faustus* de Thomas Mann. Sur une source du chapitre 14." *EG* 27: 87–91.

Jonas, Klaus. 1972. *Die Thomas-Mann-Literatur: Bibliographie der Kritik 1896-1955*. Vol. 1. Berlin: Schmidt.

Matter, Harry. 1972. *Die Literatur über Thomas Mann. Eine Bibliographie. 1898-1969*. 2 vols. Berlin: Aufbau. *Doctor Faustus*, Vol. 1: 511–70.

Meixner, Horst. 1972. "Thomas Manns *Doktor Faustus*. Zum Selbstverständnis des deutschen Spätbürgertums." *Jahrbuch der deutschen Schillergesellschaft* 16: 610–22.

Moses, Stéphane. 1972. *Une affinité littéraire: 'Le Titan' de Jean Paul et le 'Docteur Faustus' de Thomas Mann*. Paris: Klincksieck.

Oesch, Hans. 1972. "Albert Moeschingers Briefwechsel mit Thomas Mann: *Doktor Faustus* bewirkte des Komponisten Hinwendung zur Zwölftontechnik." *Schweizerische Musikzeitung* 112: 3–11.

Pritzlaff, Christiane. 1972. *Zahlensymbolik bei Thomas Mann*. Hamburg: Buske. (Hamburger Philologische Studien, Vol. 25.).

Schmidt, Gérard. 1972. *Zum Formgesetz des 'Doktor Faustus' von Thomas Mann*. Wiesbaden: Humanitas-Verlag.

Varga, István. 1972. "Das ungarische Dorf im *Doktor Faustus*." *Arbeiten zur deutschen Philologie* 6:115–22.

Brode, Hans-Peter. 1973. "Musik und Zeitgeschichte im Roman. Thomas Manns *Doktor Faustus*." *Jahrbuch der deutschen Schillergesellschaft* 17: 455–72.

Carnegy, Patrick. 1973. *Faust as Musician: A Study of Thomas Mann's Novel 'Doctor Faustus.'* London: Chatto & Windus.

Eisler, Hanns. 1973. "Notizen zu *Doktor Faustus*." In his *Materialien zu einer Dialektik der Musik*, ed. Manfred Grebs. Leipzig: Reclam. Revised edition 1987, Berlin: Verlag das Europäische Buch.

Finke, Ulrich. 1973. "Dürer und Thomas Mann." In *Essays on Dürer*, ed. C.R. Dodwell. Manchester: Manchester University Press. 121–46.

Mann, Michael. 1973. "Über Thomas Manns *Doktor Faustus*." In *Thomas Mann und die Seinen*, ed. Walter A. Berendsohn. Berne: Francke. 321–27.

Mendelssohn, Peter de, ed. 1973. *Thomas Mann. Briefwechsel mit seinem Verleger Gottfried Bermann Fischer 1932–1955*. Frankfurt am Main: S. Fischer.

Meyers, Jeffrey. 1973a. "Dürer and Mann's *Doctor Faustus*." *Art International* 17: 56–60, 63–64.

———. 1973b. "Shakespeare and Mann's *Doctor Faustus*." *Modern Fiction Studies* 19: 541–45.

Müller, Martin. 1973. "Walter Benjamin und Thomas Manns *Doktor Faustus*." *Archiv für das Studium der neueren Sprachen und Literaturen* 125: 327–330.

Pache, Walter. 1973a. "Ein Ibsen-Gedicht im *Doktor Faustus*." *Comparative Literature* 25: 212–20.

———. 1973b. "Blake's seltsame Poesien: Bildzitat und Bildwirkung in Thomas Manns *Doktor Faustus*." *Arcadia* 8: 138–55.

Vogel, Harald. 1973. "Die Zeit in Thomas Manns Roman *Doktor Faustus.* Eine Untersuchung zur polyphonen Zeitstruktur des Romans." *ZDP* 92: 511–36. Reprinted 1978 in *Zeitgestaltung in der Erzählkunst*, ed. Alexander Ritter. Darmstadt: Wissenschaftliche Buchgesellschaft. (Wege der Forschung, Vol. 447.).

Wysling, Hans, ed. 1973. "Thomas Mann, Notizen zu *Felix Krull, Friedrich, Königliche Hoheit, Versuch über das Theater, Maja, Geist und Kunst, Ein Elender, Betrachtungen eines Unpolitischen, Doktor Faustus* und anderen Werken." *Euphorion*, Supplement 5. Heidelberg: Winter.

Bonyhai, Gábor. 1974. "Handlungssystem und Wertsystem: Semiotische Randbemerkungen zur Struktur des *Doktor Faustus*." *Neohelicon* 2: 227-54.

Brügemann, Diethelm. 1974. "Säkularisation des Teufels: Kritische Anmerkungen zu einem geschichtlichen Prozeß." *Die Neue Rundschau* 85: 85–95.

Hannum, Hildegard D. 1974. "Self-Sacrifice in *Doktor Faustus*. Thomas Mann's Contribution to the Faust Legend." *Modern Language Quarterly* 35: 289–301.

Hoffmann, Gisela. 1974. *Das Motiv des Auserwählten bei Thomas Mann*. Bonn: Bouvier. (Studien zur Germanistik, Anglistik, und Komparatistik, Vol. 28.).

Honsa, William M. 1974. "Parody and Narrator in Thomas Mann's *Doctor Faustus* and *The Holy Sinner*." *OL* 29: 61–76. Reprinted in Bloom,1985: 219–226.

Magliola, Robert. 1974. "The Magic Square: Polar Unity in Thomas Mann's *Doctor Faustus*." *Hartford Studies in Literature* 6: 55–71.

Reed. Terence J. 1974. *Thomas Mann. The Uses of Tradition*. Oxford: Clarendon. 360–402.

Viswanathan, Jacqueline. 1974. "Point of View and Unreliability in Brontë's *Wuthering Heights*, Conrad's *Under Western Eyes* and Mann's *Doktor Faustus*." OL 29: 42–60.

Wooton, Carol. 1974. "Lure of the Basilisk. Chopin's Music in the Writings of Thomas Mann, John Galsworthy and Hermann Hesse." *Arcadia* 9: 23-38.

Wysling, Hans, ed. 1974. *Dokumente und Untersuchungen. Beiträge zur Thomas-Mann-Forschung*. Berne: Francke. (*Thomas-Mann-Studien*, Vol. 3.).

Zeller, Michael. 1974. *Väter und Söhne bei Thomas Mann. Der Generationsschritt als geschichtlicher Prozeß*. Bonn: Bouvier. (Bonner Arbeiten zur Deutschen Literatur, Vol. 17.).

Apter, T. E. 1975. "Thomas Mann's *Doctor Faustus*. Nihilism or Humanism?" *Forum for Modern Language Studies* 11: 59–73.

Assmann, Dietrich. 1975. *Thomas Manns Roman 'Doktor Faustus' und seine Beziehungen zur Faust-Tradition*. Helsinki: Suomalainen Tiedeakatemia.

Blomster, Wesley V. 1975. "A pietà in Mann's *Faustus*?" *Modern Language Notes* 90: 336–44.

Diersen, Ingrid. 1975. *Thomas Mann. Episches Werk-Weltanschauung -Leben*. Berlin: Aufbau. 304–84.

Ezergailis, Inta. 1975. *Male and Female: An Approach to Thomas Mann's Dialectic*. The Hague: Nijhoff.

Förster, Wolf-Dietrich. 1975. "Leverkühn, Schönberg und Thomas Mann. Musikalische Strukturen und Kunstreflexion im *Doktor Faustus*." DVLG 49: 694–720.

Gerhardt, Hans-Peter. 1975. "Kälte und Isolation in Thomas Manns Roman *Doktor Faustus*." *Faust-Blätter*, Issue 29: 995–1003.

Goll, Klaus R. 1975. "Die Dämonie einer alten Stadt. Anmerkungen zu *Doktor Faustus*." In *Thomas Mann geboren in Lübeck*, ed. Jan Herchenröder and Ulrich Thoemmes. Lübeck: Weiland. 115–24.

Heftrich, Eckhard. 1975. *Zauberbergmusik: Über Thomas Mann*. Frankfurt am Main: Klostermann.

Hoffmann, Fernand. 1975. *Thomas Mann als Philosoph der Krankheit*. Luxemburg: Institut Grand Ducal.

Hollweck, Thomas. 1975. *Thomas Mann*. Munich: List. (Literatur als Geschichte: Dokumente und Forschung, Vol. 1467.) 51–137.

Holthusen, Hans Egon. 1975. "Das Wiesengrund-Thema." *Ensemble: Internationales Jahrbuch für Literatur* 6: 89–97.

Jehl, D. 1975. "La grotesque chez Dostoïevski et Thomas Mann. Contributions à l'étude des nouvelles et du *Doktor Faustus.*" *EG* 30:148- 66.

Kern, J. P. 1975. "Zur Entstehung des *Doktor Faustus.*" *Neue Deutsche Hefte* 22: 228–44.

Klare, Margaret. 1975. "Eine literarische Reminiszenz? Thomas Manns *Doktor Faustus* und André Gides *Les Faux-Monnayeurs.*" *Arcadia* 10: 52–64.

Koopmann, Helmut, ed. 1975a. *Thomas Mann*. Darmstadt: Wissenschaftliche Buchgesellschaft.

Includes:

Elma, [Hans] J. 1975 (1965). "Dürer und Doktor Faustus." 320–50

Hamburger, Käte. 1975 (1969). "Anachronistische Symbolik: Fragen an Thomas Manns Faustus-Roman." 384–413.

Koopmann, Helmut. 1975b (1968). "Theorie und Praxis der epischen Ironie." 351–84.

———. 1975c. *Thomas Mann. Konstanten seines literarischen Werks*. Göttingen: Vandenhoeck & Ruprecht. 135–49.

Linder, Ann Planutis. 1975. "Music as Mysticism and Magic: The Presentation of Music in the Works of Marcel Proust and Thomas Mann." *Comparison*, Issue 5: 30–57.

Paeschke, Hans. 1975. "Nachschrift, in eigener Sache: Zu Dolf Sternberger: 'Deutschland im *Doktor Faustus* und *Doktor Faustus* in Deutschland.'" *Merkur* 29: 1139–40.

Pfaff, Lucie. 1975. "The Devil's Elixir: Aspects of Thomas Mann's *Doktor Faustus.*" *Faust-Blätter* 29: 1004–10.

Seidlin, Oskar. 1975. "The Open Wound: Notes on Thomas Mann's *Doctor Faustus.*" *Michigan German Studies* 1: 301–15. German version printed in 1982 in *Geschichtlichkeit der Moderne. Der Begriff der literarischen Moderne in Theorie und Deutung. Ulrich Fülleborn zum 60. Geburtstag*, ed. Theo Elm and Gerd Hemmerich. Munich: Fink. 291–306.

Smeed, J. W. 1975. *Faust in Literature*. New York: Oxford. 119–31.

Stern, Joseph P. 1975. *History and Allegory in Thomas Mann's 'Doktor Faustus. An Inaugural Lecture Delivered at University College London, 1 March 1973*. London: Lewis.

Sternberger, Dolf. 1975. "Deutschland im *Doktor Faustus* und *Doktor Faustus* in Deutschland." *Merkur* 29: 1123–39. Reprinted in Bludau, Heftrich and Koopmann, 1977: 155–73.

Vaget, Hans Rudolf. 1975. "Thomas Mann und Oskar Panizza. Zwei Splitter zu *Buddenbrooks* und *Doktor Faustus*". *Germanisch-Romanische Monatsschrift* 25: 231–37.

Voss, Lieselotte. 1975. *Die Entstehung von Thomas Manns Roman 'Doktor Faustus.' Dargestellt anhand von unveröffentlichten Vorarbeiten.* Tübingen: Niemeyer. (Studien zur deutschen Literatur, Vol. 39.).

Wiecker, Rolf, ed. 1975. *Gedenkschrift für Thomas Mann 1875–1975.* In *Text und Kontext,* Special Series, Vol. 2, ed. Rolf Wiecker. Kopenhagen: Verlag Text und Kontext.
Includes:
Maegard, Jan. "Zu Theodor W. Adornos Rolle im Mann/Schönberg-Streit." 215–22.
Mainika, Jürgen. "Thomas Mann und die Musikphilosophie des XX. Jahrhunderts." 197–214.

Wysling, Hans and Yvonne Schmidlin, eds. 1975. *Bild und Text bei Thomas Mann: Eine Dokumentation.* Berne: Francke.

Birnbaum, Henrik. 1976. *Doktor Faustus und Doktor Schiwago. Versuch über zwei Zeitromane aus Exilsicht.* Lisse: Peter de Ridder.

Hage, Volker. 1976. "Vom Einsatz und Rückzug des fiktiven Ich-Erzählers: *Doktor Faustus* — ein moderner Roman?" *Text und Kritik: Special Series, Thomas Mann,* ed. Heinz Ludwig Arnold. Munich: Verlag Text und Kritik. 88–98.

Hansen, Mathias. 1976. "Thomas Mann und Arnold Schönberg: Schöpferische Beziehungen zwischen Dichtung und Musik." *Forum: Musik in der DDR: Arnold Schönberg 1874–1951 zum 25. Todestag des Komponisten.* Berlin. (Arbeitsheft 24 der Akademie der Künste der DDR, Sektion Musik).

Hermsdorf, Klaus. 1976. "Doktor Faustus. Das Leben des deutschen Tonsetzers Adrian Leverkühn, erzählt von einem Freunde." In *Das erzählerische Werk Thomas Manns. Entstehungsgeschichte, Quellen, Wirkung,* ed. Klaus Hermsdorf et al. Berlin: Aufbau. 284–360.

Johnson, E. Bond. 1976. "Self-conscious Use of Narrative Point of View. Controlling Intelligence and Narrating Consciousness in *The Good Soldier* and *Doctor Faustus.*" In *Literary Criticism and Psychology,* ed. Joseph Strelka. University Park: Pennsylvania State UP. 137–49.

Kesting, Hanjo. 1976. "Krankheit zum Tode. Musik und Ideologie." In *Text und Kritik: Special Issue, Thomas Mann,* ed. Heinz Ludwig Arnold. Munich: Verlag Text und Kritik. 27–44.

Metscher, Thomas. 1976. "Faust und die Ökonomie. Ein literarhistorischer Essay." In his Vom *Faustus bis Karl Valentin. Der Bürger in Geschichte und Literatur.* Berlin: Argument-Verlag. (*Argument.* Special Issue 3.).

Moses, Stéphane. 1976. "Thomas Mann et Oskar Goldberg: un exemple de 'montage' dans le *Doktor Faustus.*" *EG* 31: 8–24.

Pfaff, Lucie. 1976. *The Devil in Thomas Mann's 'Doktor Faustus' and Paul Valéry's 'Mon Faust.'* Berne: H. Lang. (European University Papers, Vol. 145.).

Bludau, Beatrix, Eckhard Heftrich, and Helmut Koopmann, eds. 1977. *Thomas Mann 1875–1975. Vorträge in München-Zürich-Lübeck*. Frankfurt am Main: S. Fischer.

Includes:

Heftrich, Eckhard. 1977. "*Doktor Faustus*: Die radikale Autobiographie." 135- 54.

Heller, Erich. 1977. "Doktor Faustus und die Zurücknahme der Neunten Symphonie." 173–188. Reprinted in English in Heller,1984: 127–48.

Lange, Victor. 1977. "Thomas Mann: Tradition und Experiment." 566–85. Reprinted in Wolff, 1983: Part II, 113–33.

Ritter-Santini, Lea. 1977. "'Das Licht im Rücken': Notizen zu Thomas Manns Dante-Rezeption." 349–76.

Sternberger, Dolf. 1977. "Deutschland im *Doktor Faustus* und *Doktor Faustus* in Deutschland." 155–73.

Cotterill, Rowland. 1977. "Hesitant Allegory: Music in Thomas Mann's *Doktor Faustus*." *Comparison* 5: 58–91.

Dietzel, Ulrich, ed. 1977. *Thomas Mann-Heinrich Mann. Briefwechsel 1900-1949*. Berlin: Aufbau-Verlag.

Gilliam, H. S. 1977. "Mann's Other Holy Sinner: Adrian Leverkühn as Faust and Christ." *GR* 52: 122–47.

Gollnick, Ulrike. 1977. "Thomas Mann — Repräsentant der Nachkriegszeit?" In *Zur literarischen Situation 1945–1949*, ed. Gerhard Hay. Kronberg: Athenäum. 205–26. (Athenäums Taschenbuch 2117).

Jendreiek, Helmut. 1977.*Thomas Mann. Der demokratische Roman*. Düsseldorf: Bagel. 412–91.

Kurzke, Hermann. 1977. *Thomas-Mann-Forschung 1969–1976. Ein kritischer Bericht*. Frankfurt am Main: S. Fischer.

Lehnert, Herbert. 1977a. "Hundert Jahre Thomas Mann I. Thomas Mann — ein Klassiker? — Neues zur Biographie." *OL* 32: 97–115.

———. 1977b. "Hundert Jahre Thomas Mann II. Neue Thomas Mann Literatur." *OL* 32: 341–58.

Mádl, Antal and Judit Györi, eds.1977. *Thomas Mann und Ungarn. Essays, Dokumente, Bibliographie*. Cologne: Böhlau.

Mendelssohn, Peter de, ed. 1977. *Thomas Mann. Tagebücher: 1933–34*. Frankfurt am Main: Fischer. Subsequent volumes, all published in the same city by the same publisher, include: 1935–46 (1978); 1918–1921 (1979); 1937–1939 (1980); 1940–1943 (1982). For subsequent volumes, see Jens, 1986; 1989; 1991; 1993.

Sauerland, Karol. 1977. "*Doktor Faustus* ohne Adorno?" *Germanica Wratislaviensia* 29: 125–27.

Sautermeister, Gert. 1977. "Vergangenheitsbewältigung? Thomas Manns *Doktor Faustus* und die Wege der Forschung." *Basis* 7: 26–53.

Schröter, Klaus. 1977. "Literatur zu Thomas Mann um 1975." *Monatshefte* 69: 66–75.

Vaget, Hans Rudolf. 1977. "Kaisersaschern als geistige Lebensform. Zur Konzeption der deutschen Geschichte in Thomas Manns *Doktor Faustus*." In *Der deutsche Roman und seine historischen und politischen Bedingungen*, ed. Wolfgang Paulsen. Berne: Francke. 200–35. (Amherster Kolloquium zur deutschen Literatur, Vol. 9.).

Vom Hofe, Gerhard. 1977. "Das unbehagliche Bewußtsein des modernen Musikers. Zu Wackenroders Berglinger und Thomas Manns *Doktor Faustus*." In *Geist und Zeichen. Festschrift für Arthur Henkel zu seinem 60. Geburtstag*, ed. Herbert Anton, Bernhard Gajek, and Peter Pfaff. Heidelberg: Winter. 144–56.

Weigand, Hermann J. 1977. "Zu Thomas Manns Anteil an Serenus Zeitbloms Biographie von Adrian Leverkühn." *DVLG* 51:477–501. Reprinted 1982 in English translation in his *Critical Probings: Essays in European Literature from Wolfram von Eschenbach to Thomas Mann*, ed. Ulrich K. Goldsmith. Berne: Lang. 265–95. (Utah Studies in Literature and Linguistics, Vol. 22.).

Apter, T. E. 1978. *Thomas Mann. The Devil's Advocate*. London: Macmillan. 135- 157.

Böschenstein, Bernhard. 1978. "Ernst Bertrams *Nietzsche* — eine Quelle für Thomas Manns *Doktor Faustus*." *Euphorion* 72: 68–83.

Brandt, Helmut, and Hans Kaufmann, eds. 1978. *Werk und Wirkung Thomas Manns in unserer Epoche. Ein internationaler Dialog*. Berlin: Aufbau.

Includes:

Kneipel, Eberhard. 1978. "Thomas Manns Version der Schönbergschen Zwölftontechnik im *Doktor Faustus*. Zur Stellung von Kunst und Künstler in der spätbürgerlichen Gesellschaft." 273–83.

Wirth, Günter. 1978. "Thomas Mann und Paul Tillich." 371–79.

Gandelman, Claude. 1978. "La 'musique de sable' des Leverkühns: une métaphore nietzschiéenne cachée dans le *Doktor Faustus* de Thomas Mann." *DVLG* 52: 511–20.

Guibertoni, Anna Macchi. 1978. "Strawinsky ovvero la parodia come 'solitudine alternativa' nel *Doktor Faustus* di Thomas Mann." *Annali. Sezione germanica. Studi tedeschi* 21:107–27.

Hasselbach, Karlheinz. 1978. *Thomas Mann. Doktor Faustus. Das Leben des deutschen Tonsetzers Adrian Leverkühn erzählt von einem Freunde. Interpretation*. Munich: Oldenbourg (Interpretationen für Schule und Studium). Second revised and expanded edition 1988.

Klussmann, Paul G. and Jörg-Ulrich Fechner, eds.1978 *Thomas-Mann-Symposium Bochum 1975: Vorträge und Diskussionsberichte*. Kastellaun: Henn.

Includes:

Heftrich, Eckhard. 1978. "*Doktor Faustus* — Die radikale Autobioraphie." 1–20. Expanded version in his 1982 *Vom Verfall zur Apokalypse*, 173–288.

Klussmann, Paul G. 1978. "Thomas Manns *Doktor Faustus* als Zeitroman." 82–100. Expanded version reprinted in Wolff, 1983: Part II, 92–112.

Masini, Ferruccio. 1978. "*Doktor Faustus* im nihilistischen Spiegelbild Nietzsches oder die Enthumanisierung der Kunst." 44- 56.

Stern, Joseph P. 1978. "Geschichte und Allegorie in Thomas Manns *Doktor Faustus*." 23–41.

Mahlendorf, Ursula. 1978. "Aesthetics, Psychology and Politics in Thomas Mann's *Doctor Faustus*." *Mosaic* 11, Issue 4: 1–18.

Sandberg, Hans-Joachim. 1978. "Der Kierkegaard-Komplex in Thomas Manns *Doktor Faustus*: Zur Adaptation einer beziehungsreichen Thematik." *Text und Kontext* 6: 257–74.

Dabezies, André. 1979. "Entre le mythe de Faust et l'idéologie 'faustienne:' Thomas Mann devant Oswald Spengler." In his *Le mythe d'Étiemble. Hommages, études, et recherches*. Paris: Didier. 47–56.

Dvoretzky, Edward. 1979. "Thomas Manns *Doktor Faustus*. Ein Rückblick auf die frühe deutsche Kritik." *Blätter der Thomas-Mann-Gesellschaft* 17: 9–24.

Gersdorff, Dagmar von. 1979. *Thomas Mann und E. T. A. Hoffmann. Die Funktion des Künstlers und der Kunst in den Romanen 'Doktor Faustus' und 'Lebens-Ansichten des Katers Murr.'* Frankfurt am Main: P. Lang. (Europäische Hochschulschriften, Series 1, Vol. 326.).

Hatfield, Henry. 1979a. "*Doctor Faustus.*" In his *From the Magic Mountain. Mann's Later Masterpieces.* Ithaca, New York: Cornell University Press.108-34.

———. 1979b. "The Magic Square: Thomas Mann's '*Doctor Faustus.*' In his *Crisis and Continuity in Modern German Fiction. Ten Essays.* Ithaca, N. Y.: Cornell University Press. 166-76. (Revised version of his article of 1968).

Johnson, E. Bond. 1979. "An Unpublished Letter of Thomas Mann Concerning a Non-Source for *Doctor Faustus.*" In *Protest-Form-Tradition. Essays on German Exile Literature*, ed. Joseph P. Strekla, Robert F. Bell, and Eugene Dobson. Alabama University: Alabama. University Press. 15-34.

Jonas, Klaus W. 1979. *Die Thomas-Mann-Literatur. Bibliographie der Kritik. 1956-1975.* Vol 2. Berlin: E. Schmidt.

Kamla, Thomas A. 1979. "'Christliche Kunst mit negativem Vorzeichen:' Kierkegaard und *Doktor Faustus.* " *Neophilologus* 63: 583-87.

Mádl, Antal. 1979. "Thomas Manns Weg vom *Doktor Faustus* zum *Erwählten.*" *Arbeiten zur deutschen Philologie* 13: 209-25.

Rieckmann, Jens. 1979a. "Zeitblom und Leverkühn: Traditionelles oder avantgardistisches Kunstverständnis?" *GQ* 52: 50-60.

———. 1979b. "Zum Problem des 'Durchbruchs' in Thomas Manns *Doktor Faustus.*" *Wirkendes Wort* 29: 114-28.

Sandberg, Hans-Joachim. 1979. "Kierkegaard und Leverkühn. Zum Problem der Verzweiflung in Thomas Manns Roman *Doktor Faustus.*" *Nerthus* 4: 93-107.

Sauerland, Karol. 1979. "'Er wußte noch mehr . . .' Zum Konzeptionsbruch in Thomas Manns *Doktor Faustus*" unter dem Einfluß Adornos." *OL* 34: 130-45.

Sautermeister, Gert. 1979. "Zwischen Aufklärung und Mystifizierung: Der unbewältigte Widerspruch in Thomas Manns *Doktor Faustus.*" In *Antifaschistische Literatur*, ed. Lutz Winkler. Königstein: Scriptor. 77-125.

Stern, Joseph P. 1979. "Zwei Arten des historischen Bewußtseins in Thomas Manns *Doktor Faustus.*" *Literatur und Kritik* 14: 535-39.

Szudra, Klaus Udo. 1979. "Shakespeare-Reminiszenzen in Thomas Manns *Doktor Faustus.*" *Neophilological Quarterly* 26: 259-78.

Thoenelt, Klaus. 1979. "Selbstentfremdung als deutsches Phänomen in Thomas Manns *Doktor Faustus* und Alfred Rosenbergs *Mythus des 20. Jahrhunderts.* " In *Deutsche Exilliteratur. Literatur im Dritten Reich*, ed. Wolfgang Elfe, James Hardin, and Gunther Holst. Berne: Lang. 93-102.

Wolff, Uwe. 1979. *Thomas Mann. Der erste Kreis der Hölle. Der Mythos im 'Doktor Faustus.'* Stuttgart: Heinz. (Stuttgarter Arbeiten zur Germanistik, Vol. 6.).

Adelson, Leslie. 1980. "Heterosexuality and the Bourgeoisie in Thomas Mann's *Doktor Faustus.*" *Neue Germanistik* l: 49–58.

Aronson, Alex. 1980. *Music and Novel: A Study in 20th Century Fiction.* Towota, N. J.: Rowman and Littlefield. 182–215.

Fetzer, John F. 1980a. "Clemens Brentano's Muse and Adrian Leverkühn's Music. Selective Affinities in Thomas Mann's *Doctor Faustus.*" *Essays in Literature* 7: 115–31.

———. 1980b. "Nachklänge Brentanoscher Musik in Thomas Manns *Doktor Faustus.*" In *Clemens Brentano. Beiträge des Kolloquiums im Freien Deutschen Hochstift 1978,* ed. Detlev Lüders. Tübingen: Niemeyer.

Frank, Manfred. 1980. "'Kaum das Urthema wechselnd.' Die alte und die neue Mythologie im *Doktor Faustus.*" *Fugen. Deutsch-französisches Jahrbuch für Text-Analytik*: 9–42. Revised version of 1982 in his "*Invaliden des Apoll.*" *Motive und Mythen des Dichterleids,* ed. Herbert Anton. Munich: Fink. 78–94.

Gockel, Heinz. 1980. "Thomas Manns Faustus und Kierkegaards Don Juan." *Akten des VI. Internationalen Germanisten-Kongresses Basel 1980,* ed. Heinz Rupp and Hans-Gert Roloff, in *Jahrbuch für Internationale Germanistik* 8: 68- 75.

Hasselbach, Karlheinz. 1980. "Der leitmotivische Gebrauch von Sprachschichten und Sprachpartikeln in Thomas Manns *Doktor Faustus.*" In *Sprache und Brauchtum. Bernhard Martin zum 90. Geburtstag,* ed. Reiner Hildebrandt and Hans Friebertshäuser. Marburg: Elwert. 418- 31.

Kolago, Lech. 1980. "Nachklänge der Musikgeschichte im Roman *Doktor Faustus* von Thomas Mann." *Germanica Wratislaviensia* 36: 193–201.

Koopmann, Helmut. 1980. "Der Untergang des Abendlandes und der Aufgang des Morgenlandes." *Jahrbuch der deutschen Schillergesellschaft* 24: 300–31. Reprinted 1988 in English translation in Ezergailis: 238–65.

Mádl, Antal. 1980. *Thomas Manns Humanismus. Werden und Wandel einer Welt- und Menschenauffassung.* Berlin: Rütten & Loening.

Mayer, Hans. 1980. *Thomas Mann.* Frankfurt am Main: Suhrkamp. 270–327.

Mendelssohn, Peter de, ed. 1980. Postscript to his edition of *Thomas Mann. Gesammelte Werke in Einzelbänden. 'Doktor Faustus.'* Frankfurt am Main: S. Fischer. 685–746. Reprinted in Mendelssohn, 1982.

Newman, John K. 1980. "Classical Background to Thomas Mann's *Doktor Faustus.*" *Neohelicon* 8 : 35–42.

Palencia-Roth, Michael. 1980. "Albrecht Dürers 'Melencolia' und Thomas Manns *Doktor Faustus.*" *German Studies Review* 3: 361–75.

Porter, Laurence M. 1980. "Syphilis as Muse in Thomas Mann's *Doctor Faustus.*" In *Medicine and Literature*, ed. Enid Rhodes Peschel. New York: Neal Watson Academic Publications. 147–52.

Vaget, Hans Rudolf. 1980. "Thomas Mann und kein Ende." *Zeitschrift für deutsche Philologie* 99: 276–88.

Cerf, Steven. 1981. "Love in Thomas Mann's *Doktor Faustus* as an Imitatio Shakespeari." *Comparative Literature Studies* 18: 475–86.

Gockel, Heinz. 1981. "Thomas Manns Entweder und Oder." In *Arbeitskreis Heinrich Mann, Mitteilungsblatt.* Special Issue: *Siegfried Sudhof (1927–1980) zu gedenken*, ed. Peter Paul Schneider. Lübeck: Arbeitskreis Heinrich Mann. 87–107. Reprinted in Wolff, 1983: Part II, 134–50.

Orlowski, Hubert. 1981. "Die größere Kontroverse. Zur deutschen 'nichtakademischen' Rezeption des *Doktor Faustus* von Thomas Mann (1947–1950)." In *Erzählung und Erzählforschung im 20. Jahrhundert*, ed. Rolf Kloepfer and Gisela Janetzke-Dillner. Stuttgart: Kohlhammer. 245–55.

Schlee, Agnes. 1981. *Wandlungen musikalischer Strukturen im Werke Thomas Manns. Vom Leitmotiv zur Zwölftonreihe.* Frankfurt am Main: P. Lang. (Europäische Hochschulschriften, Reihe I, Vol. 384.).

Siefken, Hinrich. 1981. *Thomas Mann. Goethe — 'Ideal der Deutschheit.' Wiederholte Spiegelungen 1893–1949.* Munich: Fink.

Steffgnsen, Steffen. 1981. "Drei Faustgestalten." In *Dikt og idé. Festskrift til Ole Koppang på syttiuars-dagen, 18. Januar 1981*, ed. Sverre Dahl. Oslo: Germanistisches Institut. (Osloer Beiträge zur Germanistik, Vol. 4.).

Wysling, Hans, and Marianne Fischer, eds. 1981. *Dichter über ihre Dichtungen*, Vol. 14: *Thomas Mann. Teil III: 1944–1955.* Heimeran: S. Fischer.

Baron, Frank. 1982. *Faustus. Geschichte, Sage, Dichtung.* Munich: Winkler. 114–19.

Dahlhaus, Carl. 1982. "Fiktive Zwölftonmusik. Thomas Mann und Theodor W. Adorno." *Jahrbuch der Deutschen Akademie für Sprache und Dichtung*, Issue l: 33–49. Reprinted in *Musica* 37 (1983): 245–52.

Fetzer, John Francis. 1982. "Faktisches und Fiktionales über Annette Kolb. Wechselbeziehungen zwischen ihrer Darstellung des Exillebens und der Darstellung ihres Lebens durch den exilierten Thomas Mann." In *Das Exilerlebnis. Verhandlungen des vierten Symposium über Deutsche und Österreichische Exilliteratur*, ed. Donald D. Daviau and Ludwig M. Fischer. Columbia, S.C.: Camden House. 280–88.

Feuerlicht, Ignace. 1982. "Thomas Mann and Homoeroticism." *GR* 57: 89-97.

Frank, Manfred. 1982. "Die alte und neue Mythologie. Thomas Manns *Doktor Faustus*." *"Invaliden des Apoll. "Motive und Mythen des DIchterleids*, ed. Herbert Anton. Munich: Fink. 78–94.

Heftrich, Eckhard. 1982. "Radikale Autobiographie und Allegorie der Epoche: *Doktor Faustus*." In his *Vom Verfall zur Apokalypse. Über Thomas Mann*. Vol. II. Frankfurt am Main: Klostermann. 173–288.

Mendelssohn, Peter de. 1982. "*Doktor Faustus*." *Nachbemerkungen zu Thomas Mann*. Vol.1. Frankfurt am Main: Fischer Taschenbuch Verlag. 109–95. Original found in Mendelssohn, 1980.

Middell, Eike. 1982. Review of Antal Mádl, *Thomas Manns Humanismus*. *Zeitschrift für Germanistik* 3: 481–85.

Schein, Reinhold. 1982. "*Doktor Faustus*.' Thomas Manns Versuch der Interpretation der deutschen Geschichte." *German Studies in India* 6: 199–206.

Schiffer, Eva. 1982. *Zwischen den Zeilen. Manuskriptänderungen bei Thomas Mann. Transkriptionen und Deutungsversuche.* Berlin: Erich Schmidt.

Schwarze, Michael. 1982. "Ein sündiges Künstlerleben. Franz Seitz verfilmte Thomas Mann Roman *Doktor Faustus*." *Hefte der Thomas-Mann-Gesellschaft* 2: 44–47.

Seidlin, Oskar. 1982. "Die offene Wunde. Notizen zu Thomas Manns *Doktor Faustus*." In *Geschichtlichkeit der Moderne. Der Begriff der literarischen Moderne in Theorie und Deutung. Ulrich Fülleborn zum 60. Geburtstag*, ed. Theo Elm and Gerd Hemmerich. Munich: Fink. 291–306.

Seitz, Gabriele, ed. 1982a. '*Doktor Faustus.' Ein Film von Franz Seitz nach dem Roman von Thomas Mann*. Frankfurt am Main: Fischer Taschenbuch. Includes:

Blahacek, Rudolf. 1982. "In deutschem Licht." 148–51.

Klimitschek, Lotte. 1982. "Das Spiel der Ebenen." 152–57.

Schick, Lilo. 1982. "Über die Achse gesprungen." 162–66.

Seitz, Gabriele. 1982b. "Zu Thomas Manns *Doktor Faustus*." 7–30.

Seitz, Franz. 1982a. "*Doktor Faustus* — Lesefassung des Drehbuchs." 31–112.

———. 1982b. "Teufelslachen löst Lawinen aus." 113–31.

Uslar-Gleichen, Hil von. 1982. "Komparsenperspektive." 167–73.

Wilhelm, Rolf. 1982. "Musik von Kaisersaschern." 132–51.

Wiegand, Helmut. 1982. *Thomas Manns 'Doktor Faustus' als zeitgeschichtlicher Roman. Eine Studie über die historischen Dimensionen in Thomas Manns Spätwerk*. Frankfurt am Main: R. G. Fischer. (Frankfurter Beiträge zur neueren deutschen Literaturgeschichte, Vol. 1.).

Wysling, Hans. 1982. *Narzissmus und illusionäre Existenzform. Zu den 'Bekenntnissen des Hochstaplers Felix Krull.'* Berne: Francke. (*Thomas-Mann-Studien*, Vol. 5.).

Allen, Marguerite de Huszar. 1983. "Montage and the Faust Theme. The Influence of the 1587 Faustbuch on Thomas Mann's Montage Technique in *Doktor Faustus*." *Journal of European Studies* 13: 109–21.

Cobley, Evelyn. 1983. "Political Ambiguities in *Under Western Eyes* and *Doctor Faustus*." *Canadian Review of Comparative Literature* 10: 377–88.

Durrani, Osman. 1983. "Echo's Reverberations: Notes on a Painful Incident in Thomas Mann's *Doktor Faustus*." *GL&L* 37: 125–34.

Jäkel, Siegfried. 1983. *Konvention und Sprache. Eine sprachphilosophische Basis für Interpretationsexperimente demonstriert am Beispiel von Thomas Manns Roman 'Doktor 'Faustus.'* Turku: Turun Yliopisto.

Puschmann, Rosemarie. 1983. *Magisches Quadrat und Melancholie in Thomas Manns 'Doktor Faustus.' Von der musikalischen Struktur zum semantischen Beziehungsnetz*. Bielefeld: AMPAL.

Ryan, Judith. 1983. *The Uncompleted Past: Postwar German Novels and the Third Reich*. Detroit: Wayne State University Press.

Schäfermeyer, Michael. 1983. *Thomas Mann: Die Biographie des Adrian Leverkühn und der Roman 'Doktor Faustus.'* Frankfurt am Main: P. Lang. (Historisch-kritische Arbeiten zur deutschen Literatur, Vol. 4.).

Seidlin, Oskar. 1983a. "And who, if we may ask, is Johann Balhorn von Lübeck?" *Euphorion* 77: 230–32.

———.1983b. "Doktor Faustus reist nach Ungarn. Notiz zu Thomas Manns Altersroman." *Heinrich-Mann-Jahrbuch* 1: 187–204.

———.1983c. "Doctor Faustus: The Hungarian Connection." *GQ* 56: 594–607.

Sommerhage, Claus. 1983. *Eros und Poesis. Über das Erotische im Werk Thomas Manns*. Bonn: Bouvier (Bonner Arbeiten zur deutschen Literatur, Vol. 40.).

Wald, H. 1983. "Strukturprobleme der Romane F.M. Dostoevskijs und Thomas Manns. Das Paradigma der Musik in *Doktor Faustus* unter komparatistischem Aspekt." *Zeitschrift für Slawistik* 28: 693–703.

Wolff, Rudolf, ed. 1983. *Thomas Manns Dr. Faustus und die Wirkung*. Bonn: Bouvier. (Sammlung Profile, Vol. 4.)

Part I includes:

Carlsson, Anni. 1983 (1949). "Das Faustmotiv bei Thomas Mann." 84-105

Hamburger, Käte. 1983 (1969). "Anachronistische Symbolik. Fragen an Thomas Manns Faustus-Roman." 124–50.

Lukács, Georg. 1983 (1948). "Die Tragödie der modernen Kunst." 34–83.

Mayer, Hans. 1983 (1959). "Thomas Manns *Doktor Faustus*. Roman einer Endzeit und Endzeit eines Romans." 106–23.

Sontheimer, Kurt. 1983 (1961). "Thomas Mann und die Deutschen." 16-32.

Part II includes:

Dörr, Hansjörg. 1983 (1970). "Thomas Mann und Adorno. Ein Beitrag zur Entstehung des *Doktor Faustus*." 48–91.

Klussmann, Paul. 1983 (1978). "Thomas Manns *Doktor Faustus* als Zeitroman." 92–112.

Koopmann, Helmut. 1983. "*Doktor Faustus* und sein Biograph. Zu einer Exilerfahrung sui generis." 8–26. Reprinted in Koopmann, 1988, 93-108.

Kost, Rudi. 1983. "Dr. Fäustchen oder die (De-)Montage der Attraktionen. Gedanken zur *Doktor Faustus*-Verfilmung von Franz Seitz und zu Literaturverfilmungen überhaupt." 27–46.

Lange, Victor. 1983 (1977). "Thomas Mann: Tradition und Experiment." 113–50

Böhm, Karl Werner. 1984. "Die homosexuellen Elemente in Thomas Manns *Der Zauberberg*." *Literatur für Leser: Zeitschrift für Interpretationspraxis und geschichtliche Texterkenntnis* (1984):171–90.

Busch, Arnold. 1984. *Faust und Faschismus: Thomas Manns 'Doktor Faustus' und A. Döblins 'November 1918' als exilliterarische Auseinandersetzung mit Deutschland*. Frankfurt am Main: P. Lang. (Europäische Hochschulschriften, Series I, Vol. 777.).

Curtius, Mechthild. 1984. *Erotische Phantasien bei Thomas Mann*. Königstein: Athenäum.

Fischer, Erika. 1984. "Adrian Leverkühns Philosophie der Neuen Musik." *Literatur für Leser. Zeitschrift für Interpretationspraxis und geschichtliche Texterkenntnis* (1984): 162–70.

Friedrichsmeyer, Erhard. 1984. "Adrian Leverkühn. Thomas Manns lachender Faust." *Colloquia Germanica* 17: 79–97.

Gandelman, Claude. 1984. "The *Doktor Faustus* of Thomas Mann as a Drama of Iconicity." *Semiotica* 49: 27–47.

Hansen, Volkmar. 1984. *Thomas Mann.* Stuttgart: Metzler. (Sammlung Metzler, Vol. 211.).

Heller, Erich. 1984. "The Taking Back of the Ninth Symphony. Reflections on Thomas Mann's *Doctor Faustus.*" In his *In the Age of Prose. Literary and Philosophical Essays.* Cambridge, England: Cambridge University Press. 127–48.

Ingen, Ferdinand van. 1984. "Die Erasmus-Luther-Konstellation bei Stefan Zweig und Thomas Mann." In *Luther-Bilder im 20. Jahrhundert. Symposion an der Freien Universität Amsterdam,* ed. Ferdinand van Ingen and Gerd Labroisse, with the assistance of Cornelius Augustijn and Ulrich Gäbler. Amsterdam: Rodopi. (Amsterdamer Beiträge zur neueren Germanistik, Vol. 19.). 91–117.

Kluge, Gerhard. 1984. "Luther in Thomas Manns *Doktor Faustus.*" In *Luther-Bilder im 20. Jahrhundert. Symposion an der Freien Universität Amsterdam,* ed. Ferdinand van Ingen and Gerd Labroisse, with the assistance of Cornelius Augustijn and Ulrich Gäbler. Amsterdam: Rodopi. (Amsterdamer Beiträge zur neueren Germanistik, Vol. 19.). 119–39.

Lehnert, Herbert. 1984. "The Luther-Erasmus Constellation in Thomas Mann's *Doktor Fasutus.*" *Michigan Germanic Studies* 10: 142–58.

Northcote-Bade, James. 1984. "The Background to the 'Liebestod' Plot Pattern in the Works of Thomas Mann." *GR* 59: 11–18.

Traube, Franz. 1984. "Die Wirkung eines Lebens- und Geheimwerkes. *Doktor Faustus* von Thomas Mann." *Horizonte* 8, Issue 34: 23–25.

Wedekind-Schwertner, Barbara. 1984. *"Daß ich eins und doppelt bin." Studien zur Idee der Androgynie unter besonderer Berücksichtigung Thomas Manns.* Frankfurt am Main: P. Lang. (Europäische Hochschulschriften, Series 1, Vol. 785.).

Weigand, Hermann J. 1984. "Die tote Maus oder Nachtrag zur 'moralischen Verwirrung der Zeit.' Schillers Urenkel in Thomas Manns *Doktor Faustus.*" *DVLG* 58: 470–74.

Allen, Marguerite de Huzar. 1985. *The Faust Legend. Popular Formula and Modern Novel.* New York: P. Lang. (Germanic Studies in America, Vol. 53.).

Bloom, Harold, ed. 1985. *Thomas Mann.* New York: Chelsea House. Includes:

Bergsten, Gunilla. 1985. "*Doctor Faustus* as a 'Historical' Novel." 71–85. A chapter excerpted from the 1969 translation of Bergsten's original study in German of 1963, 135–63.

Honsa, William. 1985. "Parody and Narrator in Thomas Mann's *Doctor Faustus.*" 219–26. Revised version of Honsa's essay of 1974.

Schaper, Eva. "A Modern Faust. The Novel in the Ironical Key." 103–22. Schaper's essay appeared originally in 1965.

Cerf, Steven. 1985. "The Shakespearean Element in Thomas Mann's *Doktor Faustus*-Montage." *Révue de littérature comparée* 59: 427–41.

Durrani, Osman. 1985. "The Tearful Teacher. The Role of Serenus Zeitblom in Thomas Mann's *Doktor Faustus.*" *Modern Language Review* 80: 652-58.

Heftrich, Eckhard. 1985. *Von Verfall zur Apokalypse Über Thomas Mann.* Vol. 2. Frankfurt am Main: Klostermann.

Jung, Jürgen. 1985. *Altes und Neues zu Thomas Manns Roman 'Doktor Faustus:' Quellen und Modelle, Mythos, Psychologie, Musik, Theo- Dämonologie, Faschismus.* Frankfurt am Main: P. Lang. (Europäische Hochschulschriften, Series 1, Vol. 821.).

Kiremidjian, David. 1985. *A Study of Modern Parody. James Joyce's 'Ulysses,' Thomas Mann's 'Doctor Faustus.'* New York: Garland.

Kurzke, Hermann, ed. 1985a. *Stationen der Thomas-Mann-Forschung. Aufsätze seit 1970.* Würzburg: Königshausen und Neumann.

———. 1985b. *Thomas Mann. Epoche-Werk-Wirkung.* Munich: Beck. Second, revised edition 1991.

Lehnert, Herbert. 1985. "Die Dialektik der Kultur. Mythos, Katastrophe und die Kontinuität der deutschen Literatur in Thomas Manns *Doktor Faustus.*" In *Schreiben im Exil . Zur Ästhetik der deutschen Exilliteratur 1933- 1945*, ed. Alexander Stephan and Hans Wagener. Bonn: Bouvier. 95–108. (Studien zur Literatur der Moderne, Vol. 13.).

Reed, Donna K. 1985. *The Novel and the Nazi Past.* New York: P. Lang. (American University Studies, Series l, Vol. 28.).

Reinhardt, George W. 1985. "Thomas Mann's *Doctor Faustus,*' a Wagnerian Novel." *Mosaic* 18, Issue 4: 109–23.

Renner, Rolf Günter. 1985. *Lebens-Werk: Zum inneren Zusammenhang der Texte von Thomas Mann.* Munich: Fink.

Scheiffele, Eberhard. 1985. "Das Theologische, Mythologische, Religiöse als strukturbestimmendes Moment im *Doktor Faustus*." *Doitsu bungaku kenky u* 30: 30–63.

Schleiner, Winfried. 1985. "The Nexus of Witchcraft and Male Impotence in Renaissance Thought and Its Reflection in Mann's *Doktor Faustus*." *JEGP* 84: 166–87.

Steinfeld, Thomas. 1985. "Genie und Dämon in Thomas Manns *Doktor Faustus*." *Text und Kontext* 13: 80–89.

Baasner, Rainer. 1986. "Die zum Geheimnis erhobene Berechnung. Zahlensymbolik in Thomas Manns *Doktor Faustus*." *Archiv für das Studium der neueren Sprachen und Literaturen* 223: 26–44.

Ball, David J. 1986. *Thomas Mann's Recantation of Faust: 'Doktor Faustus' in the Context of Mann's Relationship to Goethe*. Stuttgart: Heinz-Dieter Verlag. (Stuttgarter Arbeiten zur Germanistik, Vol. 173.).

Beddow, Michael. 1986. "Analogies of Salvation in Thomas Mann's *Doctor Faustus*." *London German Studies* 3: 117–131.

Berman, Russell A. 1986. *The Rise of the Modern German Novel: Crisis and Charisma*. Cambridge, Mass. Harvard University Press.

Bürger, Christa. 1986. "Realismus und ästhetische Moderne. Zu Thomas Manns *Doktor Faustus*." *Heinrich-Mann-Jahrbuch* 4 : 56–68.

Dowden, Stephen D. 1986. *Sympathy for the Abyss: A Study in the Novel of German Modernism: Kafka, Broch, Musil, and Thomas Mann*. Tübingen: Niemeyer.

Fähnrich, Hermann. 1986. *Thomas Manns episches Musizieren im Sinne Richard Wagners: Parodie und Konkurrenz*, ed. and expanded by Maria Hülle-Keeding. Frankfurt am Main: H.A. Herchen.

Frenzel, Elisabeth. 1986. "Der doppelgesichtige Leverkühn. Motivverschränkungen in Thomas Manns *Doktor Faustus*." In *Gelebte Literatur in der Literatur. Studien zu Erscheinungsformen und Geschichte eines literarischen Motivs*, ed. Theodor Wolpers. Göttingen: Vandenhoeck & Ruprecht. 311–20.

Härle, Gerhard. 1986. *Die Gestalt des Schönen: Untersuchung zur Homosexualitätsthematik in Thomas Manns Roman 'Der Zauberberg.'* Königstein: Hain.

Jens, Inge, ed. 1986. *Thomas Mann. Tagebücher 1944 — 1. 4. 1946*. Frankfurt am Main: S. Fischer.

Lublich, Frederick Alfred. 1986. *Die Dialektik von Logos und Eros im Werk von Thomas Mann*. Heidelberg: Winter. (Reihe Siegen. Beiträge zur Literatur- und Sprachwissenschaft, Vol. 63.).

Roberts, David. 1986. "Die Postmoderne — Dekonstruktion oder Radikalisierung der Moderne? Überlegungen am Beispiel des *Doktor Faustus*." In *Akten des VII. internationalen Germanisten-Kongresses Göttingen 1985: Kontroversen, alte und neue*, ed. Albrecht Schöne. Vol 8. Tübingen: Niemeyer. 148–53.

Roche, Mark W. 1986 "Laughter and Truth in *Doktor Faustus*: Nietzschean Structures in Mann's Novel of Self-Cancellation." *DVLG* 60: 309–32.

Schubert, Bernard. 1986. "Das Ende der bürgerlichen Vernunft? Zu Thomas Manns *Doktor Faustus*." *ZDP* 105: 568–92.

Wißkirchen, Hans. 1986. *Zeitgeschichte im Roman. Zu Thomas Manns 'Zauberberg' und 'Doktor Faustus.'* Berne: Francke. (*Thomas-Mann-Studien*, Vol. 6).

Assmann, Dietrich. 1987. "'Herzpochendes Mitteilungsbedürfnis und tiefe Scheu vor dem Unzukömmlichen.' Thomas Manns Erzähler im *Doktor Faustus*." *Hefte der deutschen Thomas-Mann-Gesellschaft*, Issue 6/7: 87–97.

Internationales Thomas-Mann Kolloquium 1986 in Lübeck. 1987. Berne: Francke. (*Thomas-Mann-Studien*, Vol. 7)

Includes:

Koopmann, Helmut. 1987. "*Doktor Faustus* als Widerlegung der Weimarer Klassik." 92–109. Reprinted in Koopmann, 1988: 109–24

Vaget, Hans Rudolf. 1987. "Die Fürstin. Ein Beitrag zur Biographie des späten Thomas Mann." 113–38

LaCapra, Dominick. 1987. "History and the Devil in Mann's *Doctor Faustus*." In his *History, Politics, and the Novel*. Ithaca, N.Y.: Cornell University Press. 150–74.

Schwarz, Egon. 1987. "Adrian Leverkühn und Alban Berg." *Modern Language Notes* 102: 663–67.

Straus, Nina Pelikan. 1987. "'Why Must Everything Seem Like Its Own Parody?' Thomas Mann's Parody of Siegmund Freud in *Doctor Faustus*." *Literature and Psychology* 33, Issue 3–4: 59–75.

Timm, Eitel. 1987. "Thomas Manns *Doktor Faustus* im Film. Zum Problem der 'Wortmusik.'" *Carleton Germanic Papers*, Issue 15: 41–54.

Vaget, Hans Rudolf. 1987a. "Amazing Grace: Thomas Mann, Adorno, and the Faust Myth." In *Our 'Faust'? Roots and Ramifications of a Modern German Myth*, ed. Reinhold Grimm and Jost Hermand. Madison: University of Wisconsin Press. 168–89. (*Monatshefte* Occasional Volumes.).

———. 1987b. "Frau von Tolna: Agnes E. Meyer und Thomas Manns *Doktor Faustus.*" In *Zeitgenossenschaft. Zur deutschsprachigen Literatur im 20. Jahrhundert. Festschrift für Egon Schwarz zum 65. Geburtstag*, ed. Paul Michael Lützeler in collaboration with Herbert Lehnert and Gerhild S.Williams. Frankfurt am Main: Athenäum. 140–52.

Vogt. Karen Drabek. 1987. *Vision und Revision. The Concept of Inspiration in Thomas Mann's Fiction.* New York: P. Lang. (Germanic Studies in America, Vol. 55.).

Baumgarten, Reinhard. 1988. "Thomas Mann als erotischer Schriftsteller." *Forum. Homosexualität und Literatur* 4: 5–22.

Cicora, Mary A. 1988. "Wagner Parody in *Doctor Faustus.*" *GR* 63: 133–39.

Del Caro, Adrian. 1988. "The Devil as Advocate in the Last Novels of Thomas Mann and Dostoevski." *OL* 43: 129–59.

Ezergailis, Inta M. 1988. "Introduction." In *Critical Essays on Thomas Mann*, ed. Inta M. Ezergailis. Boston: Hall. 1–9.

Feuerlicht, Ignace. 1988. "Thomas Mann und die Homoerotik." *Forum Homosexualität und Literatur* 3: 29–50.

Gockel, Heinz. 1988. "Faust im Faustus." *Thomas-Mann-Jahrbuch* 1:133–48.

Grim, William E. 1988. "Diabolus in musica. Thomas Mann's *Doktor Faustus.*" In his *The Faust Legend in Music and Literature.* Lewiston, Queenstown, Canada: Edwin Mellen Press. 73–98.

Härle, Gerhard. 1988. *Männerweiblichkeit. Zur Homosexualität bei Klaus und Thomas Mann.* Frankfurt am Main: Athenäum.

Hoelzel, Alfred. 1988a. "Leverkühn, the Mermaid, and Echo. A Tale of Faustian Incest." *Symposium* 42: 3–16.

———.1988b. *The Paradoxical Quest. A Study of Faustian Vicissitudes.* New York: Lang. (New Yorker Beiträge zur Vergleichenden Literaturwissenschaft, Vol. 1.).

Kaiser, Joachim. 1988. "*Doktor Faustus*, die Musik und das deutsche Schicksal." In his *Erlebte Literatur. Vom 'Doktor Faust' zum 'Fettfleck.'* Munich: Piper. 28–55. Shortened version 1989 in his *Thomas Mann und München*, Frankfurt am Main: Fischer Taschenbuch Verlag. 25–50.

Kinzel, Ulrich. 1988. *Zweideutigkeit als System. Zur Geschichte der Beziehungen zwischen der Vernunft und dem Anderen in Thomas Manns Roman 'Doktor Faustus.'* Frankfurt am Main: Lang. (Beiträge zur Literatur und Literaturwissenschaft des 20. Jahrhunderts, Vol. 8.).

Koopmann, Helmut. 1988. "*Doktor Faustus* — Schwierigkeiten mit dem Bösen und das Ende des 'strengen Satzes.'" In his *Der schwierige Deutsche. Studien zum Werk Thomas Manns*. Tübingen: Niemeyer. 125–44.

Wehrmann, Harald. 1988. *Thomas Manns Doktor Faustus. Von der fiktiven Werken Adrian Leverkühns zur musikalischen Struktur des Romans*. Frankfurt am Main: Lang. (Europäische Hochschulschriften, Series 1: Deutsche Sprache und Literatur, Vol. 979.).

Wysling, Hans, ed. with the collaboration of Thomas Sprecher. 1988. "Thomas Mann und Heinrich Mann. Briefwechsel. Neu aufgefundene Briefe 1933–1949. " *Thomas-Mann-Jahrbuch* 1: 167–230.

Cicora, Mary A. 1989. "Beethoven, Shakespeare, and Wagner. Visual Music in *Doctor Faustus*." *DVLG* 63: 267–81.

Cobley, Evelyn. 1989. "Closure and Infinite Semiosis in Mann's *Doctor Faustus* and Eco's *The Name of the Rose*." *Comparative Literature Studies* 26: 341–61.

Hillesheim, Jürgen. 1989. *Die Welt als Artefakt. Zur Bedeutung von Nietzsches 'Der Fall Wagner' im Werk Thomas Manns*. Frankfurt am Main: P. Lang. (Studien zur deutschen Literatur des 19. und 20. Jahrhunderts, Vol. 113.)

Jens, Inge, ed. 1989. *Thomas Mann. Tagebücher 28. 5. 1946 — 31.12. 1948*. Frankfurt am Main: S. Fischer.

Kaiser, Joachim. 1989. "*Doktor Faustus*: Die Musik und das deutsche Schicksal." In *Thomas Mann und München*. Frankfurt am Main: Fischer Taschenbuch Verlag. 25–50. Also appeared 1988 in his *Erlebte Literatur*: 1988, 28–55.

Kimball, Susanne. 1989. "Thomas Mann's Protagonists and the Problem of Eros." *Germanic Notes* 19: 49–57.

Koopmann, Helmut. 1989. "'Mit Goethes *Faust* hat mein Roman nichts gemein.' Thomas Mann und sein *Doktor Faustus*." In *Faust through Four Centuries*, ed. Peter Boerner and Sidney Johnson. Tübingen: Niemeyer. 213–28.

Kreutzer, Hans J. 1989. "Fausts Weg vom Wissenschaftler zum Künstler oder Thomas Manns Deutung der deutschen Geschichte." *Zeitschrift für deutsche Studien* (1989–1990), Issue 8: 79–95.

Lehnert, Herbert. 1989. "Der Narziß und die Welt: Zum biographischen Hintergrund des *Doktor Faustus* von Thomas Mann." *OL* 44: 234–51.

Lorenz, Helmut. 1989. *Die Musik Thomas Manns in Erzählungen, Buddenbrooks, Essays, Betrachtungen eines Unpolitischen, Zauberberg, Doktor Faustus, Tagebücher*. Berlin: Copy-Center in Dahlem.

Maar, Michael. 1989. "Der Teufel in Palestrina. Neues zum *Doktor Faustus* und zur Position Gustav Mahlers im Werk Thomas Manns." *Literaturwissenschaftliches Jahrbuch* 30: 211–47.

Michelsen, Peter. 1989. "Faust und die Deutschen (mit besonderem Hinblick auf Thomas Manns *Doktor Faustus*)." In *Faust through Four Centuries*, ed. Peter Boerner and Sidney Johnson. Tübingen: Niemeyer. 229–247.

Mundt, Hannelore. 1989. *'Doktor Faustus' und die Folgen. Kunstkritik als Gesellschaftskritik im deutschen Roman seit 1947*. Bonn: Bouvier. (Abhandlungen zur Kunst-, Musik- und Literaturwissenschaft, Vol. 380.).

Parkes-Perrett, Ford B. 1989. "Thomas Mann's Silvery Voice of Self- Parody in *Doktor Faustus*." *GR* 64: 20–30.

Schmidt, Bernhold. 1989. "Neues zum *Doktor Faustus*-Streit zwischen Arnold Schönberg und Thomas Mann." *Augsburger Jahrbuch für Musikwissenschaft* 6: 149–92.

Thomas-Mann-Jahrbuch 2. 1989. Frankfurt am Main: Klostermann.

Includes:

Bahr, Ehrhard. 1989. "'Identität des Nichtidentischen:' Zur Dialektik der Kunst in Thomas Manns *Doktor Faustus* im Lichte von Theodor W. Adornos *Ästhetischer Theorie*." 102–20. English version in Lehnert and Pfeiffer, 1991: 45–60.

Dierks, Manfred. 1989. "Thomas Manns *Doktor Faustus* unter dem Aspekt der neuen Narzißmustheorien (Kohut/Kernberg — Lacan)." 20–40. English version in Lehnert and Pfeiffer, 1991: 33–54.

Fetzer, John F. 1989. "Melos-Eros-Thanatos und *Doktor Faustus*." 41–60. English version in Lehnert and Pfeiffer, 1991: 61–79.

Koopmann, Helmut. 1989. "*Doktor Faustus* — eine Geschichte der deutschen Innerlichkeit?" English version in Lehnert and Pfeiffer, 1991: 17–31.

Lehnert, Herbert. 1989a. "Nachwort: *Doktor Faustus*, ein moderner Roman mit offenem historischen Horizont." 163–77. (German adaptation of his "Introduction" in Lehnert and Pfeiffer, 1991: 1–15)

Mundt, Hannelore. 1989. "*Doktor Faustus* und die Gegenwartsliteratur." 151–62. English version in Lehnert and Pfeiffer, 1991: 199–209.

Prutti, Brigitte. 1989. "Frauengestalten in *Doktor Faustus*." 61–78. English version in Lehnert and Pfeiffer, 1991: 99–112.

Schwarz, Egon. 1989. "Die jüdischen Gestalten in *Doktor Faustus*." 79–101. English version in Lehnert and Pfeiffer, 1991: 119–40.

Vaget, Hans Rudolf. 1989. "Thomas Mann und James Joyce. Zur Frage des Modernismus im *Doktor Faustus*." 121–50. English version in Lehnert and Pfeiffer, 1991: 167–91.

Timm, Eitel. 1989. *Ketzer und Dichter. Lessing, Goethe, Thomas Mann und die Postmoderne in der Tradition des Häresiegedankens*. Heidelberg: Winter. (Beiträge zur neueren Literaturgeschichte, Vol. 88.).

Fetzer, John Francis. 1990. *Music, Love, Death and Mann's 'Doctor Faustus.'* Columbia, S. C.: Camden House.

Henius, Carla. 1990. "Die wirkliche und die erdachte Musik im Roman *Doktor Faustus* von Thomas Mann." In *Musik-Theater-Werkstatt: Die Vorträge 1989–1990*. Wiesbaden: Hessisches Staatstheater. 23–35.

Kiesel, Helmuth. 1990a. "Kierkegaard, Alfred Döblin, Thomas Mann und der Schluß des *Doktor Faustus*." *Literaturwissenschaftliches Jahrbuch* 31: 233- 49.

———. 1990b. "Thomas Manns *Doktor Faustus*: Reklamation der Heiterkeit." *DVLG* 64: 726–43.

Koopmann, Helmut. 1990a. "Der Krieg als Höllensturz: Zu Thomas Manns Kriegsberichterstattung und seinem *Doktor Faustus*." *Krieg und Literatur (War and Literature)* 2, Issue 3: 13–32.

Koopmann, Helmut, ed. 1990b. *Thomas-Mann-Handbuch*. Stuttgart: Kröner Includes:

Koopmann, Helmut 1990c. "Doktor Faustus." 475–97.

———.1990d. "Forschungsgeschichte." 941–76.

Renner, Rolf Günter. 1990 "Verfilmungen der Werke von Thomas Mann." 799–20.

Wagener, Hans. 1990. "Thomas Mann in der amerikanischen Literaturkritik." 925–39.

Wißkirchen, Hans. 1990. "Thomas Mann in der literarischen Kritik." 875–924.

Pattison, George. 1990. "Music, Madness and Mephistopheles: Art and Nihilism in Thomas Mann's *Doctor Faustus*." In *European Literature and Theology in the Twentieth Century*, ed. David Jasper and Colin Crowder. London: MacMillan. 1–14.

Pütz, Peter. 1990. "Peter Handke's *Der Chinese des Schmerzes*: The Threshold as a Place of Waiting." In *Literature on the Threshold: The German Novel in the 1980s*, ed. Arthur Williams, Stuart Parkes and Roland Smith. New York: Berg. 123–33.

Scaff, Susan von Rohr. 1990. "Unending Apocalypse: The Crisis of Musical Narrative in Mann's *Doktor Faustus*." *GR* 65: 30–39.

Vaget, Hans Rudolf. 1990. "Neue Literatur zu Thomas Mann." *GQ* 63: 281- 87.

Adolphs, Dieter W. 1991. "'Wenn der gegenwärtig tobende Krieg, so oder so, sein Ende gefunden hat . . . :' Die Bedeutung der Kriegsthematik in Thomas Manns *Doktor Faustus*." *Der Zweite Weltkrieg und die Exilanten. Eine literarische Antwort*, ed. Helmut F. Pfanner. Bonn: Bouvier. 229–37. (Studien zur Literatur der Moderne, Vol. 21.).

Böhm, Karl Werner. 1991. *Zwischen Selbstsucht und Verlangen. Thomas Mann und das Stigma Homosexualität. Untersuchungen zu Frühwerk und Jugend*. Würzburg: Königshausen und Neumann.

Fullenwider, Henry F. 1991. "Adrian Leverkühn's Corrupt Diction in Thomas Mann's *Doktor Faustus*." *Neophilologus* 75: 581–90.

Heftrich, Eckhard. 1991. "Vom höheren Abschreiben." *Thomas Mann und seine Quellen. Festschrift für Hans Wysling*, ed. Eckhard Heftrich and Helmut Koopmann. Frankfurt am Main: Klostermann. 1–20.

Hofstaetter, Ulla. 1991. "'Dämonische Dichter:' die literarischen Vorlagen für Adrian Leverkühns Kompositionen im Roman *Doktor Faustus*." *"Die Beleuchtung, die auf mich fällt, hat . . . oft gewechselt." Neue Studien zum Werk Thomas Manns*, ed. Hans Wißkirchen. Würzburg: Königshausen und Neumann. 146–88.

Jens, Inge, ed. 1991. *Thomas Mann: Tagebücher 1949–1950*. Frankfurt am Main: S. Fischer.

Lehnert, Herbert, and Peter C. Pfeiffer, eds. 1991. *Thomas Mann's 'Doctor Faustus.' A Novel at the Margin of Modernism*. Columbia, S.C.: Camden House. (Studies in German Literature, Linguistics, and Culture, Vol. 49.). Includes:

Bahr, Ehrhard. 1991. "Art Desires Non-Art: The Dialectic of Art in Thomas Mann's *Doctor Faustus* and Theodore Adorno's *Aesthetic Theory*." 145–60 (response by Helmut Schneider, 161–66).

Dierks, Manfred. 1991. "*Doktor Faustus* and Recent Theories of Narcissism: New Perspectives." 33–54 (response by Gabriele Schwab, 55–60).

Fetzer, John F. 1991. "Melos, Eros, Thanatos and *Doctor Faustus*. 61–79 (response by Martin Schwab 81–97).

Koopmann, Helmut. 1991. "*Doctor Faustus*, a Novel of German Introspection?" 17–31.

Lehnert, Herbert. 1991. "Introduction." 1–17.

Mundt, Hannelore. 1991. "*Doctor Faustus* and Contemporary German Literature." 199–209 (response by James K. Lyon, 211–13).

Prutti, Brigitte.1991. "Women Characters in *Doctor Faustus*." 99–112 (response by Richard Exner, 113–18).

Schwarz, Egon. 1991. "Jewish Characters in *Doctor Faustus*." 119–40 (response by Erich Frey, 141–43).

Vaget, Hans Rudolf. 1991. "Mann, Joyce, and the Question of Modernism in *Doctor Faustus*." 167–191 (response by David E. Wellbery 193–97).

Travers, Martin. 1991. "*Doctor Faustus* and the Historians: The Function of 'Anachronistic Symbolism.'" In *The Modern German Historical Novel. Paradigms, Problems, Perspectives*, ed. David Roberts and Philip Thomson. New York: Berg. 145–59.

Vaget, Hans Rudolf. 1991. "'Germany: Jekyll and Hyde.' Sebastian Haffners Deutschlandbild und die Genese von *Doktor Faustus*." In Thomas *Mann und seine Quellen. Festschrift für Hans Wysling*, ed. Eckhard Heftrich and Helmut Koopmann. Frankfurt am Main: Klostermann. 249–71.

Walter, Christiane. 1991. *Zur Psychopathologie der Figuren in Thomas Manns 'Doktor Faustus.'* Frankfurt am Main: P. Lang. (Europäische Hochschulschriften, Series 1, Vol.1267.)

Wysling, Hans, and Yvonne Schmidlin, eds. 1991. *Thomas Mann: Notizbücher 1–6.* Vol 1. Frankfurt am Main: S. Fischer.

Wysling, Hans, ed. 1991. "Thomas Manns unveröffentlichte Notizbücher.". *Thomas-Mann-Jahrbuch* 4: 119–35."

Barnouw, Dagmar. 1992. "Fascism, Modernity, and the Doctrine of Art from *Mario and the Magician* to *Doctor Faustus*." *Michigan Germanic Studies* 18: 48–63.

Evans, Tamara S. 1992. "Thomas Mann, Anton Webern, and the Magic Square." In *German Literature and Music: An Aesthetic Fusion 1890–1989*, ed. Claus Reschke and Howard Pollack. Munich: Fink. 159–72. (Houston German Studies, Vol. 8.).

Fetzer, John Francis. 1992. "Visconti's Cinematic Version of *Death in Venice*." In *Approaches to Teaching Mann's Death in Venice and Other Short Fiction*, ed. Jeffrey B. Berlin. New York: The Modern Language Association. 146–52.

Härle, Gerhard, ed. 1992. "*Heimsuchung und süßes Gift.*" *Erotik und Poetik bei Thomas Mann.* Frankfurt am Main: Fischer Taschenbuch Verlag.

Haile, Harry G. 1992. "Faust als nationales Symbol bei Stephen Vincent Benét und Thomas Mann." *ZDP* 111: 608–24.

Hasselbach, Ingrid. 1992. "Paradigmatische Musik. Wackenroders *Joseph Berglinger* als Vorläufer von Thomas Manns *Doktor Faustus*. "In *The Romantic Tradition ion German Literature and Music in the Nineteenth Century*, ed. Gerald Chapple, Frederick Hall, and Hans Schulte. New York: University Press of America. 95–112.

Huder, Walter. 1992. "*Doktor Faustus* von Thomas Mann als Nationalroman deutscher Schuld im amerikanischen Exil konzipiert." *Exilforschung* 10: 201–10.

Kann, Irene. 1992. *Schuld und Zeit. Literarische Handlung in theologischer Sicht. Thomas Mann-Robert Musil-Peter Handke.* Paderborn: Schöningh.

Koopmann, Helmut. 1992. Review of books by Curtius, Härle, and Böhm on Mann's sexual orientation. *Thomas-Mann-Jahrbuch* 5: 213–18.

Lehnert, Herbert. 1992. "Thomas Mann, Tagebücher 28.5.1946–31. 12. 1948 und anderes: Review Article." *OL* 47: 110–24.

Maar, Michael. 1992. "Der Flug der ausgestopften Vögel. Thomas Manns Notizen, Briefe, Quellen und Tagebücher." *Literaturwissenschaftliches Jahrbuch* 33: 299–317.

Mendelssohn, Peter de. 1992. *Der Zauberer: das Leben des deutschen Schriftstellers Thomas Mann.* Vol. 2: *Jahre der Schwebe: 1919 und 1933; nachgelassene Kapitel. Gesamtregister.* Frankfurt am Main: S. Fischer.

Potempa, Georg and Gert Heine, eds. 1992. *Thomas-Mann-Bibliographie: Das Werk.* Morsum, Sylt: Cicero Press.

Rieckmann, Jens. 1992. "Mocking a Mock-Biography: Steven Millhauser's *Edwin Mullhouse* and Thomas Mann's *Doctor Faustus*." In *Neverending Stories. Toward a Critical Narratology,* ed. Ann Fehn, Ingeborg Hoesterey, and Maria Tatar. Princeton: Princeton University Press. 62–69.

Sauer, Paul L. 1992. "Zwischen 'Außensein' und 'Dabeisein:' exilliterarische Aspekte in Thomas Manns *Doktor Faustus*." In *Die Künste und die Wissenschaften im Exil 1933–1945,* ed. Edith Böhne and Wolfgang Motzkau-Valeton. Gerlingen: Schneider. 47–69.

Tiedemann, Rolf. 1992. "'Mitdichtende Einfühlung.' Adornos Beiträge zum *Doktor Faustus* — noch einmal." *Frankfurter Adorno Blätter* 1: 9–33.

Travers, Martin. 1992. *Thomas Mann.* London: Macmillan. (Macmillian Modern Novelists). 98–114.

Vaget, Hans Rudolf. 1992a. "Deutsche Einheit und nationale Identität. Zur Genealogie der gegenwärtigen Deutschland-Debatte am Beispiel von Thomas Mann." *Literaturwissenschaftliches Jahrbuch* 33: 277–98.

——, ed. 1992b. *Thomas Mann-Agnes E. Meyer: Briefwechsel 1937–1955.* Frankfurt am Main: S. Fischer.

Wysling, Hans, and Yvonne Schmidlin, eds. 1992. *Thomas Mann. Notizbücher 7–14.* Vol. 2. Frankfurt am Main: S. Fischer.

Wysling, Hans, and Marianne Eich-Fischer, eds. 1992. *Thomas Mann. Selbstkommentare, 'Doktor Faustus' und 'Die Entstehung des "Doktor Faustus."* Frankfurt am Main: Fischer Taschenbuch-Verlag.

Assmann, Michael, ed. 1993. *Thomas Mann - Erich von Kahler: Briefwechsel 1931-1955.* Hamburg: Luchterhand.

Beyerle, Dieter. 1993. "Thomas Mann und der Teufel." In *Literarische Begegnungen: Festschrift zum sechzigsten Geburtstag von Bernhard König,* ed. Andreas Kablitz and Ulrich Schulz-Buschhaus. Tübingen: Narr. 1–16.

Böschenstein, Bernhard. 1993. "Zwei moderne *Faust*-Dichtungen: doppelter Abschied von Goethe. *Mon Faust* und *Doktor Faustus.*" *Colloquium Helveticum* 18: 39–48.

Dörr, Volker. 1993. "'Apocalypsis cum figuris:' Dürer, Nietzsche, *Doktor Faustus* und Thomas Manns 'Welt des magischen Quadrats.'" *ZDP* 112: 251–70.

Fetzer, John Francis. 1993. "Interest Never-Ending: Mignon Echoes in Thomas Mann's Echo." In *Goethe's Mignon und ihre Schwestern. Interpretationen und Rezeption,* ed. Gerhart Hoffmeister. New York: Lang. (California Studies in German and European Romanticism and in the Age of Goethe, Vol. 1.). 199–215.

Jäkel, Siegfried. 1993. "Faust und Don Juan in der Rezeption des 20. Jahrhunderts bei Thomas Mann und Max Frisch." In *Europäische Mythen der Neuzeit: Faust und Don Juan. Gesammelte Vorträge des Salzburger Symposions 1992,* ed. Peter Csobádi. Vol.1. Anif/Salzburg: Müller-Speiser.165–77.

Jens, Inge, ed. 1993. *Thomas Mann: Tagebücher 1951–1952.* Frankfurt am Main: S. Fischer.

Reed, Terence James. 1993. "Die letzte Zweiheit: Menschen-, Kunst- und Geschichtsverständnis im *Doktor Faustus.*" In *Interpretationen. Thomas Mann: Romane und Erzählungen.* Ed. Volkmar Hansen. Stuttgart: Reclam. 294–324.

Robertson, Ritchie. 1993. "Accounting for History: Thomas Mann, *Doktor Faustus.*" In *The German Novel in the 20th Century. Beyond Realism.* Ed. David Magley. Edinburgh: Edinburgh University Press. 128–48.

Runge, Doris. 1993. "Hetæra Esmeralda und die kleine Seejungfrau." In *Wagner-Nietzsche-Thomas Mann: Festschrift für Eckhard Heftrich,* ed. Heinz Gockel, Michael Neumann and Ruprecht Wimmer. Frankfurt am Main: Klostermann. 391–403.

Schillinger, Birgit. 1993. *Das kreative Chaos bei Thomas Mann und Hans Henny Jahnn: Ein Vergleich von 'Doktor Faustus' und 'Fluß ohne Ufer.'* St. Ingbert: Röhrig.

Schönhaar, Rainer. 1993. "Musik als Sprache im *Doktor Faustus:* Funktion und Verhältnis vorhandener und erfundener Kompositionen in Thomas Manns Roman." In *Europäische Mythen der Neuzeit: Faust und Don Juan. Gesammelte Vorträge des Salzburger Symposions 1992*, ed. Peter Csobádi. Vol. 2. Anif/Salzburg: Müller-Speiser. 485–506.

Seiler, Bernd W. 1993. "Ines und der Trambahnmord: eine Dresdner Skandalgeschichte in Thomas Manns *Doktor Faustus.*" In *Vergessen. Entdecken. Erhellen: literaturwissenschaftliche Aufsätze*, ed. Jörg Drews. Bielefeld: Aisthesis-Verlag. (Bielerfelder Schriften zu Linguistik und Literaturwissenschaft, 2.). 183–203.

Vaget, Hans Rudolf. 1993. 'Salome' und 'Palestrina' als historische Chiffren. Zur musikgeschichtlichen Codierung in Thomas Manns *Doktor Faustus.*" In *Wagner-Nietzsche-Thomas Mann. Festschrift für Eckhard Heftrich*, ed. Heinz Gockel, Michael Neumann, and Ruprecht Wimmer. Frankfurt am Main: Klostermann. 69–82.

Wehrmann, Harald. 1993. "'Der Roman praktiziert die Musik, von der er handelt.' Über den Versuch Thomas Manns, seinem Roman *Doktor Faustus* eine dodekaphonische Struktur zu geben." *Die Musikforschung* 46: 5–16.

Wimmer, Ruprecht. 1993. "'Ah, ça c'est bien allemand, par example!' Richard Wagner in Thomas Manns *Doktor Faustus.*" In *Wagner- Nietzsche-Thomas Mann. Festschrift für Eckhard Heftrich*, ed. Heinz Gockel, Michael Neumann, and Ruprecht Wimmer. Frankfurt am Main: Klostermann. 49–68.

Borchmeyer, Dieter. 1994. "Musik im Zeichen Saturns. Melancholie und Heiterkeit in Thomas Manns *Doktor Faustus.*" *Thomas-Mann-Jahrbuch* 7: 123–67.

Hermanns, Ulrike. 1994. *Thomas Manns Roman 'Doktor Faustus' im Lichte von Quellen und Kontexten*. Frankfurt am Main: Lang. (Europäische Hochschulschriften: Series I, Vol. 1486.).

Lublich, Frederick A. 1994. "Review Essay: 'Une mer à boire' oder die Schwanengesänge der Thomas-Mann-Forschung." *GR* 69: 177–85.

Schmitz, Heinz-Gerd. 1994. "Leverkühns Welt. Überlegungen zur Theorie der literarischen Fiktion." *OL* 49: 1–18.

Vaget, Hans Rudolf. 1994. "Musik in München. Kontext und Vorgeschichte des 'Protests der Richard-Wagner-Stadt München' gegen Thomas Mann." *Thomas-Mann-Jahrbuch* 7: 41–69.

Windisch-Laube, Walter. 1994. "Thomas Mann versus Franz Schreker?" *Thomas-Mann-Jahrbuch* 7: 71–122.

Hilgers, Hans. 1995. *Serenus Zeitblom. Der Erzähler als Romanfigur in Thomas Manns 'Doktor Faustus.'* Frankfurt am Main: Lang. (Europäische Hochschulschriften: Series I, Vol. 1500.).

Lleras, Gabriela Hofmann-Ortega. 1995. *Die produktive Rezeption von Thomas Manns 'Doktor Faustus.'* Heidelberg: Winter. (Studia Romanica, 84).

Zimmermann, Rolf Christian. 1995. "Rückwärtsgekehrte Prophetie im *Doktor Faustus*." In his *Der Dichter als Prophet. Grotesken von Nestroy bis Thomas Mann als prophetische Seismogramme gesellschaftlicher Fehlentwicklungen des 20. Jahrhunderts.* Berne: Francke. 124–54.

INDEX

Adam (biblical figure), 10
Adelson, Leslie, 96
Adolphs, Dieter W., 67
Adorno, Theodor Wiesengrund, xii, 14, 30, 31, 36, 37, 49–50, 67, 71, 75, 81, 82, 83, 89, 103, 104, 105, 106, 108, 109, 114, 126
Adorno, Theodor Wiesengrund, Works by:
  Aesthetic Theory 75,
  "Beethoven's Late Style" 50
  Dialectic of Enlightenment (with Max Horkheimer) 67
  Philosophie der neuen Musik (The Philosophy of New Music) 50, 104
Adso (narrator in Umberto Eco's *The Name of the Rose*), 86
aesthetic distance, 9
Albrecht, Ján, 51
Alexander (the Great), 12
Alexandrine, 29
allegorization, 30, 102
allegory, 22–23, 30, 93–94, 101
Allen, Marguerite de Huszar, 87, 93
almond paste (see: marzipan)
almond-shaped eyes, 99
Altenberg, Paul, 25–26, 27, 29
Amann, Paul, 18
ambiguity (ambiguous), 5, 8, 29, 40–41, 42, 43, 44, 48, 65, 70, 71, 72, 74, 75, 76, 86, 89–90, 94, 99, 102, 105, 106, 111, 113, 114, 115, 116, 123, 130, 131
ambivalence (ambivalent, "Zweideutigkeit"), 5, 8, 40–41, 47, 48, 64, 69, 70, 71, 72, 73, 74, 75, 76, 77, 82, 83, 84, 85, 88, 90, 94, 105, 115, 116, 123, 127, 129, 130–131
America (American, see also: United States), 2, 7, 65, 90, 92
American-German Review, 51
amor fati, 27
Amsterdam (University of), 91
anachronistic symbolism (anachronism), 37, 40, 62, 67

Andersen, Hans Christian, 12, 36
Andersen, Hans Christian, Works by:
  The Little Mermaid 12, 125
androgyny (androgynous), 47, 98, 99
Anglicisms, 8
Ansermet, Ernest, 119
anti-fascist (see: "fascist")
antinomy, 102
anti-Semitism (anti-Semite), 13, 75
Anton, Herbert, 26
"anxiety of influence," 125
apocalypse (apocalyptic), 22, 29, 56, 72, 93, 110
Apollonian, 41, 80
aporia, 70, 102
apostasy, 20
Apter, T. E., 62, 67, 69, 102
arabesque (sand), 80, 117
archaism (archaisms, archaic), 8, 51, 63, 65, 76–77, 79, 98, 105
archetype (archetypal), 12, 56
Archive (of Thomas Mann in Zurich) (archival), xi, xiv, 9, 10, 11, 12, 18–19, 31, 33, 34, 35, 39, 44, 55, 65, 69, 70, 77
Ariel (from Shakespeare's *The Tempest*), 85
Aronson, Alex, 102
Arzt, Matthaeus (fictional Halle student in *Doctor Faustus*), 37
Aschenbach, Gustav (protagonist of *Death in Venice*), 56–57, 103, 116
Assmann, Dietrich, 40, 93, 122
atonality (atonal), 51, 82, 105
Auden, W. H., 38
Auschwitz, 89
Austria (Austrian), 64
avant-garde (avantgardism), 32, 75, 76, 92, 115

Baasner, Rainer, 112
Babel, 9
Bachofen, Johann J., Works by:
  The Myth of the Orient and Occident 55
background music, 57, 120

Bahr, Ehrhard, 75
Balhorn, Johann, 78
Ball, David G., 87–88
Bantel, Otto, 27
Barbara (episodic figure in *Doctor Faustus*), 96
barbarism (barbaric), 3, 38, 53, 71, 72, 77, 83, 98
Barbu, Eugen, 44
Barnouw, Dagmar, 67
Baron, Frank, 87
baroque, 30, 37, 67, 103
"battle of the historians," 59, 64, 67
Baumgart, Reinhard, 49
Bavaria (Bavarian), 47
Becher, Hubert, 5
Becker-Frank, Sigrid, 36
Beckmesser (figure in Wagner's *Die Meistersinger*), 43
Beddow, Michael, 61
Beebe, William, 12
Beethoven, Ludwig van, xii, 10, 14, 34, 45, 47–48, 50, 51, 53, 83
Beethoven, Ludwig van, Works by: "Heiligenstätter Testament" (Will Written at Heiligenstadt) 14, String Quartet, Opus 132, 127, Symphony No. 9, 34, 39, 48, 71
Beissel, Johann Conrad, 51–52, 83
Benét, Stephen Vincent, Works by: "The Devil and Daniel Webster" 85–86
Benjamin, Walter, Works by: *Der Ursprung des deutschen Trauerspiels* (The Origin of the German Tragedy) 37
Berendsohn, Walter, 26
Berg, Alban, xii, 10, 83
Berger, Erich, 38
Berglinger, Joseph (fictitious Romantic composer), 28, 52, 102, 103
Bergsten, Gunilla, xv, 33-35, 36, 37, 38, 41, 42, 44, 46, 47–48, 49, 52, 54, 55, 77, 78, 79, 126
Berlin, 101
Berman, Russell A., 72

Bermann-Fischer, Gottfried, ix, 18
Bernd, Clifford A., ix
Bertram, Ernst, 18, 80, 115
Beyerle, Dieter, 123
Bianquis, Genevieve, 10
Bibliographie der deutschen Literaturwissenschaft, xiii
Bibliographie der deutschen Sprach-- und Literaturwissenschaft, xiii, xv
bibliography (bibliographies) of Mann's works, xiii, xiv, 19, 58–60
Bildungsroman, 29–30
Birnbaum, Henrik, 84
Birven, Henri, 39
bisexuality, 47, 97, 98, 116
black arts (necromancy), xi, 1, 10
Blackmur, Richard, 15
Blahacek, Rudolf, 119
Blake, William, 37–38, 57
Blake, William, Works by: "The Poison Tree" 38, "The Sick Rose" 38
Blankenagel, John C., 10–11
Blomster, Wesley, 20, 39, 57
Bloom, Harold, 125
Bludau, Beatrix, 23, 32, 38, 48, 75
Bochum, 43
Boehlich, Walter, 5
Boeninger, Helmut R., 43
Böhm, Klaus Werner, 97, 99–100
Boïtio, Arrigo, Works by: *Mefistofele* 41
Böll, Heinrich, 73
Bonwit, Marianne, 9
Bonyhai, Gábor, 31
Borcherdt, Hans Heinrich, 27
Borchmeyer, Dieter, 123, 129
bordello, 11, 78,
Böschenstein, Bernhard, 80, 125
bourgeois (bourgeoisie, burgher), 3, 4, 7, 25, 43, 49, 64, 69, 70, 96, 104, 109, 110
Brandes, Georg, 81
Brandt, Helmut, 79, 104
Braun, Hanns, 5
Brazil (Brazilian), 126
"breakthrough" (to break through),

2, 7, 22, 26, 30, 53, 61, 67, 69, 79, 87, 102, 103, 106, 110,113, 114
Brecht, Bertolt, 64, 80, 101
Breisacher, Chaim (episodic figure in *Doctor Faustus*), 12–13, 79
Brentano, Clemens, 8, 84, 98, 125
Briner, Andres, 51
Britten, Benjamin, 57, 119, 121, 130
Britten, Benjamin, Works by:
  Death in Venice 57,
  War Requiem 119, 121
Brock, Erich, 9
Brode, Hans-Peter, 22, 103
Brown, Calvin S., 39
"Büblein" (the "little lad" appearing in a Brentano fairy tale), 98
Buchel (hereditary farm of the Leverkühn family), 42, 111, 115
Buisonjé, J.C. de., 27
Bürger, Christa, 114
Bürgin, Hans, xiii, 19
Busch, Arnold, 64
Butler, Eliza M., 10
butterfly (lepidopterous), 39, 108
Buzga, Jaroslav, 50

cacophony, 110
calculation (artistic), 63, 109, 111–112
California (Southern, Pacific Palisades), xii, 1, 2, 14, 21, 128
California, University of (at Davis), ix; (at Irvine), xv, 73–76, 100, 113
Camden House, xv
Canada, 8
capitalism (capitalistic), 2, 3, 4, 25, 123
captatio benevolentiae, 43
caricature, 45, 88, 91
caritas, 16, 46
Carlsson, Anni, 11, 12, 22
Carnegy, Patrick, 47, 49–50
Cartwright, Jeffrey (narrator in Millhauser's novel), 88

Catholicism (Catholic), 4, 5, 20, 38, 62, 63
Cerf, Steven, 84–85
chapbook (see: *Doctor Faustus*, Volksbuch, chapbook of 1587)
Charney, Hanna and Maurice Charney, 36
chauvinism (chauvinistic), 22, 40, 63
chiasmus, 22, 23
Chladny (Chladni), Ernst, 80, 117
chosen (the "chosen ones," the elect), 25, 29
Christ, 62
Christian (Christianity), 4–5, 38, 39, 63, 68, 75, 81
Cicero (Ciceronian), 77
Cicora, Mary A., 82–83
cinema (film versions of Mann's works), xiii, 56–57, 85, 118–121, 129, 130
circle (as geometric form), 111
closure, 72, 74, 76, 86
Cobley, Evelyn, 86
cold war, 3, 123
coldness (coolness, frigidity), 4, 16, 52, 53, 114, 121, 127
collage, xiii, 13, 18, 51
Colleville, Maurice, 11
Cologne, 11–12
comic element (comedy, humor, wit), 28–29, 43, 45, 71, 76, 81, 91, 118
communist criticism (also: socialist, leftist, East bloc), 2, 3, 4, 22, 25, 28, 49, 51, 52, 64, 68, 69, 104, 123
Conrad, Joseph, 37
"conservative revolution," 91
consonance, 48
constructivist(ic) music (see also: dodecaphonic music, strict form, serial technique of composition, twelve-tone technique), 12, 13–14, 15, 57, 82, 103, 104, 108, 109, 128
contrafacture (contrafact), 88
Corinthians (St. Paul's First Epistle to the), 1, 17

Cotterill, Rowland, 101, 102
counterpoint (contrapuntal), 109, 120
crab form (variation of the twelve-tone row), 108, 109
Cranach, Lukas, 91
crisis (of creativity, of culture, of modernity), xii, 13, 27, 32, 38, 50, 70, 98, 106–107, 110, 117
critical theory (theorists), 72, 129
culture industry, 72
Curtius, Mechthild, 97, 98

Dabezies, André, 81
Dahlhaus, Carl, 105–106
Dante (Alighieri), 38, 114, 126
Dante, Works by:
Divine Comedy 38, 114
"dark lady" (in Shakespeare's sonnets), 85
Danube, 41
Death in Venice (the film version, see: Visconti, Luchino)
decadence (decadent), 11, 27, 31
decoding, 109
deconstruction (deconstructive criticism), 30, 34, 75, 85, 86, 129
Delanu, Andrei, 44
Del Caro, Adrian, 84
dementia, 115
democracy (democrat, democratic), 7, 64, 65, 69, 71–72
demon (demonic, see: "devil")
Denmark (Danish), 81
Deussen, Paul, 11
Deutschlin (fictitious Halle student in *Doctor Faustus*), 37
devil (diabolic, demon, demonic, bedeviled, Satan, satanic), xi, 1, 2, 3, 4, 5, 15, 16, 20, 21, 23, 24-25, 29, 30, 35, 37, 40, 41, 42, 43, 46, 51, 53, 56, 60, 62, 63, 65, 66, 67, 71, 74, 79, 81, 84, 85, 87–88, 89, 96, 98, 102, 109, 116, 117, 119, 120, 123, 127, 130
Devoto, Daniel, 51

dialectic (dialectical thinking, negative dialectic), 5, 14, 16, 22, 30, 41, 46, 65, 70, 75, 81, 85, 99, 105, 108
Dierks, Manfred, 55, 100, 113–114
Diersen, Ingrid, 10, 25
Dietzel, Ulrich, 58
Dill, H. J., 41
Dionysian, 2, 11, 32, 41, 43, 53, 80
discourse (analysis, levels of), 90, 92, 95
disease (see: syphilis)
"disinherited (mind)," 24, 30, 115
disintegration (dissolution, fragmentation), 30, 113–114
dissonance (also: discord), 48, 102
Dittmann, Ulrich, 32–33
"divine child," 12, 129
Dobbek, Wilhelm, 49
Döblin, Alfred, 64
Doctor Faustus (Volksbuch, chapbook of 1587), xii, 1, 5, 10, 34, 39–40, 48, 75, 78, 84, 87–88, 89
Doctor Zhivago (by Boris Pasternak) 84
dodecaphonic music (see also: constructivist music, strict form, twelve-tone technique, serial technique of composition), 15, 51, 53–54, 80, 105, 109, 110, 111
Doflein, Erich, 14
Don Juan, 129
Dornheim, Alfredo, 12
Dörr, Hansjörg, 50, 104
Dörr, Volker, 128
Dostoevsky, Feodor, 36, 84, 109
Dostoevsky, Feodor, Works by:
The Brothers Karamazov 84
"double autobiography," 92
double vision (double focus, bifocal vision, double optic, "doppelte Optik"), 8, 29, 54, 65, 70, 82, 118, 131
doubt, 70
Dowden, Steven P., 70
"Dreigestirn" (cosmic triumvirate,

triadic constellation), 27, 31, 48, 81
Dresden, 127
Dück, Hans-Udo, 52
Dürer, Albrecht, xiii, 53, 55–56, 111, 116, 128
Dürer, Albrecht, Works by: *Apocalypsis cum figuris* 55, "The French Disease" ("Die Franzosenkrankheit") 56, "Knight, Death and the Devil" ("Ritter, Tod und Teufel") 56, *Melencolia I* 55, 111, 116–117
Durrani, Osman, 80, 93
Dvoretzky, Edward, xiv, 59
"dynamic metaphysics," 45
"dynamics of denial," 115

East bloc criticism (see: communist criticism)
"Ecce homo," 56, 62
echo (echo effect), 37, 67
Echo (Leverkühn's nephew, the boy Nepomuk Schneidewein, who is called Echo), 5, 8, 11, 12, 47, 80, 85, 89, 96, 98, 99, 103, 126, 129
Echo (the nymph in Ovid's *Metamorphosis*), 98
Eco, Umberto, Works by: *The Name of the Rose* 86
Eden (Garden of), 88
ego (in conjunction with the "id"), 85
Egri, Péter, 36
Ehrenberg, Paul, 28, 93, 97, 126
Eich-Fischer, Marianne (see Fischer, Marianne)
Eichner, Hans, 8, 15
Eisler, Hanns, 110
"elective affinity," 76
Elma, Hans, 56
emigration (inner and outer), 68
encoding, 93, 94, 109, 125
Engel, Hans, 14
Engelberg, Edward, 14
Engelmann, Hans Ulrich, 52
England (English, Anglo-Saxon), xi, xv, 7, 8, 38, 50, 51, 57, 64, 70, 73, 74, 75, 76, 83, 100, 113, 119, 121, 129
enharmonic change, 111
Enright, Dennis J., 8, 20
Ephrata (Pennsylvania), 51
equivocation (equivocal), 5, 8, 62, 65, 68, 70, 76, 77, 88, 90, 123, 130, 131
Erasmus, Desiderius, 91
Eros, 12, 16, 46, 47, 96, 97, 98, 99, 100
erotic (eroticism, erotology; see also: love), xv, 15–16, 46, 75, 81, 93, 95–101, 102, 116, 127
"eternal feminine," 62, 71
"eternal recurrence," 13, 42
Euphorion (figure in Goethe's *Faust*), 11, 89
Europe (European), 1, 2, 6, 19, 28, 31, 63, 66, 68, 129
Eva-Ave (Eve-Ave Maria) polarity, 83
Evans, Tamara S., 103
exile, xii, 1, 3, 21, 29, 51, 64, 65, 68, 69, 76, 84, 90, 92
existential (existentialist), 29, 63, 81
eye (evil), 38
Ezergailis, Inta, 46–47, 60, 96

Faesi, Robert, 6
Fähnrich, Hermann, 82
fascism (fascist, prefascist), 2, 3, 8, 21, 25, 26, 50, 51, 60, 64, 65, 67, 72, 79, 90, 110
Fass, Barbara, 36
fatherland, 23
father-son conflict, 22
Faustina (Heinrich Heine's female Faust figure), 10
Faustus, Dr. Johann (Renaissance necromancer), xi, xii, 1, 40, 47, 54, 56
Fechner, Jörg-Ulrich, 43, 93
Fetscher, Iring, 6
Fetzer, Henriette, vix
Fetzer, John F., 84, 100–101, 130–131
Feuerlicht, Ignace, 27, 28, 54, 97
film (see: cinema)

film music (for Seitz's *Doktor Faustus*), 119, 120–121
Finke, Ulrich, 56
Finland (Finnish), xiv
First World War (see under: World War)
Fischer, Ernst, 3–4, 25, 64, 69
Fischer, Marianne (married name is Eich-Fischer), 1, 58
Fitelberg, Saul (impressario figure in *Doctor Faustus*), 71, 99, 109
Floquet, Jean-Marie, 37
"flower of evil," 65
Forman, Milos, Works by: *Amadeus* (the Mozart film), 126
formulaic fiction, 87
Förster, Wolf-Dietrich, 52
France (French, Franco), xiv, 22, 84, 126
Frank, Manfred, 114
Frankfurt School (of Critical Theory), 50
Freideutsche Position, Die (The Free German Position), 37
Freischütz, Der (see: Weber, Carl Maria von, Works by)
Frenzel, Elisabeth, 118
Freud, Siegmund (Freudian; see also: psychoanalysis), 16, 45–46, 85, 95, 100, 113, 129
Frey, Leonhard H., 52
Friedrichsmeyer, Erhard, 70–71
fugue, 128
Fullenwider, Henry F., 76–77

Gandelman, Claude, 80, 117–118
genius (genial), 4, 45, 76, 115, 119, 130
genre, 30, 71–72
Gerhardt, Hans-Peter, 52
German (language, German people), ix, xi, xv, 6, 7, 8, 20, 21, 24, 26, 39, 43, 44, 45, 48, 49, 50, 51, 54, 57, 58, 62, 63, 64, 65, 66, 67, 68, 70, 72, 74, 75, 80, 84, 86, 89, 90, 93, 97, 102, 114, 116, 117, 121, 125, 126, 127, 129, 130

German-American, 51
German Democratic Republic (East Germany), xi, 3, 14, 16, 19, 20, 25, 27, 68
Germanistik, xiii
Germanism, Germanness (see also: "ideal Germanness"), 7
Germany (German, German nation, Germanic) , xi, xiii, 2, 3, 4, 11, 16, 18, 22, 23, 27, 28, 59, 60, 63, 64, 67, 86, 89, 92, 93, 101, 102, 123, 125, 127
Germany: land of the middle, 63
Germany: two Germanies (one good, one evil), 64, 74, 80, 123
Germany: unification of, xi, 68–69, 123
Gersdorff, Dagmar von, 84
Gide, André, 37, 38
Gide, André, Works by: *Les Faux-Monnayeurs* (The Counterfeiters) 37
Gilliam, H. S., 62
Gisselbrecht, André, 49
Gleichen-Rußworm, Baron von (incidental figure in *Doctor Faustus*), 84, 92
Gockel, Heinz, 81, 88–89
God (deity), 2, 5, 16, 20, 23, 40, 62, 78, 91, 115
Godeau, Marie, 22, 47, 85
Goethe, Johann Wolfgang von, 13, 26, 30, 36, 40, 69, 86, 88, 89, 89, 122, 125
Goethe, Johann Wolfgang von, Works by: *Faust* xii, 2, 4, 5, 10, 11, 25, 30, 34, 36, 39, 40, 43 (figure of Wagner), 69, 78, 84, 87, 88, 89, 122, 125; *Torquato Tasso* 52; *Wilhelm Meisters Lehrjahre* (*Wilhelm Meister's Apprenticeship*) 12 (figure of Mignon), 30, 98
Goldberg, Oskar, 13, 79
Golik, Iwan, 52
Goll, Klaus R., 20, 78
Gollnick, Ulrike, xiv

Index

Grabbe, Christian Dietrich, Works by:
   Don Juan and Faust 10
grace (salvation, redemption), 5, 23, 24, 25, 27, 39, 40, 45, 53, 61, 62, 68, 70, 75, 78, 80, 83, 86-87, 88, 89–90, 91, 103, 105, 106, 111, 123
Grail (the Holy), 26
Grass, Gunter, 22, 73
Grass, Gunter, Works by:
   Die Blechtrommel (The Tin Drum) 22
Graz, 95
Greece (Greek), 12, 80
Gregorius, 96
Greiner, Martin, 15
Gretchen (figure in Goethe's *Faust*), 11, 87
Gronicka, André von, 7, 16, 27, 54, 74
(the) grotesque, 124
Guilbertoni, Anna Macchi, 36
guilt (culpability), 62–63, 68, 86
Györi, Judit, 41
Gypsies, 78

Haffner, Sebastian, Works by:
   Germany: Jekyll and Hyde 80
Hage, Volker, 44
hagiography (hagiographic), 43, 87, 93
Haile, Harry G., 85–86
Halle, 37
Hamburger, Käte, 40, 62, 67
Handke, Peter, Works by:
   Der Chinese des Schmerzes (translated into English as: *Across*) 129
Hannum, Hildegard D., 20
Hansen, Mathias, 105
Hansen, Volkmar, 60
Hardin, James, ix
Härle, Gerhard, 97, 99
Harris, Frank, Works by:
   The Man Shakespeare and His Tragic Life Story 38
harmony, harmonic (musical), 83, 92, 110, 111, 114, 131

Hartwig, Thomas, 4
Hasselbach, Ingrid, 103
Hasselbach, Karlheinz, 60–61
Hatfield, Henry, xiii, 8, 15, 19, 28, 53–54, 111
Hausmann, Manfred, 21
Heftrich, Eckhard, 23, 29, 30, 32, 38, 48, 75, 79, 93–95, 106
Hegel, Georg F. W., 117
Heidegger, Martin, 29
Heimann, Bodo, 50, 104
Heine, Gert, 58
Heine, Heinrich, 8
Heine, Heinrich, Works by:
   Der Doktor Faust. A Dance Poem (the figure of Faustina appears in *Doctor Faust. Ein Tanzpoem*)10
Heintel, Erich, 11
Helena (Helen of Troy, a figure in Goethe's *Faust*), 11
hell (hellish), 5, 12, 37, 66, 114
Heller, Erich, xiv, 7, 20, 24–25, 30, 39, 44, 48, 51
Hellersberg-Wendriner, Anna, 20–21
Henius, Carla, 102
Henning, Hans, 39
Henning, Margrit, 43–44
Hennings, Elsa, 10
Henze, Eberhard, 44
heresy (heretic, heretical), 61
Hermanns, Ulrike, 126
hermaphrodite (hermaphroditism), 98
hermeneutic, 105
Hermes, 12
Hermsdorf, Klaus, 27, 28–29
Herz, Gerhard, 14
Hesse, Hermann, 14, 80
Hesse, Hermann, Works by:
   Das Glasperlenspiel (Magister Ludi, also called: The Glass Bead Game) 14
Hetæra Esmeralda (also referred to as "femme fatale," the good-evil prostitute, and by the German musical notation H-E-A-E-Es), 11, 12, 16, 39,

47, 56, 57, 61–62, 83, 84, 85, 96, 99, 112, 119, 125
heterosexuality, 15, 46, 85, 96
high G of the cello At the conclusion of *Dr. Fausti Weheklag*"), 5, 25, 106
"higher copying" (Mann's designation for "montage"), 79, 106
Hilgers, Hans, 127
Hillesheim, Jürgen, 81
Hilscher, Eberhard, 8–9, 25
Hirschbach, Frank, 16, 46, 96
historicism, 64
historicity, 64
historiography, 64, 67
history of ideas, 9, 21, 24
Hitler, Adolf (Hitlerian), 2, 21, 31, 65, 67, 91, 94
Hoelzel, Alfred, 83, 88, 96
Hoffmann, Ernst Theodor Amadeus, 10, 84
Hoffmann, Ernst Theodor Amadeus, Works by: *Lebensansichten des Katers Murr* (The Philosophy of Life of Murr the Cat) 84 (see also Kreisler, Johannes)
Hoffmann, Fernand, 45–46
Hoffmann, Gisela, 29
Hofmannsthal, Hugo von, Works by: "Letter to Lord Chandos" 9
Hofstaetter, Ulla, 85
Höhler, Gertrud, 57
Hollingdale, Reginald, 27
Hollweck, Thomas, 19
holocaust, 28, 59, 68
Holthusen, Hans Egon, 4–6, 7, 19–20, 24–25, 61, 71, 76, 102
Holthusen, Wilhelm, 55
homoeroticism (homosexuality), xv, 15–16, 28, 46, 85, 93, 95, 96, 97, 99–100, 116
homophony, 48, 128
Honsa, William M., 44
hope (hope beyond hopelessness), 5, 9, 16, 53, 62, 68, 81, 89, 90
Horkheimer, Max, Works by:

Dialektik der Aufklärung (Dialectic of the Enlightenment) 67
hubris (pride, arrogance), 12, 113
Huder, Walter, 68
Hülle-Keeding, Maria, 82
humanism (humanist, humanistic), xii, 1, 3, 7, 11, 31, 32, 33, 34, 38, 43, 45, 53, 62, 68, 69-70, 72, 80, 86, 88, 91, 92, 110, 114, 127
humor (see: comic element)
Hungary (Hungarian), xiv, 3, 41, 69, 78–79, 127
Hwang, Hyen-Su, 27
Hyphialta (reference to a female figure in *Doctor Faustus*), 11

Ibsen, Henrik, 37
ice flowers (ice configurations), 118, 119
icon (inconicity), 117–118
id (Freudian), 85
"ideal Germanness," 88, 89
idée fixe, 111
identity (of opposites, similarity of the dissimilar or non-identical), 14, 40–41, 75, 86, 112
identity (hidden, secret), xii, 11, 12, 23, 41, 43, 91, 92, 94, 99, 108
ideology (ideological), etc.), ix, 2–4, 9, 51, 65, 66, 67, 68, 69, 74, 81, 123
imitatio, 13, 54, 76, 88
"implied reader," 127
impotence, 97
improvisation (artistic), 63
incest (incestuous), 96
infinite regress, 124
Ingen, Ferdinand van, 91
initiation, 129
insanity, 88, 115
inspiration, 62, 71, 116
Institoris, Ines (figure in *Doctor Faustus*), 85, 127
instrumentum diaboli, 83
Internationales Thomas Mann Kolloquium 1986 in Lübeck, 88

intertextuality (intertext, intertextual), 7–8, 13, 32, 34, 36, 52, 72, 77, 84, 85, 89,
introspection, 74
inverted crab (a form of the serial or row technique of composition), 108, 109
inwardness (interiority), 49, 61, 70, 72, 74, 91
irony (ironic, ironicize), 5, 7, 21, 22, 24, 27, 32, 38, 44, 48–49, 64, 65, 70, 77, 80–81, 83, 89, 92, 94, 97, 104, 105, 118, 130
Irvine (see: California, University of, at Irvine)
Italy (Italian), xiv, 41, 103

Jahnn, Hans Henny, Works by: *Fluß ohne Ufer* (River Without Banks), 124
Jäkel, Siegfried, 76, 129
Japan (Japanese), xiv
Jean Paul (Richter), 37
Jehl, D., 36
Jendreiek, Helmut, 71–72
Jens, Inge, 18, 58, 95, 122
Jews (Jewish, Judaism), 13, 51, 74, 75
Johnson, E. Bond, 78, 91
Jonas, Ilsedore, 19, 41
Jonas, Klaus, xiii, 19, 58
Jørgensen, Aage, 34
Joyce, James, 36, 75, 83
Joyce, James, Works by: *Ulysses* 44, 72–73
Jung, Jürgen, 60
Jung, Ute, 50

Kafka, Franz, Works by: The Metamorphosis (*Die Verwandlung*), 130
Kahler, Erich (von), 4, 10, 122
Kaiser, Joachim, 101
Kaisersaschern (fictitious German city in *Doctor Faustus*), 56, 63–64, 78, 79, 119
Kalma, Thomas A., 81
Kann, Irene, 62–63
Karst, Roman, 27

Karst, Theodor, 51
Kaschperl (dog in *Doctor Faustus*), 41
Kastalien (from Hermann Hesse's novel *Magister Ludi*), 14
Kaufmann, Alfred, 16, 45
Kaufmann, Fritz, 14, 21
Kaufmann, Hans, 104
Kaye, Julian, 37
Kerényi, Károly, 12, 41
Kern, J. P., 27
Kesting, Hanjo, 50–51
Kielmeyer, Otto, 6
Kierkegaard, Søren, 5, 45, 61, 62, 80, 81
Kierkegaard, Søren, Works by: *Don Juan* 81, *Either / Or* 81
Kiesel, Helmuth, 62, 71
Kilchberg (Switzerland), 18, 35, 36
Kimball, Susanne, 96
Kinzel, Ulrich, 71
Kiremidjian, David, 72–73
Kirsch, Edgar, 40
kitsch, 6, 92
Klare, Margaret, 37
Klein, Johannes, 6
Kleist, Heinrich von, 36
Klimitschek, Lotte, 119
Kluge, Gerhard, 91
Klussmann, Paul G., 22, 43, 93
Kneipel, Eberhard, 104
Knopf, Alfred A., xi, 7
Kohlschmidt, Werner, 11
Kohut, Heinz, 95, 100, 113
Kolago, Lech, 104
Kolb, Annette, 84
Kolb, Hans-Ulrich, 37
Koopmann, Helmut, xiv, 18, 23, 29, 32, 38, 48, 49, 60, 66, 68, 74, 75, 81, 88, 89, 92, 96, 100, 107, 108, 118, 122
Kost, Rudi, 119
Kreisler, Johannes (fictional composer in E. T. A. Hoffmann's novel *Lebensansichten des Katers Murr*), 10, 28
Krenek, Ernst, 104
Kretzschmar, Wendell (Leverkühn's

musical mentor in *Doctor Faustus*), 51
Kreutzer, Hans J., 64
Kreuzer, Helmut, 37
Krey, Johannes, 14
Kridwiß Circle, 111
Krieger, Murray, 28
Kross, Siegfried, 52
"Kulturnation" (a nation with a tradition of culture), 68
Kumpf, Ehrenfried (university professor in *Doctor Faustus*), 11, 37, 45, 91, 109
Kundry (seductive figure in Wagner's *Parsifal*), 83
Kunne-Ibsch, Elrud, 42
Kurzke, Hermann, xiv, 23, 58, 59

Lacan, Jacques, 95, 100, 113, 114
LaCapra, Dominick, 66
Lange, Victor, 32, 44, 75
Last Judgment, 21, 66
laugh, laughter (of Leverkühn), 37, 70–71, 80, 119
leftist criticism (see: communist criticism)
Lehnert, Herbert, xiv, xv, 19, 20, 44–45, 59, 73–77, 83, 86, 90–91, 100, 106, 113
Leipzig, 120
leitmotif, xii, 26, 76, 82, 107–108
Lenau, Nikolaus, Works by:
Faust 10
Lenz, Siegfried, 73
Leonard, Kurt, 10
Lesser, Jonas, 6
Lessing, Gotthold E., 37, 120
Leverkühn, Adrian, Works by:
Apocalypsis cum figuris 22, 106, 116, 119, 128
Chamber music, 106
Chronology of and models for Leverkühn's compositions, 108, 128
Dr. Fausti Weheklag' (The Lamentation of Dr. Faustus) 5, 9, 14, 16, 25, 34, 71, 83, 103, 105, 106, 110, 113, 114
Love's Labour's Lost 38, 85

Violin Concerto 85, 106
Leverkühn, Elsbeth (the composer's mother), 28, 47, 55
Leverkühn, Jonathan (the composer's father), 31, 55, 86, 108, 117
Leverkühn (Schneidewein), Ursula (sister of the composer), 96
Levin, Harry, 56
Lewalter, Christian E., 5
libido, 113
Library of Congress, 79
"Liebestod" (love-death), 81–82
"light in the night," 16, 58, 89, 105–106, 121
Linder, Ann Planutis, 53
Lindsay, James M., 7
"literarization of music," 110
Little Mermaid (see Andersen, Hans Christian, Works by)
Lleras, Gabriela Hoffmann-Ortega, 126
Locarno Pact, 22
logocentrism (logocentric), 43
Logos, 98–99
London, 49
Lorenz, Helmut, 101
Los Angeles (Pacific Palisades), 1
love (see also: Eros, erotic), xiv, 5, 23, 24, 25, 28, 38, 46–47, 52, 70, 74, 75, 84–85, 87, 89, 97–101, 110, 127
Lowe-Porter, Helen Tracy, xi, xiii, 7, 8
Lübeck, 56, 78, 88
Lublich, Frederick A., 97, 98–99, 122–123
Lüders, Eva M., 11
Lukács, Georg, 3, 25, 64, 70, 71, 105, 114
Luther, Martin (Lutheranism), 11–12, 44–45, 87, 90–91, 109
Lyon, James K., 52

Maar, Michael, 36, 58–59, 103
Maatje, Frank C., 34
Mádl, Antal, 41, 69, 70, 72
madness (insanity), 102
Maegard, Jürgen, 50

Maenads, 114
magic (and music), 48, 53–54, 87, 96, 101, 105, 111–112
Magician (a nickname ascribed to Thomas Mann), 131
"magic square," 31, 53, 54, 55, 104, 111, 116–117, 128
Magliola, Robert, 31
Magnus, Simon, 10
Mahlendorf, Ursula, 115
Mahler, Gustav, xii, 10, 36, 57, 83, 103, 116
Mahler, Gustav, Works by: *Kindertotenlieder* 103, *Das Lied von der Erde* 103, Symphony No. 3, 36, 57, Symphony No. 5, 57, Symphony No. 8, 36
Maier, Hans A., 8
Mainika, Jürgen, 50
Mainzer, Hubert, 42
Maja (in Indian philosophy, the deceptive world of phenomena), 131
Manardi, Giovanni, 12
Mann, Erika, 8, 18, 106
Mann, Fridolin (Frido), 80, 126
Mann, Katia, 97
Mann, Klaus, 38, 99
Mann, Klaus, Works by: *André Gide and the Crisis of Modern Thought* 38
Mann, Michael, 22, 27, 47, 80
Mann, Thomas:
 birth of, xiii
 centenary (commemorative) celebrations for, xiii–xv, 19, 23–24, 77
 correspondence of, xi, 9, 10, 18–19, 27, 36, 49, 58–59, 72, 78, 79–80, 100, 122
 death of, xi, xv, 3, 9, 16, 18, 23, 24, 45, 96, 112
 diaries of, xi, 10, 18, 35, 36, 46, 58, 65, 66, 72, 77, 90, 95, 97, 98, 100, 101, 103, 112, 122
 notes and notebooks of, xi, 1, 9, 18, 35, 55, 58, 72, 100
 private library of, xi, 34, 55
Mann, Thomas, Works by (English title given first):
 The Beloved Returns (*Lotte in Weimar*) 88, Buddenbrooks (*Buddenbrooks*) xvi, 101, The Confessions of Felix Krull, Confidence Man (*Die Bekenntnisse des Hochstaplers Felix Krull*) 24, 98, 112–113, Death in Venice (*Der Tod in Venedig*) 46–47, 54, 57, 103, 116, 129, Doctor Faustus, The Life of the German Composer Adrian Leverkühn as Told by a Friend (*Doktor Faustus. Das Leben des deutschen Tonsetzers Adrian Leverkühn, erzählt von einem Freunde*):
 autobiographical background of (autobiography), xii, 10–13, 30, 42–47, 53, 58, 90–101, 116, 126–127; biographical background of (biography), xii, 2, 6, 12–13, 14–15, 22, 27, 30, 39, 41, 42–47, 77, 78, 79–80, 81, 83, 90–101, 102, 114–115, 126–127, 130; film version of, xi, 57, 118–121; form of, 30–31: genesis of, 2 geographical aspects of (geography, topography), 25, 35, 41, 77, 78–79, 102, 116, 126; historical dimensions of (see also under: Germany), xi, 1, 3, 5, 7, 9, 11, 20, 21–23, 55, 63–69, 123, 126
 influence of (on later works), 59
 life-work context, 7, 8, 9, 23–27, 69, 91–102, 123–124
 manuscript versions of, 59
 omissions (deletions) from, 8, 20, 34, 78, 89
 prototypes (friends and acquaintances as figures in the novel), 78, 79–80,
 sources of, xii, xvi, 10–13, 18, 24, 33–41, 44, 51–52, 60, 77–

90, 102, 126–127
structure of (structural analysis), xii, xiii, xv, 7, 13, 15, 26, 30–31, 33, 34, 40, 43–44, 46, 52, 53, 54, 55, 62, 68, 75, 76, 77, 80, 82, 107–112, 118
stylistic aspects of, 2, 7, 8-9, 26, 32–33, 36, 59, 61, 76–77, 78, 80, 84, 106, 117
translation into English, 1, 8
visual component of, xiii, 55–57, 116–121, 130–131
Essays (and expository prose), 64, 66, 72, 95, 101
Fontane in His Old Age ("Der alte Fontane") 54
The Holy Sinner (*Der Erwählte*) 8, 24, 62
The Joseph Novels 122
Luther's Wedding ("Luthers Hochzeit") 45
The Magic Mountain (*Der Zauberberg*) xvi, 29, 65, 98, 99, 101, 108
Mario and the Magician (*Mario und der Zauberer*) 67
Nietzsche's Philosophy in the Light of our Experience ("Nietzsches Philosophie im Lichte unserer Erfahrung") 10
The Observations of a Non-Political Man (*Betrachtungen eines Unpolitischen*) 44, 101
The Story of a Novel. The Genesis of 'Doctor Faustus'(Die Entstehung des 'Doktor Faustus': Roman eines Romans) xii, 10, 11, 35, 36, 37, 41, 50, 57, 58, 81, 94, 95 ,106
Tonio Kröger (*Tonio Kröger*) 42, 52, 79
Tristan (*Tristan*) 49
"margin of modernism," xv, 73, 75
"Markusbrot" (baked male figures made of marzipan), 99
Marlowe, Christopher, 10, 88
Marlowe, Christopher, Works by: The Tragical History of Dr.
Faustus 10
Martens, Armin, 97
Martin, Alfred von, 11
Marx, Karl (Marxism, Marxist), 3, 4, 22, 25, 49, 68, 69, 70, 110
marzipan, 99, 101
Masini, Ferruccio, 43
mathematics (and music), 48, 73, 103, 108–109, 111, 117, 128
Matter, Harry, xii, 19
Mayer, Hans, 3, 22, 25, 69, 103
mediate (mediation, mediator), 24, 42, 61, 63, 75, 98, 129
medieval (see Middle Ages)
Meixner, Horst, 22
melancholy (and also: Melancholy), 111, 116–117, 123, 129
Melencolia I (see Dürer, Works by)
melocentrism (melocentric), 43
Melos–Eros–Thanatos (constellation of music, love, and death), 100–101
Mendelssohn, Peter de, ix, 5–6, 18, 58, 77, 124
meningitis, 96
Mephistopheles (Mephistophelian), 89, 102, 120
Merrick, Joan, 7–8
Metscher, Thomas, 64
Metzler, Ilse, 43
Meyer, Agnes E., 75, 79–80, 122
Meyer, Herman, 36
Meyers, Jeffrey, 38–39, 56
Michelangelo (Buonarroti), 66
Michelson, Peter, 66
Middell, Eike, 25, 70
Middle Ages (medieval), x, 5, 8, 10, 12, 30, 43, 63, 67, 87, 93, 112, 116, 119
Mignon (a figure in Goethe's *Wilhelm Meister's Apprenticeship*), 12, 98, 129
Milch, Werner, 6
Miller, Leslie L., 54
Millhauser, Steven, Works by: *Edwin Mullhouse: The Life and Death of an American Writer (1943–1954), by Jeffrey Cartwright* 86

mimicry, 108, 117–118
Mittenzwei, Johannes, 49
Modern Language Association, xii
modernism (modern, modernity, modernist; see also: avant-garde), ix, xi, xii, xv, 1, 2, 3, 9, 10, 13, 14, 15, 22, 24–25, 27, 32, 38, 39, 40, 44, 47, 48, 49, 50, 52, 55, 57, 61, 62, 63, 67, 70, 72, 73, 74, 75–76, 77, 82, 83, 84, 87, 89, 92, 93, 94, 98, 102, 103, 105, 109, 110, 112, 115, 129, 131
modulation (musical), 111
"Mon Faust" (see: Valéry, Paul, Works by)
monody, 48, 128, 131
montage, xiii, 7–8, 13, 18, 33, 34, 35, 37, 42, 44, 51, 56, 57, 79, 80, 81, 84, 106, 118, 119
Montesi, Gotthard, 4
Monteverdi, Claudio, 34, 67
Monteverdi, Claudio, Works by:
Lamento 34
mosaic, 35, 37, 53
Moses, Stéphane, 37, 79
Mozart, Wolfgang Amadeus, Works by:
Don Juan (*Don Giovanni*) 81
Müller, Joachim, 20, 36
Müller, Martin, 37
Müller-Blattau, Joseph, 14
Müller-Seidel, Walter, 32
multivalence (see also: polyvalence), 73, 74
Mundt, Hannelore, 73
Munich, 23, 32, 103, 127
music, xi, 3, 13–15, 26, 47–54, 101–112
music drama (Wagnerian), 82, 127
music history, xii, 47–54, 83, 125
musicians, xii, 13–15, 47–54, 81–83, 84, 102–103
musicology, xi, 47–54, 128
music theory, xi, xii, 47–54
musicalization of literature, xii, 15, 30, 34, 52–53, 57, 82, 107–111
Myers, David, 46

mysticism, 29
myth (mythical, mythology, mythological), 4, 10, 12, 13, 16, 21, 26, 27, 28, 30, 32, 40, 41, 42, 44, 54, 55, 56, 60, 62, 65, 66, 67, 72, 74, 75, 80, 86, 88, 94, 107–108, 110, 112, 114, 115, 117, 128–129
myth and psychology, xi, 26, 54–55, 112–116, 128
myth plus psychology, xiii, 16, 54–55, 115–116, 128
narcissism (narcissistic, Narcissus), 90, 95, 96, 97, 112–113, 116, 128

narratology (see also: Zeitblom, as narrator), 44, 92, 93, 129
National Socialism (Nazi; see also: fascist), xii, 2, 3, 6, 29, 51, 63, 64, 65, 66, 67, 68, 75, 80, 82, 91, 114, 127
nationalism, 66
Naturalism, 35
Naumburg, 56
necromancy (see: black arts)
negative dialectic, 31
Nemerov, Howard, 27
neoclassicism, 51
Nepo, Nepomuk Schneidewein (see: Echo)
Nepomuk, Johannes von, 37
Nestroy, Johann Nepomuk, 124
New Criticism (New Critics, close reading, intrinsic method), 25, 100
Newman, John K., 83
New York, xi
Nielsen, Birgit, 54
Nietzsche, Friedrich, xii, 10, 11, 24, 27, 31, 36, 42–43, 44, 45, 48, 53, 55, 56, 63, 67, 71, 75, 78, 80, 81, 90, 92, 94, 101, 115, 117, 126, 127, 128
Nietzsche, Friedrich, Works By:
The Case of Wagner (*Der Fall Wagner*), 81; Thus Spake Zarathustra (*Also sprach Zarathustra*) 36

nihilism (nihilistic), 5, 24, 27, 43, 69, 91
Noble, Cecil A., 45–46
Northcote-Bade, James, 81–82
Novalis (the German Romantic author Friedrich von Hardenberg), 40
number symbolism, 53, 104, 108–109, 111–112, 128
numinous, 61
Nuremberg, 56

Oates, Joyce Carol, 27
objective correlative, 47, 67, 74, 111
Oedipus (Oedipal), 115, 128
Oesch, Hans, 49
onomatopoeia, 52
"open wound," 70
opera (operatic), 119
Oplatka, Andreas, 51
Orlowski, Hubert, xiv, 43, 59, 87, 93
Orpheus, 114
Orton, G., 8, 76
Oswald, Victor A., 12, 39, 112
Otto III (Emperor), 63
Ovid, Works by:
    Metamorphosis 98
Pache, Walter, 37–38, 57
pact (compact with the devil), x, 2, 15, 23, 24, 25, 29, 35, 46, 67, 89, 116, 121
Paeschke, Hans, 5
Palencia-Roth, Michael, 116
Palestrina (the city in Italy and the name of the composer), 41, 81, 103, 109, 120, 121, 130
Palestrina (see: Pfitzner, Hans, Works by)
Panizza, Oskar, 37
Panofsky, Erwin, 116
paradox (paradoxical), 40, 62, 70, 73, 86, 105
Parkes-Perret, Ford B., 93
parody, 15, 27, 29, 32, 38, 65, 70, 72–73, 77, 82, 83, 85, 87
Pasternak, Boris, 84
Pasternak, Boris, Works By:

Doctor Zhivago, 84
Pater, Walter, xii
pathogenesis, 64
pathology (pathological), 4, 50, 97, 115
Pattison, George, 102
pedagogy (the teaching of *Doctor Faustus*), 6, 27–28, 60–61
pederastic, 99
Pennsylvania, 51, 83
Pentateuch, 12
persiflage, 7
perspectivism, 31, 42, 63, 118, 124
Peterson, John, 20
Petriconi, Hellmuth, 54
Petsch, Robert, 34
Pfaff, Lucie, 36
"pfeiffen" (to whistle), 41
Pfeiffer, Peter C., xiv, 73–77, 83, 86, 100, 113
Pfeiffering (or Pfeffering: fictitious Bavarian village in *Doctor Faustus*), 41, 42, 111, 115
Pfitzner, Hans, Works by:
    Palestrina 125
philo-Semitism (philo-Semite), 13, 75
philosophy (philosophers, philosophical), xi, xii, 4–6, 14, 19, 20–21, 63, 78, 80–81, 82, 106
Piana, Theo, 25
Pickard, P. M., 16
pietà, 39, 57
Plard, Henri, 36
point of view, 91, 104
Poland (Polish), xiv, 104
politics (political), xv, 21, 26, 32, 51, 53, 63, 64–65, 66, 67, 68, 86, 88, 102, 115
Politzer, Heinz, 34
polyperspectivism, 29, 74
polyphony (polyphonic), 6, 25, 52–53, 82, 108, 109, 114, 128, 131
polyvalence (see also: multivalence), 42, 48, 74, 107
Pongs, Hermann, 27
Porter, Laurence M., 96

Poser, Hans, 27
positivist approach, 77, 106, 124
postmodernism, ix, 73, 104, 131
"Postscript" (to *Doctor Faustus*), 53
Potempa, Georg, 58
"prefigurative patterning," 55, 62, 117
primary work of art, 72
"Princess" ("die Fürstin," Mann's designation for Agnes E. Meyer), 79
Princeton University, 2, 79
Pringsheim, Klaus, 14
Pritzlaff, Christiane, 53, 111
program music, 102
Prospero (a major figure Shakespeare's *The Tempest*), 85
Protestantism (Protestant), 4, 11, 21, 38, 45
Prutti, Brigitte, 74–75
psychiatric (psychiatry), 116
psychic (psyche), 40, 67, 91, 95, 97, 114, 115, 129, 130
psychoanalysis (psychoanalytical), 16, 45–46, 54, 74, 95, 101, 112, 115, 129
psychology (psychological, psychologist), xiii, 16, 26, 54, 55, 60, 74, 94, 95, 112, 115, 128, 129
psychopathology (psychopathological), 112, 115
Puknat, E.M., 38
Puknat, Siegfried, 38
Puschmann, Rosemarie, 104, 111–112
Pütz, Peter, 31–32, 35, 42, 129
Pythagoras, 128

"radical autobiography," 93–94
Raleigh, John Henry, 8
rascal (see: rogue)
reader response, 76
"reciprocal illumination of the arts" (see also: Walzel), 15, 48, 107
redemption (see: grace)
Reed, Carroll, 10
Reed, Donna, 65
Reed, Terence J., 31–32, 35, 103, 123
Reformation (reformer, see also: Luther), 11, 45, 47, 56, 87
regression (psychological), 115
Rehm, Walter, 55
Reinhardt, George W., 82, 83
Reisiger, Hans, 126
Reiss, Gunter, 30, 36
"relationship (is everything"), xiii, 15, 48, 107, 131
religion (see: theology)
Renaissance, ix, 1, 3, 10, 37, 55, 56, 96, 116
Renner, Rolf Günter, 95, 118
"repeated mirrorings," 88
repression, 97
Reuter, Gabriele, 37
Rey, William, 16, 20, 45
rhetoric (rhetorical), 22, 43, 69, 76–77, 82, 85
Rice, Philip B., 14
Ridley, Hugh, xiv
Rieckmann, Jens, 86, 92, 106–107
Riemenschneider, Tilman, 37
Rilla, Paul, 3
Ritter-Santini, Lea, 38
Robertson, Ritchie, 123
Roche, Mark W., 80–81
Rochocz, Hans, 4
rogue figure (see also: "Schelm"), 28–29, 70–71
Romance (languages), 126
Romanticism (Romantic, Romantics, Romanticized), ix, 4, 10, 15, 22, 24, 25, 28, 29, 30, 37, 47, 51, 54, 62, 65, 66, 73, 82, 84, 91, 92, 98, 102, 103, 114, 117
rondo, 82
Rose, Marilyn Gaddis, 52
Rosenberg, Alfred, Works by: *Mythus des 20. Jahrhunderts* (Myth of the Twentieth Century) 114
row composition (see: serial technique of composition)
Runge, Doris, 125
Rupprecht, Erich, 27
Russia, (Russian, Russians), xiv, 51

Ryan, Judith, 65

Sachs, Arieh, 20
Sagave, Pierre-Paul, 11, 39, 44
Salomé (see: Strauss, Richard, Works by)
salvation (see: grace)
Samiel, 78
Sammael, 78
Sandberg, Hans Joachim, 81
sand configurations, 80, 117
Satan (see: devil)
Sator (see also: "magic square"), 104
Saturday Review of Literature, 15
Saturn (Saturnian), 123, 129
Sauer, Paul L., 68
Sauerland, Karol, 75, 105
Sautermeister, Gert, xiv, 59, 70
Scaff, Susan von Rohr, 110–111
Schädlich, Michael, 20
Schäfermeyer, Michael, 92–93
Schaper, Eva, 49
Scharfschwerdt, Jürgen, 29–30
Scheible, J., 34
Scheiffele, Eberhard, 62
Schelling, Friedrich W., 114
"Schelm" (rascal, rogue), 70
"Schema" (schemata, schematic), 26
Scher, Stephen P., 49
Scherrer, Paul, 33
Scheuerl, Jeanette (female figure in *Doctor Faustus* modeled on the writer Annette Kolb), 84
Schick, Lilo, 119
Schiffer, Eva, 59, 78
Schildknapp, Rüdiger (translator figure in *Doctor Faustus*), 51, 126
Schiller, Friedrich, 84
Schillinger, Birgit, 124
Schimansky, Gerd, 20
schizoid, 116
schizothymia, 116
Schlee, Agnes, 107–108
Schlegel, Friedrich, 114, 124
Schleiner, Winfried, 96
Schleppfuß, Eberhard (diabolic university teacher in *Doctor Faustus*), 96, 109, 120
Schmidlin, Yvonne, 55, 58, 116
Schmidt, Gérard, 30–31
Schmitz, Heinz-Gerd, 124
Schneidewein, Nepomuk (see: Echo)
Schoeps, Hans-Joachim, 37
scholarship (surveys of criticism, inventories of research, also "Forschungsberichte"), 19, 38, 59–60, 122–123
Schönberg, Arnold, xii, 2, 13, 14–15, 49, 50, 53–54, 73, 75, 82, 103, 104–106, 108, 109, 110
Schönberg, Arnold, Works by:
  A Survivor of Warsaw 104
Schönhaar, Rainer, 128
Schoolfield, George C., 28, 96, 102

Schopenhauer, Arthur, 14, 21, 24, 27, 31, 48, 81, 113
Schopenhauer, Arthur, Works by:
  Die Welt als Wille und Vorstellung (The World as Will and Idea) 14, 21, 113
Schrecker, Franz, Works by:
  Die Gezeichneten (The Marked Men), 126
Schubert, Bernhard, 71
Schuh, Willy, 15
Schulz, H. Stefan, 5
Schumann, Robert, xii, 10, 45, 83
Schwarz, Egon, 74, 75, 83
Schwarze, Michael, 118–119
Schweigestill, Else (maternal figure in *Doctor Faustus*), 28, 39, 47
Schwerdtfeger, Rudi (concert violinist in *Doctor Faustus*), 28, 41, 47, 79, 85, 126, 127
Schwerte, Hans, 39
Second World War (see under: World War)
Seghers, Anna, 36
Seidlin, Oskar, 39, 70, 78–79, 80, 125
Seiferth, Wolfgang, 7
Seiler, Bernd W., 127
Seitz, Franz (director of the film *Doktor Faustus*), 57, 118–121

Index

Seitz, Gabriele, 119, 122
Sell, Friedrich, 7
semiotics (semiotic), 31, 86, 117–118, 124, 129
Sender, Ramón J., 7
serenity (cheerfulness), 71, 123, 129
serial technique of composition (see also: constructivist music, dodecaphonic, twelve-tone technique, strict form), xii, 2, 13–14, 15, 48, 50, 53–54, 67, 76, 82, 100, 104, 108–109, 110, 111, 128
sexism, 74–75
sexual indeterminacy, 129
sexuality (see: erotic, love)
Shakespeare, William, 38–39, 84–85
Shakespeare, William, Works by: *Love's Labour's Lost* (see also: Leverkühn, Adrian, Works by) 38–39, 85; Sonnets 85; *The Tempest* 12; sickness (see: syphilis)
"sickness unto death" (Kierkegaard), 51
Siefken, Hinrich, 22, 88
Simon, Ulrich, 20
Sinn und Form, 44, 49
Smeed, J.W., 40
socialist criticism (see: communist criticism)
Socratic education, 72
solipsism (solipsistic), 96
Sommerhage, Claus, 97–98, 99
sonata form, 82, 128
Sontheimer, Kurt, 21
Sørensen, Bengt Algot, 54
Söter, István, 53
space (spatial suspension), 110–111
Spain (Spanish), xiv
speaking unspokenness, 9
speculating in the elements, xi, 40, 117
Spengler, Oswald, 80, 81
Spirit-Life complex (in Mann's work), 97
Sprecher, Thomas, 58
Staiger, Emil, 6

Starzycki, Andrzej, 53
Stein, Jack M., 14, 49
Steinfeld, Thomas, 71
sterility (artistic), 16, 53, 56, 64, 66
Stern, Joseph P., 22–23, 27
Sternberger, Dolf, 23
Stevenson, Robert Louis, Works by: *Dr. Jekyll and Mr. Hyde* 80
Stewart, John L., 14, 50
Stout, Harry L., 37
Straus, Nina Pelikan, 85, 93
Strauss, Richard, Works by: *Salomé* 95, 125
Stravinsky, Igor, 36, 50
Stresau, Hermann, 26, 27
strict form ("strenger Satz," no free note; see also: constructivist music, dodecaphonic music, strict style, twelve-tone technique), 12, 15, 34, 41, 48, 85, 106–107, 117
sublimation, 97, 115
Suhl, Abraham, 8, 76
Suhrkamp, xi
superman (Nietzsche's concept of), 63
surrealistic, 118
swastika, 111
Sweden, xi
Switzerland (Swiss), 5, 6
symbiosis (symbiotic relationship), 113, 128–129
syphilis (venereal disease, sexually transmitted disease), xi, 1, 2, 4, 9, 11, 15, 16, 27, 32, 38, 42, 45–46, 53, 56, 62, 96, 96, 115, 127
Szudra, Klaus Udo, 85
"taking back" (Beethoven's Symphony No. 9, Goethe's *Faust*, etc.), 18, 30, 34, 39, 47, 71

Tasso, Torquato, 52
Tauber, Adalbert, 55
Taubes, Jacob, 12
terrorism (in Germany), 21
Teutonic, 65
theology (theological, theologian,

religion, religious, metaphysics), xi, 2, 4–6, 7, 9, 19–20, 28, 38, 40, 44–45, 52, 53, 60, 61–63, 70, 102, 105, 113, 114, 123
Thieß, Frank, 21
Third Reich (see: National Socialism), 21, 65, 123
Thirlwall, John C., 8
Thoenelt, Klaus, 114
Thomas, R. Hinton, 24
Thomas Mann Circle (East German), 44
Thomas-Mann-Handbuch, 60
Thomas-Mann-Jahrbuch, xv, 73, 74–75, 83, 100, 113
Thomas-Mann-Studien, 33–34
threshold ("Schwelle"), 75, 129, 131
Tiedemann, Rolf, 106
Tillich, Paul, 35, 37, 79, 81
time, 34, 52–53, 62–63, 108
Times (London), 49
Times Literary Supplement, 7
Timm, Eitel, ix, 61, 120–121
Timpe, Williram, 97
Tolna, Frau von (unseen benefactress of Leverkühn in *Doctor Faustus*), 12, 39, 41, 62, 79–80, 83, 112
tone poem, 110
"tone setter" (a literal translation of the dated German term for composer "Tonsetzer" in the German title of *Doctor Faustus*), 117
tradition (traditional, convention), 28, 31–32, 35, 43, 44, 51, 63, 75, 76, 92, 103, 107, 110
transcendence (world without, transcend, transcendent), 4–6, 19–20, 24–25, 30, 37, 61, 76,102, 103, 110, 123
"transvaluation of all values," 43
Travers, Martin, 66–67, 124
triad (triumvirate, triadic, tripartite, triangular; see also: "Dreigestirn"), 8, 43, 49, 63, 81, 84–85, 92, 100

tritone (interval in music), 119, 120

Trommler, Frank, 22, 69
Tuska, Jon, 27
twelve-tone technique (or row; see also: dodedcaphonic, serial technique of composition, strict style,), 13, 15, 49–50, 51, 53–54, 68, 76, 104, 105, 107, 108, 110, 117, 128

United States (see: America), 7, 51, 79, 86
Upsala, 34
Uslar-Gleichen, Hil von, 119

Vaget, Hans Rudolf, xiv, 37, 38, 58, 59, 61–62, 63–64, 68–69, 75–76, 78–79, 79–80, 83, 86–87, 89, 122, 125, 127
Valéry, Paul, 36
Valéry, Paul, Works by:
  "Mon Faust" 10, 125
Vansittart, Robert G., 64
Varga, István, 41
venereal disease (see: syphilis)
Venice, 103
Vienna, 82
"Viergestirn" (quadratic or quadruple constellation), 81
viola d'amore (Zeitblom's instrument), 93
Visconti, Luchino, 57, 118
Visconti, Luchino, Works by:
  Death in Venice (film version of Mann's novella) 57, 118, 129
"visible music," 80
visual element (visual component), xiii, 55–57, 116–122
Viswanathan, Jacqueline, 37
Vogel, Harald, 52–53, 108
Vogt, Karen Drabek, 71
Volksbuch (see under *Doctor Faustus*, Volksbuch, chapbook of 1587)
vom Hofe, Gerhard, 102
Voss, Lieselotte, xv, 33, 35–36, 41, 42, 54, 77, 78, 126

Wackenroder, Wilhelm Heinrich, 52, 102, 103
Wagener, Hans, xiv, 60
Wagner (figure in Goethe's *Faust*), 43
Wagner, Richard (Wagnerian), 27, 31, 43, 48, 49, 51, 73, 75–76, 81–83, 86, 107, 127–128
Wagner, Richard, Works by:
Die Meistersinger 43 (Beckmesser), 49;
Parsifal 82, 83
Der Ring des Nibelungen (The Ring of the Nibelung) 92,
Tristan und Isolde 81–82, 92
Wald, H., 109–110
Walter, Bruno, 51, 103
Walter, Christiane, 115–116
Walzel, Oskar (coined the phrase "reciprocal illumination of the arts"), 107
warmth (human warmth, heat), 46, 52, 53, 114, 117, 127
Washington Post, 79
Weber, Carl Maria von, Works by:
Der Freischütz 78
Webern, Anton, 83, 104
Webern, Anton, Works by:
Concerto for Nine Instruments 104
Wedekind-Schwertner, Barbara, 98
Wegener, Herbert, 18
Wehrmann, Harald, 108–109, 111, 128
Weigand, Hermann J., 83–84, 92
Weimar, 11, 22, 65, 69
Weimar classicism, 5, 88, 89
Welter, Marianne, 27
Wenzel, Georg, 19, 27, 40, 49
whistling ("pfeiffen"), 42
White, Andrew, 27
White, James Fellows, 8, 12
White, John J., 55
Wiecker, Rolf, 50
Wiegand, Helmut, 64–65
Wiemann, H., 27
Wilhelm, Rolf, 57, 119, 121, 130
Wilhelminian era, 3

Williams, William D., 27
"willing (unwilling) suspension of disbelief," 53, 54, 128
Willnauer, Franz, 27
Wilmont, Nikolai, 51
Wimmer, Ruprecht, 127
Windisch-Laube, Walter, 126
Winfried (fictional student group in *Doctor Faustus*), 37, 79
Wirth, Günter, 79
Wißkirchen, Hans, xiv, 60, 65–66
witchcraft, 96
Wolf, Hugo, xii, 10, 45, 83
Wolff, Hans M., 24, 25
Wolff, Rudolf, 59, 92, 119
Wolff, Uwe, 114
Women (their role in *Doctor Faustus*), 76
Wooton, Carol, 51
word music, 120
World War (First World War, 22, 65–66; Second World War, xi, xii, 1, 2, 63, 69, 89)
Wysling, Hans, xv, 1, 19, 33, 34, 51, 55, 58, 112, 113, 116

Yeats, William Butler, 30

Zagreb, 49
Zeitblom, Serenus, xii, 1, 16, 23, 34, 38, 42, 43, 70, 72, 85, 88, 91, 93, 101, 114, 115, 117, 122, 127
Zeitblom, Serenus (as narrator), xii, 1, 4, 9, 11, 25, 30, 32, 33, 43–44, 53, 62, 63, 65, 68, 70, 71, 76–77, 82, 86, 87, 88, 89, 91–93, 94, 96, 98, 105–106, 108, 110, 115, 118, 121, 127
Zeller, Michael, 22
Zimmermann, Rolf Christian, 124
Zmegac, Viktor, 47, 49
Zuckerkandl, Victor, 14
Zurich, xi, 10, 18, 33, 34, 35, 44, 55, 65, 69
Zweig, Stefan, 91